Islamic Finance and Economic Development

Also by Munawar Iqbal and Philip Molyneux

THIRTY YEARS OF ISLAMIC BANKING: History, Performance and Prospects

Also by Philip Molyneux and Munawar Iqbal

BANKING AND FINANCIAL SYSTEMS IN THE ARAB WORLD

Also by Munawar Iqbal and David Llewellyn (editors)

ISLAMIC BANKING AND FINANCE: New Perspectives on Profit-Sharing and Risk

Also by Munawar Iqbal (editor)

DISTRIBUTIVE JUSTICE AND NEED FULFILMENT IN AN ISLAMIC ECONOMY

ISLAMIC BANKING AND FINANCE: Current Developments in Theory and Practice

ISLAMIC ECONOMIC INSTITUTIONS AND THE ELIMINATION OF POVERTY

ISLAMIC PERSPECTIVES ON SUSTAINABLE DEVELOPMENT

Also by Munawar Iqbal and Rodney Wilson (editors)

ISLAMIC PERSPECTIVES ON WEALTH CREATION

Also by Ziauddin Ahmed, Munawar Iqbal and M. Fahim Khan (editors)

MONEY AND BANKING IN ISLAM

FISCAL POLICY AND RESOURCE ALLOCATION IN ISLAM

Also by Munawar Iqbal and Habib Ahmed (editors)

POVERTY IN MUSLIM COUNTRIES AND THE NEW INTERNATIONAL ECONOMIC ORDER

Also by Munawar Iqbal and Tariqullah Khan (editors)

FINANCIAL ENGINEERING AND ISLAMIC CONTRACTS

Islamic Finance and Economic Development

Edited by

Munawar Iqbal
Chief, Islamic Banking and Finance Division
Islamic Research and Training Institute
Islamic Development Bank
Jeddah, Saudi Arabia

and

Ausaf Ahmad
Head, Special Assignments Unit
Islamic Research and Training Institute
Islamic Development Bank
Jeddah, Saudi Arabia

palgrave
macmillan

Islamic Research and Training Institute
A Member of the IDB Group

University of Bahrain

International Association for Islamic Economics

First published 2005 by
PALGRAVE MACMILLAN
Houndmills, Basingstoke, Hampshire RG21 6XS and
175 Fifth Avenue, New York, N.Y. 10010
Companies and representatives throughout the world

PALGRAVE MACMILLAN is the global academic imprint of the Palgrave Macmillan division of St. Martin's Press, LLC and of Palgrave Macmillan Ltd. Macmillan® is a registered trademark in the United States, United Kingdom and other countries. Palgrave is a registered trademark in the European Union and other countries.

ISBN-13: 978–1–4039–4718–5
ISBN-10: 1–4039–4718–X

This book is printed on paper suitable for recycling and made from fully managed and sustained forest sources.

A catalogue record for this book is available from the British Library.

Library of Congress Cataloging-in-Publication Data
International Conference on Islamic Economics and Finance (5th : 2003 : Manama, Bahrain)
Islamic finance and economic development / [edited by] Munawar Iqbal and Ausaf Ahmad.
p. cm.
Papers from the 5th International Conference on Islamic Economics and Finance, held Oct. 7–9, 2003 in Manama, Bahrain, organized by the International Association for Islamic Economics, the Islamic Research and Training Institute, and the University of Bahrain.
Includes bibliographical references and index.
ISBN 1–4039–4718–X
1. Banks and banking—Islamic countries—Congresses. 2. Finance—Islamic countries—Congresses. 3. Islamic countries—Economic conditions—Congresses. I. Iqbal, Munawar. II. Ausaf Ahmad. III. Islamic Research and Training Institute. IV. International Association for Islamic Economics. V. Jami'at al-Bahrayn. VI. Title.
HG3368.A6I575 2003
332.1'0917'67—dc22 2005049810

Transferred to digital print 2007

Printed and bound in Great Britain by
CPI Antony Rowe, Chippenham and Eastbourne

Contents

List of Tables and Figures

Tables

Figures

Preface

The International Association for Islamic Economics, the Islamic Research and Training Institute of the Islamic Development Bank and the University of Bahrain organized the Fifth International Conference on Islamic Economics and Finance under the patronage of the Bahrain Monetary Agency (BMA) during 7–9 October 2003 in Manama, Bahrain. The theme of the Conference was 'Sustainable Development and Islamic Finance in Muslim Countries'. All papers submitted to the Conference were refereed before the Conference. On the basis of the referee reports, the Academic Committee for the Conference selected 28 papers, which were presented and discussed during the Conference.

Those papers and comments are being published in four volumes. The present volume is one of them. The text deals with the role of Islamic finance in promoting growth and development. Over the last 30 years, Islamic banking has emerged as a viable and efficient model of financial intermediation. This text highlights some of the benefits that this new model of financial intermediation can bring to society. It points out some crucial prerequisites for Islamic finance to be an engine of growth and identifies the areas where more research and development is needed. It underlines the fact that while Islamic banking fulfils the religious requirements of a large portion of the global population, it widens the choice set for all. By doing so, it increases the efficiency of the resource allocation process. It presents some interesting case studies that bring to light certain features of Islamic finance and their relationships with growth, economic and financial stability, allocative efficiency and social justice.

In the process of preparing this volume, we benefited from the advice and assistance of several people. First and foremost, we are grateful to Dr Mohammed Omer Zubair, Chairman of the Steering Committee for the Conference, for providing inspiration and guidance throughout the process of preparing both for the Conference itself and the publication of the papers presented there. We are grateful to all members of the Academic Committee, especially its Chairman, Dr Muhammad Umer Chapra, and the referees of the papers for their valuable advice and comments which helped to improve the quality of papers. In several cases, the papers have been revised after the Conference in the light of the discussions held during the Conference. All contributors have been very cooperative, for which we are grateful. Thanks are also due to Mr Shaikh Amanul Hoque, Mr Jaleel Asghar, Mr Rasulul Hacque, and Mr Sajjad Qurban for secretarial assistance and for meticulously going through several drafts to ensure accuracy and consistency of style.

MUNAWAR IQBAL
Chief, Islamic Banking and Finance Division
Islamic Research and Training Institute

AUSAF AHMAD
Head, Special Assignments Unit
Islamic Research and Training Institute

Glossary of Arabic Terms

Aḥādīth	Plural of *ḥadīth*. For meaning, see below.
Amānah	Trust.
Amīr	Leader, ruler.
Awqāf	Plural of *waqf*. For meaning, see below.
Āyah	1. A verse of *Qur'ān*. 2. Sign.
Bay'bi thaman al-'ājil	Another term used for *bay'mu'ajjal*.
Bay'mu'ajjal	Sale on credit (i.e., a sale in which goods are delivered immediately but payment is deferred).
Fatāwā	Plural of *fatwā*. Religious verdicts by *fuqahā'*.
Fiqh	Refers to the whole corpus of Islamic jurisprudence. In contrast with conventional law, *fiqh* covers all aspects of life, religious, political, social, commercial or economic. The whole corpus of *fiqh* is based primarily on interpretations of the *Qur'ān* and the *Sunnah* and secondarily on *ijmā'* (consensus) and *ijtihād* (individual judgement). While the *Qur'ān* and the *Sunnah* are immutable, *fiqhī* verdicts may change due to changing circumstances.
Fiqhī	Relating to *fiqh* (see above).
Fuqahā'	Plural of *faqīh* meaning jurist, who gives rulings on various juristic issues in the light of the *Qur'ān* and the *Sunnah*.
Ḥadīth	Sayings, deeds and endorsements of the Prophet Muhammad (peace be upon him) narrated by his Companions.
Ḥalāl	Things or activities permitted by the *Sharī'ah*.
Ḥanafī	A school of Islamic jurisprudence named after Imam Abu Ḥanīfa.
Ḥarām	Things or activities prohibited by the *Sharī'ah*.
Ḥimā	Reserves.
Ḥisbah	Literally, it means reward, calculation. Technically, it refers to an institution that existed through most of Islamic history for implementing what is proper and preventing what is improper. The main role of *al-ḥisbah* was the regulation and supervision of markets to ensure proper market conduct by all concerned.

Ijārah	Leasing. Sale of usufruct of an asset. The lessor retains the ownership of the asset with all the rights and the responsibilities that go with ownership.
Ijārah muntahiyyah bil-tamlīk	Lease ending in ownership.
Ijārah wa iqtinā'	Lease ending in ownership.
Infāq	Spending. In the literature of Islamic economics, it usually refers to spending in the way of Allah.
Istiṣnā' (used as a short form for *bay'al-istiṣnā'*)	Refers to a contract whereby a manufacturer (contractor) agrees to produce (build) and deliver a well-described good (or premise) at a given price on a given date in the future. As against *salam*, in *istiṣnā'* the price need not be paid in advance. It may be paid in instalments in step with the preferences of the parties or partly at the front end and the balance later on as agreed.
Ju'ālah	Performing a given task against a prescribed fee in a given period.
Khalīfah	Vicegerent.
Khums	Literally means one-fifth. Technically refers to the 20 per cent rate of *zakāh* applicable to certain forms of wealth.
Malikī	A school of Islamic jurisprudence named after Imam Malik.
Maqāṣid al-Sharī'ah	Basic objectives of the *Sharī'ah*. These are protection of faith, life, progeny, property and reason.
Mu'āmalāt	Relationships/contracts among human beings as against *'ibādāt*, which defines the relationship between God and His creatures.
Mu'āwaḍāt	Contracts of exchange of value with value.
Muḍārabah	A contract between two parties, capital owner(s) or financiers (called *rabb al-māl*) and an investment manager (called *muḍārib*). Profit is distributed between the two parties in accordance with the ratio upon which they agree at the time of the contract. Financial loss is borne only by the financier(s). The entrepreneur's loss lies in not getting any reward for his services.
Muḍārib	An investment manager in a *muḍārabah* contract.
Muḥtasib	Ombudsperson.

Murābaḥah	Sale at a specified profit margin. The term, however, is now used to refer to a sale agreement whereby the seller purchases the goods desired by the buyer and sells them at an agreed marked-up price, the payment being settled within an agreed time frame, either in instalments or in a lump sum. The seller bears the risk for the goods until they have been delivered to the buyer. *Murābaḥah* is also referred to as *bayʿmu'ajjal.*
Musāqah	A contract in which the owner of a garden agrees to share its produce with someone in an agreed proportion in return for the latter's services in irrigating and looking after the garden.
Mushārakah	Partnership. A *mushārakah* contract is similar to a *muḍārabah* contract, the difference being that in the former both the partners participate in the management and the provision of capital, and share in the profit and loss. Profits are distributed between the partners in accordance with the ratios initially set, whereas loss is distributed in proportion to each one's share in the capital.
Muzāraʿah	A contract whereby one party agrees to till the land owned by the other party in consideration for an agreed share in the produce of the land.
Qarḍ or *Qarḍ ḥasan*	A loan extended without interest or any other compensation from the borrower. The lender expects a reward only from God.
Qimār	Gambling.
Qur'ān (also written as *Al-Qur'ān*)	The Holy Book of Muslims, consisting of the revelations made by God to the Prophet Muhammad (peace be upon him). The *Qur'ān* lays down the fundamentals of the Islamic faith, including beliefs and all aspects of the Islamic way of life.
Qurūḍ Ḥasanah	Plural of *qarḍ al-ḥasan.*
Rabb al-māl	Capital owner (financier) in a *muḍārabah* contract.
Rabūbiyyah	An attribute of God, meaning His being the ultimate sustainer of all.
Ribā	Literally, it means increase or addition or growth. Technically it refers to the 'premium' that must be paid by the borrower to the lender along with

	the principal amount as a condition for the loan or an extension of its maturity. Interest as commonly known today is regarded by a predominant majority of *fuqahā'* to be equivalent to *ribā*.
Ṣadaqah	An act of charity.
Salam	The short form of *bay' al-salam*.
Shāfi'ī	A school of Islamic jurisprudence named after Imam Shāfi'ī.
Sharī'ah	Refers to the corpus of Islamic law based on Divine guidance as given by the *Qur'ān* and the *Sunnah* and embodies all aspects of the Islamic faith, including beliefs and practices.
Shirākah	Partnership. Technically, it is equivalent to *mushārakah*.
Ṣukūk	Plural of *ṣakk* which refers to a financial paper showing entitlement of the holder to the amount of money shown on it. The English word 'cheque' has been derived from it. Technically, *ṣukūk* are financial instruments entitling their holders to some financial claims.
Sunnah	The Sunnah is the second most important source of the Islamic faith after the *Qur'ān* and refers to the Prophet's (peace be upon him) example as indicated by his practice of the faith. The only way to know the Sunnah is through the collection of *aḥādīth*, which consist of reports about the sayings, deeds and endorsements of the Prophet (peace be upon him).
Sūrah	A chapter of *Al-Qur'ān*.
Takāful	An alternative for the contemporary insurance contract. A group of persons agree to share certain risk (for example, damage by fire) by collecting a specified sum from each. In case of loss to anyone of the group, the loss is met from the collected funds.
Tawḥīd	Belief in the unity of God both in terms of person as well as in His attributes.
Tazkiyah	Purification, growth.
Ummah	The nation of Muslims.
Wakālah	Contract of agency. In this contract, one person appoints someone else to perform a certain task on his behalf, usually against a fixed fee.

Waqf — Appropriation or tying up a property in perpetuity for specific purposes. No property rights can be exercised over the corpus. Only the usufruct is applied towards the objectives (usually charitable) of the *waqf*.

Zakāh — The amount payable by a Muslim on his net worth as a part of his religious obligations, mainly for the benefit of the poor and the needy. It is an obligatory duty on every adult Muslim who owns more than a threshold level of wealth.

Notes on the Contributors and Editors

Contributors

Habib Ahmed, Economist, Islamic Economics Cooperation and Development Division, Islamic Research and Training Institute, Islamic Development Bank, Jeddah, Saudi Arabia.

Said Al-Hallaq, Department of Economics, Yarmouk University, Irbid, Jordan.

Mabid Ali Al-Jarhi, Consultant, Monetary and Financial Economics, and President, International Association for Islamic Economics, 28 Omer Tosson Street, Agouza, Giza, Egypt.

Khalid A. Al Meshal, Associate Professor, Deptartment of Economics, Imam Muhammad University, PO Box 84167, Riyadh 11671, Saudi Arabia.

Ahmed S. Bamakhramah, Professor, Department of Economics, Faculty of Economics and Administration, King Abdulaziz University, Jeddah, Saudi Arabia.

Abdelkader Chachi, Researcher, Islamic Economics Research Center, King Abdulaziz University, PO Box 80214, Jeddah 21589, Saudi Arabia.

Yadollah Dadgar, Chairman, Islamic Economics Department, Tarbiat Modarres University, PO Box 14115-316, Tehran, Islamic Republic of Iran.

Humayon Dar, Department of Economics, Loughborough University, Loughborough LE11 3TU, United Kingdom.

Karim Eslamloueyan, Assistant Professor, Department of Economics, Shiraz University, Eram Square, Shiraz 71944, Islamic Republic of Iran.

Zubair Hasan, Department of Economics, Kulliyyah of Economics and Management Sciences, International Islamic University, Jalan Gombak 53100, Kuala Lumpur, Malaysia.

Abul Hassan, Department of Economics and Finance, University of Durham, 23–26 Old Elvet, Durham DH1 3HY, England.

Morteza Heidari, Management and Planning Organization, Shokreih Bolv., Hamedan, Postal Code 65167, Islamic Republic of Iran.

Javed Hussain, Director of MPhil/PhD Programmes, Business School, University of Central England, Perry Barr, Birmingham B42 2SU, UK.

Mariani Abdul Majid, Lecturer, Faculty of Economics, Universiti Kebangsaan Malaysia, 43600 Bangi, Selangor Darul Ehsan, Malaysia.

Sherifa Marafi, Project Analyst, The Industrial Bank of Kuwait, Kuwait City, PO Box 3146, 13032 Safat, Kuwait.

Victor Murinde, Reader in Finance and Director, Corporate Finance Research, Department of Accounting and Finance, The Birmingham Business School, Edgbaston, Birmingham B15 2TT, United Kingdom.

Nor Ghani Md. Nor, Lecturer, Faculty of Economics, Universiti Kebangsaan Malaysia, 43600 Bangi, Selangor Darul Ehsan, Malaysia.

Ridha Muhammad Saadallah, Faculté des Sciences Economiques et de Gestion de Sfax, Route de l'Aerodrome, BP 1088, Sfax 3018, Tunisia.

Abulhasan M. Sadeq, Vice Chancellor, Asian University of Bangladesh, Dhaka 1230, Bangladesh.

Kazem Sadr, Professor, Shahid Beheshti University, School of Economics and Political Sciences, Tehran 19834, Islamic Republic of Iran.

Fatin Faezah Said, Lecturer, School of Economics, Faculty of Economics and Business, Universiti Kebangsaan Malaysia, 43600 Bangi, Selangor, Malaysia.

Shamim Ahmad Siddiqui, Department of Economics, Brunei University, Jalan Tungku Link, Gadong BE1410, Negara Brunei Darussalam.

Sayyid Tahir, Professor of Economics, International Islamic University, Islamabad, Pakistan.

Iraj Toutounchian, Department of Economics, Az-zahra University, Tehran, Islamic Republic of Iran.

Editors

Munawar Iqbal was born in Pakistan (1950). He holds an MA (Economics) degree from McMaster University and a PhD from Simon Fraser University, Canada. He has worked as Senior Research Economist, Pakistan Institute of Development Economics, Islamabad; Dean, Faculty of Social Sciences, International Islamic University, Islamabad; Director, International Institute of Islamic Economics, Islamabad; and Economic Adviser, Al-Rajhi Banking and Investment Corporation, Saudi Arabia, before joining the Islamic Research and Training Institute (IRTI). Currently he holds the position of Chief of Research, Islamic Banking and Finance Division, IRTI, of the Islamic Development Bank (IDB), Jeddah, Saudi Arabia. He is also Editor of *Islamic Economic Studies*, the professional journal of IRTI. He has published more than 30 research papers and books on Islamic economics and banking. Some of his recent publications include: *Islamic Banking and Finance: New Perspectives on Profit Sharing and Risk* (co-ed., Edward Elgar); *Islamic Banking and Finance: Current Developments in Theory and Practice* (Islamic Foundation); *Islamic Banking: Answers to Some Frequently Asked Questions* (co-authored), Occasional Paper No. 4, IRTI; *Financing Public Expenditure: An Islamic Perspective* (co-authored), Occasional Paper No. 7, IRTI; *Thirty Years of Islamic Banking: History, Performance and Prospects* (co-authored, Palgrave Macmillan); *Banking and Financial Systems in the Arab World* (co-authored, Palgrave Macmillan). E-mail: munawariqbal@isdb.org

Ausaf Ahmad was born in Lucknow, India, in 1945. He obtained his Master's degree in economics with distinction from Lucknow University in 1969 and an MPhil in Regional Development from Jawaharlal Nehru University, Delhi. He obtained a PhD degree in economics from Northern Illinois University in 1977 on a Fulbright Scholarship. Before joining the Islamic Research and Training Institute of the Islamic Development Bank in 1984, he was associated with departments of economics at many Indian universities in different capacities. He has carried out research projects for the Indian Council of Social Science Research, the International Labour Office, and the King Abdulaziz University. The main areas of his research interest are the economics of development, public finance, monetary policy and Islamic banking. His research work includes 17 books and 30 research papers which have been published in India and abroad. Some of his works have been translated into other languages including Urdu, Hindi, Arabic, French and Italian. His main works include *Saving Behaviour in a Metropolitan Economy; Development Issues of the Third World; Development and Problems of Islamic Banks; Lectures on Islamic Economics* (jointly edited with Kazim Awan); *Indian Muslims: Issues in Social and Economic Development; Structure of Deposits in Selected Islamic Banks*; and *Islamic Financial Instruments for the Development of Infrastructure* (jointly edited with Tariqullah Khan).

List of Abbreviations

2SLS	Two-Stage Least Squares
ABM	Association of Banks in Malaysia
ADF	Augmented Dickey–Fuller
AFTA	ASEAN Free Trade Agreement
AIC	Akaike Information Criterion
ARDL	Autoregressive Distributed Lag
ASEAN	Association of South East Asian Nations
BIMB	Bank Islam Malaysia Berhad
BMI	Bank Markazi Iran (Iranian Central Bank)
BMMB	Bank Muamalat Malaysia Berhad
CFIs	conventional financial institutions
DAC	developed and advanced countries
DEA	Data Envelopment Analysis
ECM	Error Correction Model
EMS	Environmental Management Systems
FfD	Financing for Development
GATS	General Agreement on Trade and Services
GDP	Gross National Product
GNP	Gross National Product
HQC	Hannan–Quinn Criterion
IBBL	Islami Bank Bangladesh
IBK	Industrial Bank of Kuwait
ICOR	Incremental Capital–Output Ratio
IDB	Islamic Development Bank
IFB	Interest-Free Banking
IFBL	Interest-Free Banking Law
IFF	Interest-Free Finance
IFIs	Islamic Financial Institutions
IIED	International Institute for Environment and Development
IIIE	International Institute of Islamic Economics
IRTI	Islamic Research and Training Institute
JIB	Jordan Islamic Bank
KD	Kuwaiti Dinar
KFAS	Kuwait Foundation for Advancement of Science
KFH	Kuwait Finance House
LIBOR	London Inter-Bank Offer Rate
NGOs	Non-Governmental Organizations
NORM	Neutral Omni-partial Rule-Making

ODA	Official Development Assistance
ODS	Office of Development Studies
OIC	Organization of the Islamic Conference
OLS	Ordinary Least Squares
PIC	Petrochemical Industries Corporation
PLS	Profit and Loss Sharing
RM	Malaysian Ringgit
S&Ls	Savings and Loans Associations
SBC	Schwarz Bayesian Criterion
SD	Sustainable Development
SMEs	Small and Medium Enterprises
TMCL	Time Multiple Counter Loan
UN	United Nations
UNCED	United Nations Conference on Environment and Development
UNCTAD	United Nations Conference on Trade and Development
UNDP	United Nations Development Programme
UNEP	United Nations Environment Programme
WACC	Weighted Average Cost of Capital
WBCSD	World Business Council for Sustainable Development
WCED	World Commission on Environment and Development
WSSD	World Summit on Sustainable Development
WTO	World Trade Organization

1
Introduction

Munawar Iqbal and Ausaf Ahmad

There is overwhelming theoretical and empirical evidence that financial sector development plays an important role in enhancing growth. There are many channels through which financial institutions affect growth. Banks in particular perform some very important functions for society and, in the process, significantly influence major economic variables. Out of these functions, two are especially important: one is intermediation between ultimate savers and borrowers, and the other is the administration of the payments mechanism.

In any economy, there is a need to transfer funds from savers to investors because people who save are frequently not the same people who have the ability to exploit the profitable investment opportunities. This transfer is effected either by means of direct finance through securities markets or through the process of financial intermediation in the financial markets, with the latter being more important. The importance of financial intermediation can be seen by the fact that around two-thirds of new investment passes through this process in most countries, especially the less developed ones. Thus, development and financial intermediation are very closely linked to each other and financial sector development is a prerequisite for economic development.

Financial intermediation enhances the efficiency of the saving/investment process by reducing transaction costs and eliminating the mismatches inherent in the needs of surplus and deficit units of an economy. Since the savers and investors are usually different units, they require a considerable amount of information about each other. This information is not free, and thus the process of channelling funds from savers to investors involves transaction costs. Moreover, due to asymmetric information, it also gives rise to the problems of adverse selection and moral hazard. Financial intermediaries can benefit from economies of scale and hence reduce the transaction costs of transferring funds from surplus units to the deficit units. For the same reason, they are also in a better position to tackle the problems arising from asymmetric information.

The process of financial intermediation also removes some mismatches in the tastes, maturity terms and size of the funds needed by the two sides. The surplus units are often small households who save relatively small amounts and the deficit units are the firms who often need relatively large amounts of cash. Financial intermediaries remove this size mismatch by collecting small savings and packaging these to make them suitable to the needs of the users. In addition, users of funds in general need funds for relatively long-term deployment, which cannot be met by individual suppliers of funds. This creates a mismatch between the maturity and liquidity preferences of individual savers and users of funds. The intermediaries resolve the conflict again by pooling small funds. Moreover, the risk preferences of small suppliers and large users of funds are also different. Small savers are generally considered to be risk-averse and prefer safer placements whereas the fund users deploy the funds in risky projects. Therefore, the funds cannot be directly supplied. The role of the intermediary again becomes crucial. They can substantially reduce this risk through portfolio diversification. Furthermore, small savers cannot efficiently gather information about investment opportunities. Financial intermediaries are in a much better position to collect such information, which is crucial for making the investment successful.

The role and functions of financial intermediaries outlined above are indeed economically useful and socially desirable, but unfortunately interest plays a central role in performing most of these functions. Islamic financial intermediation endeavours to replace interest by other modes and instruments both for mobilizing savings and for putting those savings to productive use. The functions that the banks perform are important whether the economy concerned is secular or Islamic; people need banking services. Conventional banking uses interest rates to provide these services. Now, since the banking services are needed but interest is prohibited, Islamic economies have to find alternative ways of performing various banking functions.

It is worth noting here that the Islamic teachings about zero rates of interest are not an aberration. There is a strong school of economists who argue that interest-based finance is sub-optimal on purely economic grounds. Despite the fact that the rate of interest operates in conventional economies as a price, monetary economists insist that a zero nominal interest rate is a necessary condition for optimal allocation of resources.[1] The reason is simple. After switching from metallic to fiat money, adding one marginal unit of real balances costs the community no real resources. Therefore imposing a positive price on the use of money would lead traders to economize on the use of money, in their efforts to minimize their transaction costs. They would therefore use some real resources instead of money.

However, when the rate of interest is zero, traders will have no incentive to substitute real resources for money. More real resources can therefore be directed to consumption and investment. When this matter was investigated within general equilibrium models, it was found that a zero interest rate is both necessary and sufficient for allocative efficiency.[2]

Looking at it from the equity perspective, the results of the operations of a certain production enterprise in which such loans are to be invested are by no means certain. Therefore guaranteeing in advance a fixed return on a loan without taking into consideration the *actual* results of the operations of the borrowing enterprise would load all the business risk on the entrepreneur. The arrangement would be fairer if the financier were to participate in the actual profit or loss of the enterprise, whatever the case may be.

Different models of financial intermediation

The above discussion shows that financial intermediation enhances the efficiency of the saving/investment process by eliminating the mismatches inherent in the needs of surplus and deficit units with respect to size, duration, liquidity and risk profiles. The process involves the creation of a variety of financial assets and liabilities with different characteristics to cater for the different needs of savers and the ultimate users of funds. There are a number of ways in which such financial assets can be created. The process involves finding mechanisms to price these assets in such a way that the market can function efficiently, and different players on the market (including savers, investors and the financial institutions) can be appropriately rewarded. The usual form of commercial banking is based on pure financial intermediation, whereby banks borrow from savers and then lend to enterprises or individuals. They make their profit from the margin between the rates of interest for borrowing and lending. Commercial banks are prohibited from trading and their shareholding is severely restricted to a small proportion of their net worth.

A second model of financial intermediation is what is known as universal banking. Universal banks are allowed to hold equity and also to carry out operations such as trading and insurance, which usually lie beyond the sphere of commercial banking. Universal banks are better equipped to deal with information asymmetry than their commercial counterparts. They finance their business customers through a combination of shareholding and lending. In Anglo-Saxon countries, commercial banking dominates, while in Germany, Switzerland, the Netherlands and Japan, universal banking is more popular.

Before proceeding further, a few observations on the two models of financial intermediation within the conventional banking framework mentioned above may be helpful. Commercial banking is based on a pure financial intermediation model, whereby banks mainly borrow from savers and then lend to enterprises or individuals. They make their profit from the margin between the borrowing and lending rates of interest. They also provide banking services, such as letters of credit and guarantees. A proportion of their profit comes from the low-cost funds that they obtain through demand deposits. Commercial banks are prohibited from trading and their shareholding is severely restricted to a small proportion of their net worth.

As a result of the fractional reserve system they produce derivative deposits, which allow them to multiply their low-cost resources. The process of bank lending is, however, subject to some problems that can make it inefficient. Borrowers usually know more about their own operations than lenders. Acting as lenders, banks face this information asymmetry. Because borrowers are in a position to hold back information from banks, they can use the loans they obtain for purposes other than those specified in the loan agreement, exposing banks to unknown risks. They can also misreport their cash flows or declare bankruptcy fraudulently. Such problems are known as moral hazard. The ability of banks to secure repayment depends a great deal on whether the loan is effectively used for its purpose to produce enough returns for debt servicing. Even at government level, several countries have borrowed billions of dollars, used them unproductively for other purposes and ended up with serious debt problems. Banks can ascertain the proper use of loans through monitoring but it is either discouraged by clients or is too costly, and hence not commercially feasible. Thus the purpose for which the loan is given plays a minimal role in commercial banking; it is the credit rating of the borrower that plays a more important role.

By contrast, universal banks are allowed to hold equity and also carry out operations such as trading and insurance, which usually lie beyond the sphere of commercial banking. Universal banks are better equipped to deal with information asymmetry than their commercial counterparts. They finance their business customers through a combination of shareholding and lending. Shareholding allows universal banks to sit on the boards of directors of their business customers, which enables them to monitor the use of their funds at a low cost. The reduction of the monitoring costs reduces business failures and adds efficiency to the banking system.

Based on these arguments, many economists have preferred universal banking because of its greater efficiency. They have pointed out several advantages for the use of universal banking as compared to commercial banking, including the fact that, because they operate in a world marred by asymmetric information, banks would greatly benefit from reducing the risks emanating from moral hazard and adverse selection. By providing equity as well as non-equity finance simultaneously, they can monitor the performance of firms obtaining finance at much lower costs than commercial banks. Because of cheaper monitoring, banking theory indicates that universal banking would be exposed to lower levels of moral hazard and adverse selection.

In addition, by sitting on the firms' board of directors, banks could influence corporate governance in the whole productive sector, leading to general improvements in macroeconomic performance. Empirical work done on universal banking has found that universal banks face lower risks than commercial banks during both upturns and downturns. It was also found empirically that the risk differential between universal and commercial banks gets wider and more significant during downturns. This is rather significant, as downturns usually represent difficult times for banks to carry through.

Islamic banking is another way of performing financial intermediation. It is closer to the Swiss–German universal banking model than the Anglo-Saxon commercial banking model. An Islamic bank is a deposit-taking institution whose functions include all currently known banking activities. On the liabilities side, it mobilizes funds on the basis of *muḍārabah* (profit-sharing) or *wakālah* (as an agent charging a fixed fee for managing funds). On the assets side, it makes finance available on a profit-and-loss sharing basis or through the purchase of goods (in cash) and their sale (on credit) or other trading, leasing and manufacturing activities. It plays the role of an investment manager for the owners of deposits, except demand deposits which are treated as interest-free loans from the clients to the bank and are guaranteed to be repaid in full. Such deposits share in neither risk nor reward. Equity holding as well as commodity and asset trading constitute an integral part of Islamic banking operations. It is in this sense that Islamic banks are similar to the universal banks operating in several European countries. An Islamic bank shares its net earnings with its depositors (other than demand depositors) in a way that depends on the size and time-to-maturity of the deposits.

Historically, the role of a financial intermediary in the Islamic economy is found in the principle of *al-muḍārib udārib*, a practice which has existed in Islamic history since early centuries. It can be expressed as, 'the one who mobilizes funds on a profit-sharing basis extends these funds to the users on the same basis'. Similarly, in leasing, the lessee who possesses the usufruct may sell this against a higher price (rent), and create additional value. In the early Islamic period, most caravan trades were financed by *muḍārabah* (trust financing). In trading, it is possible to purchase something on order at a given price and resell it to the orderer of purchase at a higher price. This has given rise to a new financial product known as *murābaḥah*. It is worth noting that the Islamic concept of financial intermediation is interwoven with the production and exchange of real goods and services.

Islamic banking and development

When Islamic banks came on the scene some 30 years ago, they were seen to be some sort of religious institutions. However, the serious research work done during the last quarter of a century and the actual practice by hundreds of Islamic financial institutions around the globe has shown that Islamic banking is a viable and efficient method of financial intermediation. Like traditional banks, Islamic financial institutions are simply profit-seeking businesses. While Islamic banking fulfils the religious requirements of Muslims, it also broadens the choice-set available to others by offering both finance for sales and low-risk products (i.e., buying and selling) as well as products based on sharing risks and returns. In addition to providing more choices to clients, this mix of fixed and variable return modes has a number of healthy effects for the efficiency and stability of the system. Al-Jarhi (Chapter 2) mentions several of these. Other writers have also pointed out many potential benefits of Islamic banking.[3] A tentative list of potential benefits from the emergence of Islamic banking may include the following points:

1 The range of contracts available to savers and entrepreneurs is widened. The menu ranges from low risk trade-linked products to high risk-sharing contracts.
2 The financial system is enriched by the establishment of financial institutions with different modus operandi. This diversity enhances the stability of the financial system because the behavioural characteristics of different types of banks are likely to vary.
3 Competition among alternative banking models is expected to increase the efficiency of the financial system.
4 The financial needs of Muslims can be met in accordance with their faith. Since the public's acceptance of the services provided by the industry play a vital role in creating stable and efficient markets, plurality and inclusiveness are important for the development of financial markets.
5 The allocation of financial resources on the basis of profit-and-loss sharing (PLS) gives maximum weight to the profitability of investment as compared with creditworthiness in the conventional system. Such an allocation of resources is expected to be more efficient than one based on interest.
6 As a result of PLS contracts, the liabilities side of the balance sheet tends to become symmetrical with the assets side. This helps to make Islamic banks less vulnerable to external shocks and insolvency.
7 The liability of investment depositors to share bank losses motivates them to be more vigilant about the operations of their banks and to demand greater transparency and more effective audit. Banks are also under pressure to evaluate their clients' projects more carefully and to monitor the risks more effectively.

8 Since (in the case of both profit-sharing and sale-based contracts) bank assets are created in response to investment opportunities in the real sector of the economy, and all financing is linked to commodities or assets, the real factors related to the production of goods and services (rather than speculative manoeuvres) become the prime determinants of the rates of return.
9 Debt creation in Islamic finance is generally not possible without the backing of goods and services. Monetary expansion would thus tend to take place in step with the growth of the real economy. This is expected to control inflationary pressures. Destabilizing speculation would also be significantly curtailed as would the erratic and mass movement of short-term funds.
10 Like 'ethical funds', Islamic banks do not provide finance to projects considered socially undesirable. That introduces greater social responsibility.

Several elements in the above list point to the fact that Islamic banking takes a broader view of the concept of development. In this regard, it may be worth noting that the concept of 'sustainable development' (SD) also does the same. The advancement of sustainable development philosophy has changed the neo-classical economic paradigm in several ways. Hassan and Chachi (Chapter 4) draw our attention to the fact that the concept of sustainable development has a strong link with values. In this sense it is a major departure from the value-neutral neo-classical paradigm towards the value-based Islamic economic paradigm. Neo-classical philosophy placed undue reliance on market forces. A market economy can be efficient in allocating resources to meet individual preferences and lead to higher rates of growth; but the market will not necessarily deliver other objectives that a society may have, such as social justice. Justice in society expands concern for immediate family and nearest neighbours to concern for the common good. It insists that all members of society be included in this common 'good' and that society's institutions be structured accordingly. Financial institutions are among the most important institutions to be reformed. Hasan and Chachi stress that Islamic financial institutions can help to achieve this balance between allocative efficiency and distributional equity and that social justice as a moral value is inseparable from sustainability.

The distribution of credit in an Islamic banking system is expected to be more equitable than in an interest-based economy, the reason being that in the case of profit-sharing the banks are interested in the results of the project. Of course, they are concerned with the safety of the capital itself but, in an interest-based system, the safety of the capital gets almost all the weight in the decision to provide the finance. Because the rate of interest is fixed, the banks' main concern is that they get their principal as well as the interest back. In a profit-sharing arrangement, the banks as well as the entrepreneurs will try to maximize their profit, so their interests are mutual. They are working for the same objective (i.e., getting a better return which they will share). Thus both allocative efficiency and equity are promoted. Even where a person's credibility may be low, if the potential of the project is high, the banks may be willing to finance that project because they will get a better return on their investment. Therefore, small savers and small entrepreneurs who belong to the lower and middle classes have the opportunity of getting finance from the banks. In an interest-based system most of the funds flow to large industries, multinational corporations and big industrialists. Small savers and small middle-class entrepreneurs do not get sufficient finances even for their very best projects. The distribution of credit in an interest-based system is skewed in favour of the rich and big industrialists, whereas in a profit-sharing system bank finances will be more equitably distributed.

Like Hassan and Chachi, Dadgar (Chapter 6) emphasizes the fact that an economic system should be seen as a unitary system with linkages among social, economic, political, cultural and religious factors. The development process will not be sustainable if non-economic factors are not given their due importance. The injunction against *ribā* is so deeply rooted in the religious feelings of a large majority of Muslims that a financial system based on interest cannot unleash its full growth potential. Pious Muslims still have reservations in dealing with interest-based commercial banks and, if circumstances force such dealings, they prefer only to open current accounts. This, on the one hand, leaves surplus resources hoarded outside the financial sector and, on the other hand, leads to the 'exclusion' of a large number of people from the development process. A major point brought forth by Dadgar is that Islamic banking is an integrating factor for the whole system of the Islamic economy in which all the economic functions carried out in product and factor markets are sustainable by their very nature. Islamic financial institutions help the economy to follow a course of growth which would be sustainable. The tax and social security system, along with government budget and private sector investment activities, are all carried out in a way that leads the economy to obtain the maximum level of income and at the same time preserve the quality of life and environmental capital for future generations.

However, one must not overlook the fact that, in order to be growth-enhancing, any financial system must contain some crucial features. Ahmed (Chapter 3) attempts to identify the factors of economic growth and then link the financial sector to those factors. He attempts to construct an index for the contribution of the Islamic financial system to various financial factors of growth. He then assesses the potential of the Islamic financial system to meet different financial needs that will bring about growth. He identifies the strengths and weaknesses of the Islamic financial system, and concludes that while, theoretically, the Islamic financial system is well suited to growth-enhancing functions, at present (being in its infancy) it lacks a comprehensive set of operational institutions and instruments as compared to conventional systems. He suggests some areas in which further research and innovation are required. These include working capital needs, housing finance and incentive-compatible profit-sharing finance, something which is generally conceived by Muslim scholars to be most growth enhancing.

Commenting on the contribution of Ahmed, Dar points out that working capital financing should not pose a significant problem to Islamic banks if they increase their investment portfolio in favour of equity financing. In fact, in an equity-based relationship between a bank and a business, working capital financing may not arise as a problem at all. He proves his point through a numerical example. However, no one will disagree with Ahmed's view that in order to have a more meaningful contribution to growth, the Islamic financial system has to develop institutions and instruments that serve the current and future financial needs of various segments of society.

Dar also reminds us that Muslims perceive Islamic banking and finance as a social enterprise and expect it to play a socially responsible role in the development process. Hence there is a need to develop a model of Islamic banking that combines the efficiency of modern banking with the passion of charity to provide financing for development. He points to the fact that, in Islamic history, institutions such as *waqf* and *zakāh* have played an important role in the development process. These institutions can perform a financial institutional function if properly remodelled. He then presents a model of Islamic banking that combines modern banking practices with the institutions of *waqf* and *zakāh*.

The efficiency of the financial system is an important determinant of its contribution to overall growth as well as the soundness of the economic system. Over the last two decades, many financial systems have experienced severe currency and banking crises. Such crises occurred in the US banking sector in 1985–92, Mexico in 1994–95, and Asia in 1997–98 (Mishkin, 2001). One of the major features of these crises was the lack of efficiency in these systems, as well as the lack of adequate regulations to enhance efficiency. For example, it is believed that among the reasons for the Asian crisis was the severity of the moral hazard problem. Banks had been provided with implicit guarantees, which distorted incentives towards making risky loans. These types of loans, which in the case of East Asia were typically loans made to the real estate sector, created a boom in asset prices. When the asset market crashed, many banks faced insolvency problems because borrowers were unable to repay their loans. It is important that there should be studies evaluating financial systems from an efficiency perspective to judge the health of the financial system and its suitability to finance productive investment. Abdul Majid, Nor and Said (Chapter 5) do that for the case of Malaysia and provide a comparative analysis of the efficiency of Islamic and conventional banks. Using the stochastic frontier cost function approach, they have calculated efficiency scores for some conventional and Islamic banks to determine their relative positions on the efficiency ladder. Their results show that Islamic banks are at least equally efficient when compared to conventional banks despite the fact that the opportunity set available to the managers of Islamic banks is smaller in the sense that conventional banks can adopt any business strategy available to Islamic banks, but not vice versa.

Hussain and Marafi (Chapter 8) look at another aspect of efficiency of Islamic finance. In a heterogeneous banking environment, as in Kuwait where Islamic finance co-exists with conventional finance, co-financing of projects is to be expected; therefore, they evaluate the cost-effectiveness of Islamic finance when combined with conventional finance. They analyse a deal, structured for Equate Petrochemical Company, Kuwait, which was co-financed by Islamic and conventional financial institutions. The study compares aspects of Islamic project finance with conventional banking practices, examines the appropriateness of Islamic financing for industrial projects, and questions whether Islamic finance combined with conventional finance would reduce the weighted average cost of capital of a project. Their empirical results failed to find any benefits of combining Islamic with conventional finance. They then try to identify possible deterrents and stimulants for the development of the Islamic financial system to enhance its contribution to growth.

They feel that the co-existence of Islamic and conventional finance is useful and could generate more competition and thus bring about more efficient allocation of resources. Co-financing could also increase the use of profit-sharing modes, such as *mushārakah*, which are considered to be more growth enhancing. Since *mushārakah* is a rather risky proposition, a substantial contribution by a conventional financier would act as a vote of confidence for the project and would encourage Islamic financiers to enter into a co-financed deal based on *mushārakah*.

Commenting on the study, Saadallah argues that co-existence of the two financial systems in the same country or region may facilitate the structuring of co-financed deals. However, it is neither a sufficient condition for co-financing nor a necessary condition for the survival of the Islamic financial system. A priori, the two systems may co-exist and yet function independent of each other. The supposedly positive effect on competitiveness and efficiency is related to the distribution of market power in the banking industry rather than to its heterogeneous nature. A fully and exclusively Islamic banking industry may theoretically reach a high level of competitiveness if it is formed of a large number of Islamic financial institutions, each having a moderate market share. The argument that the survival of the Islamic financial system is conditional on the heterogeneity of the industry is also unacceptable. Being prohibited, *ribā* could not be a necessary and long-lasting component of an Islamic financial system. Co-existence may be accommodated as a transitory arrangement but, ultimately, an Islamic system completely purified from *ribā* should be able to survive on its own.

Another aspect of the health of a financial system is the extent to which macroeconomic variables can be controlled by policy variables. In the monetary policy sphere, the reliability of M1 (narrow monetary base) and M2 (broad money) in controlling and predicting changes in macroeconomic aggregates is considered important to ensure stability of the monetary system. The study by Eslamloueyan and Heidari (Chapter 7) is an attempt to see if the move towards a fully Islamized financial system puts any constraints on monetary controllability. Using an Autoregressive Distributed Lag (ARDL) approach, they estimate two models to investigate the link between the monetary policy and monetary aggregate/economic goals in Iran after implementing the non-interest banking system there. The models have been estimated for the narrow and broad definitions of money. The results show that the new banking system adopted in 1984 has not reduced the impact of money base growth on the growth rate of M1. More specifically, the estimation results of the M1 controllability model show that the non-interest form of banking adopted in Iran has not decreased the slope of money base growth. It means that M1 has not become less controllable in the new banking system. Rather, the results indicate that there is a significant positive shift in the intercept of the controllability model after the adoption of the interest-free banking system. In that sense, M1 has become even more controllable in the new banking arrangement. When M2 is used for policy purpose, the results of the estimated model show that the degree of controllability of M2 has not changed after the implementation of the new monetary arrangement. With respect to reliability, their results show that the introduction of the non-interest banking system has not resulted in any loss of reliability in predicting economic aggregates through monetary variables.

Hallaq (Chapter 9) presents an interesting case study on the contribution that a single Islamic bank, the Jordan Islamic Bank, has made to the Jordanian economy. He has used a Two-Stage Ordinary Least Square model to capture the direct and indirect effects for the Jordan Islamic Bank (JIB) of the growth of real per capita income (as a proxy for the rate of economic growth) during 1980–2000. The statistical results showed that both changes in total investment and net transfers from abroad proved to have a positive and significant impact on the change in real per capita income. The total credit provided by conventional banks proved to be insignificant, even though it shows a positive coefficient. This can be explained by the fact that a large portion of such credits goes to the service sector. Thus their direct effect on real per capita income was small and insignificant. Coming to the specific impact of the change in the JIB financing and investment as a percentage of total credit by conventional commercial banks on the investment level, it was found to be positive but insignificant. This is expected since most of the JIB financial operations are short or medium term, so that the bank has to hold high levels of cash to meet any contingency in an emergency situation. The indirect effect of total financing and investment by JIB as a percentage of total credit was relatively small (0.048), compared to that by conventional banks (0.50). However, this contribution made by a single Islamic bank should be looked at as a good start given the fact that it has only 20 years' experience compared to the much greater experience of conventional banks.

Commenting on Hallaq's study, Bamakhramah rightly points out that it is not enough to conclude that Islamic banks promote economic growth; it is more important to identify which mode or modes of financing contribute most to growth. Islamic banks differ from conventional banks in that their spectrum of financing is more varied. Their investments are more diversified in terms of maturity, liquidity and risk, ranging from the relatively short-term, more liquid and less risky mode of *murābaḥah* to the longer-term, less liquid and more risky mode of equity (or direct *mushārakah*) financing. Each mode differs in its effect on the capital accumulation capability and resource utilization efficiency of the banks, and thus the economic growth of the relevant country also varies. The effect of a bank's activities on economic growth will therefore depend on which modes of finance and investment the bank undertakes most and how much each one of these modes contributes to economic growth.

Broadly speaking, Islamic financial transactions are of two kinds: one is based on a fixed charge on capital, and the other is based on profit-sharing. At present, the modes of financing being used by most Islamic banks are dominated by fixed-return modes such as *murābaḥah* and leasing. Even though such modes are clearly distinguishable from interest-based modes since transactions with these modes are always done through real commodities, they do not yield the full benefits in terms of promoting growth with equity which is expected of an Islamic financial system. Specialists in Islamic financial theory had counted on Islamic banks providing a significant amount of profit-sharing finance. This would have had economic effects similar to direct investment and would have produced a strong economic development impact. However, due to some practical difficulties (see Iqbal, Ahmad and Khan, 1998, pp. 49–52), profit-sharing finance has remained negligible in the operations of Islamic banks.

Financing modes such as *murābaḥah* are serving a useful purpose: they provide investors with high liquidity at low risk. Unfortunately, until a proper institutional set-up is built and the necessary products, including those for managing risk, are developed, it may not be possible for Islamic banks to increase drastically the use of risky modes. However, Islamic banks can be encouraged to provide more profit-sharing finance, if arrangements are made to reduce the costs involved by appropriate institutional arrangements as well as financial engineering consistent with the preferences of fund users. The benefits of direct investment in terms of economic development may not always be fully reflected in the rate of return. They are felt by society as a whole. It may, therefore, pay to support the involvement of Islamic banks in profit-sharing finance. Until such arrangements are made, banks will not increase their risk exposure to any large extent. In the short run, therefore, the emphasis should move to a greater reliance by businesses on equity and smaller reliance on credit. For this purpose attempts should be made to increase the number of equity institutions such as mutual funds, unit trusts, and equities (Iqbal, 2001, pp. 39–40).

Conclusion

While the theoretical development and actual practice of hundreds of Islamic financial institutions under different regimes around the globe has proved the viability of the Islamic banking model, the contributions in this volume show that they are far from yielding their full potential. This is due to the fact that they still face a number of unfavourable factors and do not have the supporting institutional set-up in place. The commercial, banking and company laws in most Islamic countries are fashioned on the Western pattern. Those laws contain provisions that narrow the scope of activities of Islamic banking within conventional limits. Muslim countries, which have some Islamic banking presence, have either passed new laws permitting Islamic banking or have modified existing commercial banking laws to make room for Islamic banking, but the number of such countries is very small. In a large number of Muslim countries, neither of these two situations exists. Existing banking laws in most Muslim countries appear to be in conflict with the precepts of Islamic banking. For instance, *murābaḥah* has emerged as a legitimate and successful technique of Islamic banking, but in many countries financial intermediaries are forbidden to undertake direct trade. Moreover, while parties can structure their agreements according to an Islamic contract, the enforcement of those agreements in courts may require extra efforts and costs. Those conditions, among others, mean that special laws for the introduction and practice of Islamic banking need to be put in place.

The monetary authorities in most developing countries have so far not followed any consistent policy towards non-banking financial institutions, of which interest-free financial institutions are a part. In recent years, there has been tremendous expansion in the number and size of business of these institutions, which calls for modernization of regulation. The central banks usually control the non-banking financial institutions in a stringent manner. The equity and liquidity norms of these institutions in most countries appear to be too tight. The lack of an appropriately modified supervisory framework is hindering the growth of the Islamic financial industry and deserves serious attention.

In most countries Islamic banks are put under the supervision of the central bank of the country and are given the same treatment as is given to conventional commercial banks. Some countries issue special Islamic Banking Acts to govern the operations of specific Islamic banks and their relationship with the central bank.[4] Some others issue laws that set general rules for the operations of Islamic banks side-by-side with conventional banks.[5] Central banks subject Islamic banks to the same controls, conditions and regulations that they apply to the interest-based banks. However, there are certain factors which mean that Islamic banks should be treated on a different footing. Some of these factors are listed below:

1 Islamic banks, like all other commercial banks, are required to keep some of their deposits with central banks. Central banks usually pay interest on those deposits which Islamic banks cannot accept. An alternative is needed to ensure that Islamic banks get a fair return on their deposits with the central banks.
2 Central banks function as lenders of last resort to commercial banks, providing loans at times of liquidity crunch. Although most Islamic banks function under the supervision of central bank, they cannot legitimately benefit from such a facility because such funds are usually provided on the basis of interest. It is understandable that such assistance cannot be free of cost. However, there is a need to devise and implement an interest-free framework for such assistance. One possibility is using a profit-sharing mechanism whereby profit can be calculated on 'daily-product' basis.[6] Another suggestion is to build a 'common pool' for Islamic banks under the supervision of central banks to provide relief to one another in case of liquidity problems on cooperative basis.[7]
3 Legal reserves imposed on deposits with conventional banks are meant to meet possible withdrawals, whose rates vary between demand, saving and time deposits. This may apply to the same extent only in case of Islamic banks' demand deposits. However, the *muḍārabah* deposits are like bank equity. Therefore, Islamic banks should not be required to maintain reserves against them just as equity capital is not subject to those reserves.[8]
4 In countries where the central bank conducts open-market operations, Islamic banks are not able to participate in these operations because of the interest-based nature of the securities bought and sold. Thus Islamic banks are constrained by the fact that financial assets which could be liquidated quickly are not available to them. This introduces some rigidity into the asset structure of Islamic banks.
5 Lack of understanding of the correct nature of Islamic financing techniques may also be partially responsible for rather inappropriate policies of the central banks towards Islamic banks. This is particularly true of *mushārakah* and *muḍārabah*. In debt financing, granting a loan by a bank

is a one-off activity, no matter what the size of the loan. But *mushārakah* and *muḍārabah* are on-going activities and the participation of an Islamic bank in these activities continues as long as the project financed is in operation. This may have important implications for reporting as well as control and regulation of Islamic banks by the central banks.

It would be a fair conclusion to say that Islamic banking adds a healthy dimension to the international financial scene. If given a level playing ground, it could play a more effective role in the fulfillment of socio-economic goals of Muslim countries and the international community.

Notes

1. Friedman (1969).
2. Wilson (1979) and Cole and Kocherlakota (1998).
3. See for example, Mirakhor (1997).
4. This was done in the cases of establishment of Islamic banks in Jordan and Egypt.
5. As in Malaysia, Turkey and the United Arab Emirates.
6. Council of Islamic Ideology (1980).
7. Chapra (1985).
8. For further arguments in favour of this proposal, see Chapra (1985), p. 161.

References

Chapra, M. Umer (1985), *Towards a Just Monetary System*, Leicester: The Islamic Foundation.

Cole, Harold L. and Narayana Kocherlakota (1998), 'Zero Nominal Interest Rates: Why they're good and how to get them', *Federal Reserve Bank of Minneapolis Quarterly Review* (Spring), 22, 2–10.

Council of Islamic Ideology (1980), *Report of the Council of Islamic Ideology on the Elimination of Interest from the Economy*, Islamabad: Council of Islamic Ideology.

Friedman, Milton (1969), 'The Optimum Quantity of Money', in *The Optimum Quantity of Money and Other Essays*, Chicago, IL: Aldine, pp. 1–50.

Iqbal, Munawar (ed.) (2001), *Islamic Banking and Finance: Current Developments in Theory and Practice*, Leicester: The Islamic Foundation.

Iqbal, Munawar, Ausaf Ahmad and Tariqullah Khan (1998), *Challenges Facing Islamic Banking*, Occasional Paper No. 2, Jeddah: Islamic Research and Training Institute, Islamic Development Bank.

Mirakhor, Abbas (1997), 'Progress and Challenges of Islamic Banking', *Review of Islamic Economics*, 4 (2), 1–11.

Mishkin, Frederic S. (2001) 'Financial Policies and the Prevention of Financial Crises in Emerging Market Countries', *NBER Working Paper* No. 8397 and also in Martin Feldstein (ed.), *Economic and Financial Crises in Emerging Market Countries*, Chicago, IL: University of Chicago Press.

Wilson, Charles (1979), 'An Infinite Horizon Model with Money', in Jerry R. Green and José Alexandre Scheinkman (eds), *General Equilibrium, Growth, and Trade*, New York: Academic Press, 81–104.

2

Islamic Finance and Development

Mabid Ali Al-Jarhi

Financial development and growth

Development economics is supposed to show us why some countries are *developed* while others are *developing*, and then how the latter can catch up with the former. 'Financial development' is an important component of the overall development strategy. A theory of financial development can be based on the costs associated with the provision of external finance,[1] which are related to information asymmetries between borrowers and lenders. Firms with limited financial resources can obtain higher returns through their access to financial intermediaries. Their superior performance provides incentives to more firms to access external finance, as their net worth rises relative to debt. Growth in the finance industry reduces the costs of financial intermediation and raises the overall return on investment.

A recent investigation of the relationship between finance and development asserts that qualitative developments in the banking sector are significantly and positively related to economic growth, confirming common beliefs.[2] However, a rise in the amount of credit by itself has no bearing on economic growth. An Islamic economist would point out that bank credit under the commercial banking regime is used only rarely to finance directly developmental activities. In other words, one may argue that it is the quality, not the quantity, of credit that counts.

Other economists stress the positive correlation between real economic development and stock market activity.[3] They point to the loss of resources due to informational frictions in the capital market as a major obstacle to growth.[4] They stress the possibility of *underdevelopment traps* in which real and financial sectors display little co-evolution.

Contrary to the popular belief that debt and equity represent alternative sources of corporate finance, recent evidence suggests that they act more as complements to each other.[5] The cost of pure debt and pure equity finance rises with the level of development. At some point, lenders find it optimal to complement the use of debt with the use of equity as a double-edged strategy for dealing with a double (rather than single) moral hazard problem.[6] Several contributions have confirmed the relationship between financial market development and growth,[7] in line with the theory. A study estimates that equity liberalization leads to an increase in annual real economic growth by 1 per cent over a period of five years.[8]

Some economists examine the direction of causality between financial development and economic growth.[9] Several conclusions come out of such investigation. First, financial development generally leads to economic growth. Second, Granger causality from financial development to economic growth (and vice versa) exists. Third, financial deepening contributes to economic growth more in developing countries than in industrial countries. Fourth, the longer the sampling interval, the larger is the effect of financial development on economic growth. Fifth, financial deepening propels economic growth through faster capital accumulation and productivity growth. Furthermore, empirical evidence points towards the existence of an independent effect exerted by bank efficiency on real growth, which corroborates the presence of a Schumpeterian channel, emphasizing the allocative function of banks.[10]

There are four views regarding the relationship between the financial structure and economic growth: the intermediary-based view, the market-based view, the financial services view, and the law and finance view.[11] The first two views suggest that financial markets and intermediaries are substitutes, while the last two suggest that they are complements.

The *intermediary-based* view emphasizes the importance of intermediaries in project identification, resource mobilization, monitoring firms and managing risks. Intermediary-based systems, especially in countries at an early stage of development, are more effective in fostering growth than market-based financial systems. In this respect, universal banking, which is very close to Islamic banking, appears to be especially effective in development finance. The *market-based* view stresses the role of markets in diversifying and managing risks while arguing that financial intermediaries can extract information rents from firms. Mature and relatively safe firms depend mostly on market (and specifically bond) financing.[12] Financing through financial markets is suitable for industries faced with continuous technological advances.[13] The *financial services* view suggests that financial intermediaries may provide services complementary to those provided by markets. It emphasizes the importance of the overall level and quality of financial services and the necessary environment for better-functioning intermediaries and markets.[14] The *law and finance* view is, in fact, an extension of the financial services view.[15] It emphasizes the legal environment and the enforcement of contracts. It claims that the legal system plays a crucial role in determining the growth-stimulating nature of financial services. Obviously, no financial intermediary, market or instrument can exist without an appropriate legal framework. This view reinforces this idea which is based on common sense. Many economists have empirically investigated these views,[16] and some have found support for one or more of them.[17] It appears to be still too early to give a vote of confidence to one view, and more research is needed on all aspects of the issue of finance and development.

The nature of Islamic finance

Turning to Islamic finance, let us start by describing what is meant by an Islamic financial institution. An Islamic bank, like other banks and financial institutions, provides fund owners as well as fund users with profitable opportunities. It provides *owners of funds* with opportunities to place their financial resources profitably; it also provides finance to enterprises either through sharing directly in the net results of their activities or through financing their purchases/leases of assets, goods, and services.

Islamic banks are supposed to hold equity in corporations and sit on their boards of directors. They use the information obtained from their vantage point to reduce risk from information asymmetry and to fine-tune their finance directed to the same corporations. In addition, they trade in goods and services, provide insurance, and operate in financial markets. In other words, they operate like *universal* rather than commercial banks.

Islamic non-banking financial institutions collect funds without taking deposits and use Islamic modes of financing to provide finance to entrepreneurs. They mobilize funds through selling stocks, mutual shares, and a variety of instruments (*ṣukūk*) with a wide choice of risk-sharing and maturities. They have even greater flexibility to deal with equity and partnership than ordinary commercial banks, as they are not encumbered with guaranteed demand deposits. The advantages of financing working capital requirements for enterprises in which they hold equity can therefore be more pronounced than in universal banking.

Islamic modes of finance can be grouped into three main categories: (i) equity and profit sharing, (ii) credit purchase, and (iii) leasing. Equity finance entails providing funds to enterprises in return for a share in their prospective net returns as well as in management. Meanwhile, profit-sharing finance implies providing finance for shorter periods with and without sharing in management.

Credit purchase provides goods and services for spot delivery in return for a non-negotiable debt instrument that promises payment of their value plus a *mark-up* at a specified future date. An extension is granted in case of temporary insolvency at no cost to borrowers. Delinquent debtors can be subjected to penalty. Alternatively, the financing institution can pay the value of the goods and services spot and get them delivered at some specified time in the future. In this case, the debt instrument would be written in terms of goods and services.

Leasing (operational lease[18]) finance implies that the financing institution purchases a durable asset and leases it to a customer in return for regular payments, reflecting the cost of holding and maintaining the asset which is transferred to the possession of the finance recipients.

The advantages of Islamic finance

Benefiting from several contributions in the Islamic finance literature, one can list several advantages of Islamic finance.[19] The most important among these are described below.

Islamic finance is more efficient

The first is that Islamic finance is more efficient at the macroeconomic level, as it avoids using interest-based lending. Monetary economists have established that a zero nominal interest rate is a necessary condition for the optimal allocation of resources (Friedman, 1969). The reason is simple. Adding one marginal unit of real balances costs the community no real resources. Therefore, imposing a positive price on the use of money would lead traders to economize on the use of money, in their efforts to minimize their transaction costs. They would therefore use some real resources instead of money. However, when the rate of interest is zero, traders will have no incentive to substitute real resources for money. More real resources can therefore be directed to consumption and investment. In general equilibrium models, a zero interest rate is both necessary and sufficient for allocative efficiency (Wilson, 1979; Cole and Kocherlakota, 1998).[20]

Conventional economics, however, does not propose an institutional restructuring to avoid trading present against future money, but suggests a policy of steady deflation instead (Ireland, 2000). Islamic finance, meanwhile, does propose an institutional change to replace the interest-based monetary system. The rate of interest is replaced by the rate of profit on equity and profit-sharing finance, by mark-ups on credit-purchase finance and by rental rates on leasing finance. While the time-value of money is maintained, there is no need to handle the complicated questions of how to bring the rate of interest down to zero in order to reach the optimal allocation of resources. In other words, Islamic finance is a short-cut to efficiency in the financial sector.

Islamic finance makes the economic system more stable

With both assets and liabilities being subject to amounts of risk-sharing sufficiently balanced to protect the banks from runs on funds, Islamic finance makes the banking system as a whole more stable. Conventional banks carry liabilities, including demand, time and saving deposits, which they fully guarantee. Their assets, however, are mainly risky debt. Default on the asset side of a bank, if it happens in significant proportions, would imply inability to meet the bank's obligations on the liability side. Such default can be expected at times of crises, whether it be bank-specific or macroeconomic in nature.

An Islamic bank guarantees only demand deposits. Meanwhile, investment deposits are placed on a profit-and-loss sharing basis. When such a bank faces macroeconomic or bank-specific crises, investment depositors automatically share the risk. The bank is less likely to fall and bank runs are less probable. It can therefore be said that an Islamic banking system is relatively more stable when compared to conventional banking (Khan, 1986).

In conventional finance, present money is traded against future money in debt or bond markets, which are highly integrated at both the national and international level. Bond markets provide an easy and automatic mechanism through which short-term funds flow at will from one country to another. Much of those flows follows factors that are only nebulously related to economic fundamentals, threatening national economies with instability and *contagion*. The experiences of the Southeast Asian economies and others have motivated some economists to propose placing restrictions on capital movements.

In contrast, debt is created in Islamic finance through selling goods and services on credit. The resulting debt instruments are not readily tradable. We can visualize the existence of a credit market for each commodity and service in which the demand and supply to buy it on credit determines a mark-up rate. Such credit markets would be fully segmented; there is no room for sudden and mass movements of funds. Possibilities of instability and contagion would therefore be remote and the need to choke capital movements through imposing restrictions would lose its justification.

Islamic finance controls excessive credit creation and speculation

It has been noted above that Islamic finance never provides present money in return for future money. All Islamic modes of finance involve money on the one hand and goods and/or services on the other. Monetary flows through Islamic financial modes would have to be tied directly to commodity flows. In other words, Islamic finance removes the dichotomy between financial and real activities. Obviously, this leaves little room for excessive credit expansion, as the finance provided by financial institutions to business units is automatically earmarked for specific uses.

Speculative activities related to interest rate expectations would no longer be a factor. Changes in spending would automatically be reflected in changes in the demand and supply of goods and services, causing the quantities of output produced to respond more quickly to market forces. In other words, markets would be more likely to operate efficiently and smoothly. It is therefore interesting to note that Islamic finance, though non-conventional, supports market forces and mechanisms more than does conventional finance.

Islamic finance reduces moral hazard and adverse selection problems

Since Islamic banks operate as universal banks, they are likely to be more efficient in monitoring and surveillance, thereby reducing the risks of adverse selection and moral hazard (Calomiris, 2000). A bank would be exposed to *adverse selection* when it fails to choose the finance applicants who are most likely to perform. This can be avoided by careful screening of finance applicants. When a bank provides equity and debt finance simultaneously, it will have more access to information than when only debt finance is provided, rendering screening more effective and adverse selection less probable.

Reducing the possibilities of moral hazard requires monitoring the firm that obtains finance (Aoki, 1994). Equity finance provides the bank with access to the information necessary to practise monitoring, giving universal banks an extra edge in monitoring their borrowers (Dewenter and Hess, 1997).

Equity finance also reduces the firm's incentives to substitute riskier for safer assets. Meanwhile, debt finance would reduce the firm's incentives to hide its profits. Furthermore, when the firm faces problems, the bank, as an equity holder, will assist in order to protect its investment.

In summary, banking theory indicates that universal banking would be exposed to lower levels of moral hazard and adverse selection. In addition, by sitting on the firms' boards of directors, banks could influence corporate governance in the whole productive sector, leading to improvements in economic performance.

Empirically, it has been found that if banks use a combination of debt and equity finance, this seems to carry several advantages to both banks and firms, confirming the theoretical findings. Banking theory would indicate that banks would be relatively more exposed to adverse selection during economic upturns and to moral hazard during downturns. Applied research has found that universal banks face lower risks than commercial banks during both upturns and downturns. In addition, the risk differential between universal and commercial banks gets wider and more significant during downturns (Dewenter and Hess, 1998).[21]

Islamic finance is more growth-promoting

As they operate like universal banks, Islamic banks and financial institutions can reduce the cost of industrialization and increase the profitability of firms. Several economists believe that universal banking can be credited in part for industrial development and economic growth in Germany and

Japan, thanks to economies of scope and greater efficiency that allowed more finance at lower costs, thereby promoting industrial investment.[22] In particular, German banks have been maintaining close, long-term relationships with industrial firms, which influenced banks' attitudes towards multi-period optimization (Fohlin, 1998).

Da Rin and Hellmann (2002) develop a new theory of the role of banks in promoting industrialization in emerging economies, starting from a 'big push' model where there are two Pareto-rankable equilibriums. A bank can induce the economy to move from low to high equilibrium by mobilizing a 'critical mass' of firms. Banks will only play a catalytic role if they are sufficiently large to invest in a critical mass of firms and have enough market power to recoup their costs. The costs of mobilizing the critical mass are reduced if banks are allowed to own equity through which they can have a share in the value they create. This means that universal banks will find it easier to promote investments in new industries.

In order to act as a catalyst, an investor needs to be large enough to mobilize a critical mass of entrepreneurs, as well as possess enough market power to make profits from the other entrepreneurs who start new firms, so as to recoup the cost of coordination. When the leader finances entrepreneurs with equity, he participates in the profits obtained in the emerging market, thereby internalizing partially the externality that is at the root of the coordination problem. This reduces the cost of subsidizing entrepreneurs in the critical mass and makes coordination easier. The decrease in the coordination cost also means that the competitive fringe can be larger.

Given that Islamic banks operate according to the rules of universal rather than commercial banking, we can ask which system gives better support to economic development. In this regard, we can intuitively conclude that the practice of universal banking by Islamic banks puts their financing activities right at the heart of the development process. Bankers in this case become both partners in, and financiers of, entrepreneurial efforts to develop the economy. Empirical findings seem to confirm such an intuition.

Calomiris (2000), through his study of pre-First World War Germany, has found that universal banking served to reduce the cost of financing industrialization in Germany relative to the corresponding levels in other countries where commercial banking was prevalent. He also found that the financial sector reached a higher level of allocative efficiency in the former than in the latter. We can therefore safely conclude that banks operating as universal banks give better support to development efforts.

It is widely accepted that economic development requires mobilization of vast financial resources, both internally and externally. Any financial resources left hoarded would imply unrealized potential for economic development. As Islamic teachings emphatically prohibit trading present for future money at a rate of interest, many Muslims hold their funds outside the banking and financial sector, thereby missing an opportunity to apply those funds to the development process. Islamic finance opens the door to the effective use of much-needed financial resources within many Islamic countries that would be otherwise kept idle. In addition, it provides Muslims with a way through which they can participate in the development process without sacrificing their religious beliefs. Muslim minorities in other countries, whose banking systems do not provide Islamic financial products, suffer from *cultural exclusion*. Some of those Muslims may have to keep their savings outside the financial system, thereby contributing to idle financial resources in their countries.

Islamic finance is more 'inclusive' and widens risk-sharing

The Islamic monetary system contributes to the integrity of the whole economic system, so that its parts are closely intertwined with each other. Conventional finance can be likened to a *spectator's game* where a few skilled players stay in the arena while a big crowd watches from outside. Islamic finance, meanwhile, is similar to *participatory sports*, where everyone is playing and no one is concerned with merely watching. In addition, there is a moral side to Islamic finance that seems to be in the back of everyone's mind.

Risk is known to be one of the most important considerations in making investment. Those who finance investment share a good part of the risks involved with those who carry out actual investment activities. Conventional finance leaves risk to be borne by specialists. Banks and financial institutions provide investors with loans guaranteed by collateral. In this fashion, they keep themselves apart from certain kinds of risk, such as those attached to production, marketing and distribution, and limit their exposure to risk to collateral only.

Islamic finance allows savers who deposit their funds to share with banks the risks associated with choosing the right investment. Banks and financial institutions advancing funds share risk with those receiving finance, including producers, traders, and so on. Islamic finance with *proper corporate governance* allows depositors some influence on banks' investment decisions and allows banks and financial institutions a share in the decision-making process at the firm level by sitting on the boards of directors of firms receiving funds. In this way, risks as well as decision-making are spread over a much larger number and wider variety of concerned people. Risk-sharing is balanced by sharing in decision-making. This allows for wider involvement in economic activities, so that people will eventually feel they are partners rather than spectators.

The benefit of wider involvement goes beyond the mere feeling of partnership. The economic system itself becomes more compact with wider involvement. The real and financial sector, banks and savers, investors and fund owners are all strongly glued to each other. This finally leads to an economic system with a high degree of integrity that can withstand shocks.

Islamic finance is more conducive to poverty alleviation

Islamic finance provides more equity. Islamic financial institutions, if given the right tools, can contribute to the efforts taken by the whole society to reduce poverty. Islam prescribes a tax-subsidy approach to reducing poverty. A levy called *zakāh* is paid by the wealthy (those whose wealth exceeds a certain minimum level) in proportion to their property. *Zakāh* proceeds are earmarked for certain uses, including income and wealth maintenance for the poor. *Income maintenance* is provided within narrow limits to those incapable of work, and *wealth maintenance* is provided to the rest of the poor. The latter policy entails giving the poor productive assets, which they can use to produce goods and services and sell them for profit. Such redistribution is mostly directed towards making the poor more productive, which in turn contributes to economic development. Income maintenance would involve regular (monthly) payments to the needy. Wealth maintenance, meanwhile, involves transferring to the poor a combination of productive resources which would be capable of generating sufficient income to maintain at least one household. Wealth maintenance can be implemented through the establishment of micro enterprises that would be owned and operated by the poor. The experience of Islamic banking and financial institutions in project financing should come in handy in eradicating poverty and increasing equity through proper use of *zakāh* proceeds.

Conventional lending gives utmost attention to the ability to repay loans. To ascertain such ability, it relies overwhelmingly on the provision of collateral and guarantees. In this framework, the rich would have most access to finance. In contrast, Islamic finance providing funds on equity or profit-sharing basis would be more concerned about profitability and rate of return and less concerned about collateral. Those who are not wealthy, but who have worthy investment projects, would have a better chance of obtaining finance.

Islamic finance provides more sustainability to the financial industry

Conventional debt has certain characteristics that could place debtors in difficulties if circumstances do not allow them to repay in time. Interest is compounded and debtors are often subjected to penalty rates of interest, which are higher than regular rates. Interest-based financing lacks a great deal of sustainability. Creditors have to stop every few years to give debtors relief in terms of rescheduling and forgiveness. Sometimes this also includes floating low-quality debt at a lower market value and swapping it with equity.

Debt created through Islamic finance has characteristics with which debt crises are less likely to occur. In particular the total value of debt, which includes the spot value of commodities purchased on credit as well as an implicit mark-up, is set from the very beginning. The total value of debt can be repaid in instalments, without an increase in its total value, as there is no compounded interest to pay on the outstanding balance. When debtors face unavoidable circumstances that would make them temporarily insolvent, they are often granted grace periods with no penalty fees. Therefore, we can conclude that Islamic finance is sustainable and less liable in itself to cause undue hardship to debtors.

Quite often, conventional debt cannot be repaid because it was not used for its prescribed purpose. Conventional loans are usually offered without ways or mechanisms to assure their use for certain purposes.[23] In contrast, Islamic debt is created through acquiring goods and services on credit. In other words, the loan is used from the very beginning for its prescribed purpose. Default resulting from improper use of borrowed funds would therefore be less likely. Since Islamic finance is asset-based (i.e., it is used to acquire real assets) it is much less likely to lead to debt crises. Such asset-based finance directly contributes to the ability of the economy to meet its internal and external financial obligations.

Notes

1. Khan (1999).
2. Koivu (2002).
3. Blackburn, Bose and Capasso (2001); Atje and Jovanovic (1993); Demirgüç-Kunt and Levine (1996a, 1996b); Levine and Zervos (1996, 1998).
4. McKinnon (1973) and Shaw (1973).
5. Demirgüç-Kunt and Levine (1996a, 1996b); Demirgüç-Kunt and Maksimovic (1996).
6. An increase in the size of the stock market is typically associated with an increase in the volume of debt in many economies. Such evidence has been regarded as a puzzle. Boyd and Smith (1996, 1998) resolve the puzzle by postulating an increase in the cost of pure debt finance as an economy develops. Eventually, equity emerges as a complementary means of raising funds.
7. See Cameron (1967), King and Levine (1993), Demirgüç-Kunt and Maksimovic (2001), Rajan and Zingales (1998), Bekaert, Harvey and Lundblad (2000), and Rousseau and Wachtel (1998).
8. Bekaert, Harvey and Lundblad (2001).
9. Calderón, César and Lin Liu (2002).
10. Fisman and Love (2002).
11. Dolar and Meh (2002).
12. Petersen and Rajan (1994); Bolton and Freixas (2000).
13. Allen and Gale (1999, 2000).
14. Levine (1997, 2002).
15. La Porta *et al.* (1997, 1998).
16. Goldsmith (1969), Levine (2002).
17. Demirgüç-Kunt and Levine (2001).
18. This is called 'operational lease', as opposed to 'financial lease'. In the former, the lessor bears all risk attached to the asset until its title is transferred to the lessee, while in the latter the lessee assumes all risks from the very beginning.
19. Jarhi al- and Iqbal (2001).

20. Though these theoretical results are dependent on some simplifying assumptions, they are robust in a variety of models (Correia and Teles, 1997). They imply that the long-forgotten Christian and Jewish teachings, as well as those of Islam and Hinduism, which prohibit the charge of interest on loans are not an aberration. It is amazing to see such religious teaching stay valid after so many centuries.
21. There are several reservations and doubts expressed by some economists regarding the advantages of universal as compared to commercial banking. However, when placed under scrutiny, they are found to be generally groundless (Jarhi al-, 2003).
22. For a theoretical analysis of the relationship between finance and growth, see Greenwood and Smith (1997).
23. In cases where a loan is earmarked for the purchase of commodities, a conventional bank would find it cheaper to enforce earmarking through a sale-finance contract.

References

Allen, F. and D. Gale (1999), 'Diversity of Opinion and Financing of New Technologies', *Journal of Financial Intermediation*, 8, 68–89.

Allen, F. and D. Gale (2000), *Comparing Financial Systems*, Cambridge, MA: MIT Press.

Aoki, Masahiko (1994), 'Monitoring Characteristics of the Main Banking System: An Analytical and Developmental View', in M. Aoki and H. Patrick (eds), *Japanese Main Bank System*, New York: the Oxford University Press.

Atje, R. and B. Jovanovic (1993), 'Stock Markets and Development', *European Economic Review*, 37, 632–40.

Bekaert, G., C. Harvey and C. Lundblad (2000), 'Emerging Equity Markets and Economic Development', *Working Paper No. 7763*, Cambridge, MA: National Bureau of Economic Research.

Bekaert, Geert, Campbell R. Harvey and Christian Lundblad (2001), 'Does Financial Liberalization Spur Growth?', *Working Paper No. 8245*, Cambridge, MA: National Bureau of Economic Research. Also available at http://www.nber.org/papers/W8245.

Blackburn, Keith, Niloy Bose and Salvatore Capasso (2001), 'Financial Development, Financing Choice and Economic Growth', *Discussion Paper Series, Number 007*, Manchester: Centre for Growth and Business Cycle Research, School of Economic Studies, University of Manchester. Also available at http://www.ses.man.ac.uk/cgbcr/discussi.htm.

Bolton, P. and X. Freixas (2000), 'Equity, Bonds, and Bank Debt: Capital Structure and Financial Market Equilibrium under Asymmetric Information', *Journal of Political Economy*, 1,082, 324–51.

Boyd, J. H. and B. D. Smith (1996), 'The Co-Evolution of Real and Financial Sectors in the Growth Process', *World Bank Economic Review*, 10, 371–96.

Boyd, J. H. and B. D. Smith (1998), 'The Evolution of Debt and Equity Markets in Economic Development', *Economic Theory*, 12, 519–60.

Calderón, César and Lin Liu (2002), 'The Direction of Causality between Financial Development and Economic Growth', *Working Paper Number 184*, Santiago: Central Bank of Chile.

Calomiris, Charles W. (2000), 'Universal Banking and the Financing of Industrial Development', in Gerard Caprio, Jr and Dimitri Vittas (eds), *Reforming Finance: Some Lessons from History*, Cambridge and New York: Cambridge University Press.

Cameron, R. (1967), *Banking in the Early Stages of Industrialization: A Study in Comparative Economic History*, New York: Oxford University Press.

Cole, Harold L. and Narayana Kocherlakota (1998), 'Zero Nominal Interest Rates: Why they're good and how to get them', *Federal Reserve Bank of Minneapolis Quarterly Review*, 22, 2–10.

Correia, Isabel and Pedro Teles (1997), 'The Optimal Inflation Tax', *Discussion Paper No. 123*, Minneapolis: Institute for Empirical Macroeconomics, Federal Reserve Bank of Minneapolis.

Da Rin, Marco and Thomas Hellmann (2002), 'Banks as Catalysts for Industrialization', *Journal of Financial Intermediation*, 11 (4), 366–97.

Demirgüç-Kunt, A. and R. Levine (1996a), 'Stock Market Development and Financial Intermediaries: Stylized Facts', *World Bank Economic Review*, 10, 291–321.

Demirgüç-Kunt, A. and R. Levine (1996b), 'Stock Markets, Corporate Finance and Economic Growth: An Overview', *World Bank Economic Review*, 10, 223–39.

Demirgüç-Kunt, A. and R. Levine (2001), 'Bank-Based and Market-Based Financial Systems: Cross-Country Comparisons', in A Demirgüç-Kunt and Ross Levine (eds), *Financial Structure and Economic Growth: A Cross-Country Comparison of Banks, Markets, and Development*, Cambridge, MA: MIT Press, pp. 81–140.

Demirgüç-Kunt, A. and V. Maksimovic (1996), 'Stock Market Development and Financing Choices of Firms', *World Bank Economic Review*, 10, 341–69.

Dewenter, Kathryn L. and Alan C. Hess (1997), 'Risks and Returns in Relationship and Transactional Banks: Evidence from Banks' Returns in Germany, Japan, the U.K., and the U.S.', *Working Paper Number 97*, Philadelphia, PA: The Wharton Financial Institutions Center.

Dewenter, Kathryn L. and Alan C. Hess (1998), 'An International Comparison of Bank's Equity Returns', *Journal of Money Credit and Banking*, 30 (3) (August, Part 2), 472–92.

Dolar, Veronika and Césaire Meh (2002), 'Financial Structure and Economic Growth: A Non-Technical Survey', *Working Paper Number 2002–24*, Ottawa, Ontario: Bank of Canada.

Fisman, Raymond and Inessa Love (2002), 'Trade Credit, Financial Intermediary Development and Industry Growth', *Working Paper Number 8960*, Cambridge, MA: National Bureau of Economic Research.

Fohlin, Caroline (1998), 'Relationship Banking, Liquidity, and Investment in the German Industrialization', *Journal* of *Finance*, 53 (5), 1737–58.

Friedman, Milton (1969), 'The Optimum Quantity of Money', in *The Optimum Quantity of Money and Other Essays*, Chicago, IL: Aldine, pp. 1–50.

Goldsmith, Raymond W. (1969), *Financial Structure and Development*, New Haven, CT: Yale University Press.

Greenwood, Jeremy and Bruce D. Smith (1997), 'Financial Markets in Development, and the Development of Financial Markets', *Journal of Economic Dynamics and Control*, January, 145–81.

Ireland, Peter N. (2000), *Implementing the Friedman Rule*, Cambridge, MA: National Bureau of Economic Research.

Jarhi al-, Mabid Ali (2003), 'Islamic Finance An Efficient and Equitable Option', http://www.wfdd.org.uk/articles-talks/mabid.pdf.

Jarhi al-, Mabid Ali and Munawar Iqbal (2001), *Islamic Banking: Answers to Some Frequently Asked Questions*, Jeddah: Islamic Research and Training Institute.

Khan, Aubhik (1999), 'Financial Development and Economic Growth', *Working Paper Number 99–11*, Philadelphia, PA: Federal Reserve Bank of Philadelphia.

Khan, Mohsin S. (1986), 'Islamic Interest-Free Banking: A Theoretical Analysis', *IMF Staff Papers*, 33 (1), 1–27.

King, R. G. and R. Levine (1993), 'Finance and Growth: Schumpeter Might be Right', *Quarterly Journal of Economics*, 108 (3), 717–37.

Koivu, Tuuli (2002), 'Do Efficient Banking Sectors Accelerate Economic Growth in Transition Countries?', *BOFIT Discussion Paper Number 14/2002*, Helsinki: Bank of Finland, Institute for Economies in Transition.

La Porta, R., F. Lopez-de-Silanes, A. Schleifer and R. W. Vishny (1997), 'Legal Determinant of External Finance', *Journal of Finance*, 52 (3), 1,131–50.

La Porta, R., F. Lopez-de-Silanes, A. Schleifer and R. W. Vishny (1998), 'Law and Finance', *Journal of Political Economy*, 106 (6), 1, 113–55.

Levine, Ross (1997), 'Financial Development and Economic Growth: Views and Agenda', *Journal of Economic Literature*, 36, 688–726.

Levine, Ross (2002), 'Bank-Based or Market-Based Financial Systems: Which is Better?' *NBER Working Paper No. 9138*, September.

Levine, R. and S. Zervos (1996), 'Stock Market Development and Long-Run Growth', *World Bank Economic Review*, 10, 323–39.

Levine, R. and S. Zervos (1998), 'Stock Markets, Banks and Economic Growth', *American Economic Review*, 88, 537–57.

McKinnon, R. I. (1973), *Money and Capital in Economic Development*, Washington, DC: Brookings Institution.

Petersen, M. A. and Rajan, R. G. (1994), 'The Benefits of Lending Relationships: Evidence from Small Business Data', *Journal of Finance*, 49 (March), 3–37.

Rajan, R. and L. Zingales (1998), 'Financial Dependence and Growth', *American Economic Review*, 88 (3), 559–86.

Rousseau, P. and P. Wachtel (1998), 'Financial Intermediation and Economic Performance: Historical Evidence from Five Industrialized Countries', *Journal of Money Credit and Banking*, 30 (4), 657–78.

Shaw, E. S. (1973), *Financial Deepening in Economic Development*, New York: Oxford University Press.

Wilson, Charles (1979), 'An Infinite Horizon Model with Money', in Jerry R. Green and José Alexandre Scheinkman (eds), *General Equilibrium, Growth, and Trade*, New York: Academic Press, pp. 81–104.

3

The Islamic Financial System and Economic Growth: An Assessment

Habib Ahmed

Views on the role of the financial system on economic growth vary. However, it is generally agreed that financial sector development plays an important role in the overall development of an economy. One way to study the role of the financial system in the economy is to examine its functions and the implications of these functions on growth. Islamic financial practices, being in their infancy, do not have a comprehensive financial structure to perform all the financial functions in the economy. This chapter evaluates the extent to which the Islamic financial system performs growth-enhancing functions. The role of Islamic financial institutions in achieving economic growth is assessed, first by discussing the factors of economic growth, and then the role of Islamic financial institutions and instruments in facilitating growth factors is analysed. This chapter identifies the gaps in the contemporary Islamic financial system in providing financial factors of growth in order to indicate where the focus of future research and practice is required for the development of a comprehensive Islamic financial system that may be conducive to economic growth.

Introduction

Theoretical and empirical studies indicate that the financial sector plays an important role in the overall development of an economy. Many economists have maintained that the development and efficiency of the financial system are closely linked to economic growth and have pointed out various channels through which the financial system affects economic growth (McKinnon, 1973; Shaw, 1973; Levine, 1997; Tsuru, 2000). Most of the empirical studies on the subject find a positive relationship between the development of the financial sector and economic growth (see King and Levine, 1993a, 1993b; Levine, Loayza and Beck, 1999; Khan and Senhadji, 2000). One way to study the role of the financial sector in the economy and its impact on growth is to examine the functions the sector performs and the implications that these functions have for growth.

Being nascent, the Islamic financial system lacks a comprehensive set of operational institutions and instruments as compared to their conventional counterparts. Honohan (2001) questions the scope of the Islamic financial system and its role in facilitating growth. He maintains that an Islamic financial system which relies on popular financial instruments may be weaker in delivering the financial services needed to facilitate economic growth. Due to a limited menu of financial instruments, the Islamic financial system may not be able to allocate resources optimally in the economy. He contends that this may be reflected in the inability of the financial system to perform growth-enhancing functions, particularly with respect to monitoring managers and reduction of risks.

The picture does not appear to be very encouraging in countries that have tried to implement the Islamic financial system. For example, studies on Sudan, one of the two countries that have an Islamic financial system, indicate that there has been financial disintermediation in the country during 1992–7. Furthermore, the financial sector has failed to mobilize resources for investment and does not appear to have contributed to growth in the economy (see Kireyev, 2001; Hussein, 2004). Similarly, the reversal of the judgment on eliminating *ribā* in Pakistan by the Sharīʿah Appellate Bench of the Supreme Court also shows the difficulties of implementing a comprehensive Islamic financial system.[1]

There is a need to analyse and evaluate the role of the Islamic financial system in facilitating economic growth. In this chapter we attempt to do just that. To study the role of the financial system in inducing growth we look at, among others, the problems of financing firms and consumers in an economy. We identify the factors of economic growth, and link the financial sector to these factors. We then assess if the Islamic financial system can meet the differing financial needs of the firms and the consumers to bring about growth. In doing so, we identify the strengths and weaknesses of the Islamic financial system and suggest the areas on which further research and innovations are required.

The chapter is organized as follows. The following section discusses the contribution of the financial sector to growth. We derive the financial factors of growth by examining, among others, the corporate finance functions that financial institutions perform. The third section outlines different financial institutions in a conventional economy and examines how they contribute to growth by providing different financial services. In the next section, we investigate the Islamic financial system's contribution to different factors of growth. This will be studied at the institution, activity and product/instrument levels. After identifying the gaps in the contemporary Islamic financial sector in providing different financial factors that affect growth, the penultimate section outlines the policies and strategies that may help develop a comprehensive Islamic financial system conducive to economic growth. The final section concludes the chapter and identifies the areas where the focus of future research in Islamic finance is required.

The financial sector and economic growth

The linkages between the financial sector, the financial factors of growth and economic growth are shown in Figure 3.1. In this section, we examine the link between financial factors and economic growth (shown by Arrow B in Figure 3.1). In the next section, we will discuss the role of financial sector in providing the financial factors of growth (shown by Arrow A in Figure 3.1).

Owners of resources (labour, capital, and raw materials) sell the factors of production to firms in the input markets. The firms use these inputs to produce products that are sold in the product markets. At the micro level, a need for cash arises in production because the production process involves a lag between input use and the final sale of output. This implies unsynchronized cash flows where firms pay before receiving revenue from the sale of their products, necessitating financing in the input market. Similarly, in the product market, the consumers need financing to purchase high-value durable goods and assets as the income and savings of a household may not be enough to purchase durable goods and assets, and a need may arise to finance the purchase of these items.

To understand the determinants of growth, consider a typical production function showing the relationship between inputs and output as given by

$$Y = f(L, K, \mid T) \text{ and } Y_i > 0,\ Y_{ii} < 0 \tag{3.1}$$

where Y is the output, L is the labour, K is the capital, T represents the technology, and Y_i and Y_{ii} are the first and second derivatives of output with respect to input i ($i = L$ and K). Equation (3.1) states that, given the level of technology (T), the output produced (Y) increases at a decreasing rate when either labour (L) or capital (K) increases. In order to identify these sources, empirical work uses the Cobb–Douglas production function framework. The growth equation derived by taking the logarithmic derivative of this function is written as

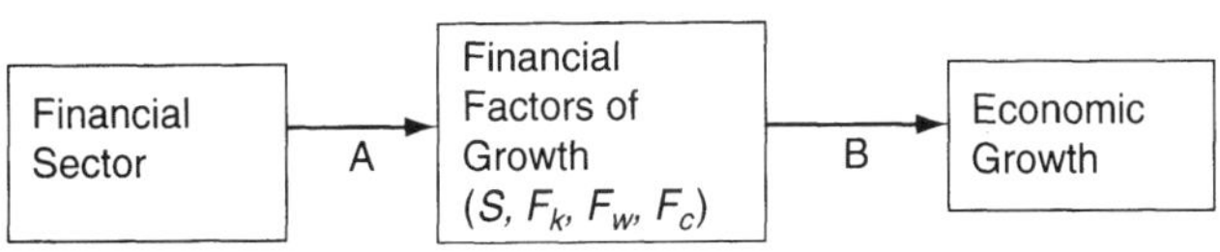

Figure 3.1 Financial sector and economic growth: linkages

$$d\ln Y = \ln A + \alpha d\ln L + \beta d\ln K + \varepsilon \tag{3.2}$$

where *d* and *ln* are the total differentiation and natural logarithm operatives respectively, *A* represents the constant, and ε is the error term. The growth literature attributes output growth to three sources: increases in the factors of production (labour and capital), increasing returns to scale, and technical progress. The coefficients of labour and capital (α and β respectively) show the relative effects of the two factors of production, while the sum of coefficients reveals the returns to scale effect, and the effect of technological change is found as the residual.[2]

Note that the production function above shows the relationship of real variables. In reality, firms face cash constraints that can limit the use of capital and labour affecting the production and growth of output adversely. In order to understand the relationship between the financial sector and economic growth, we examine the role of finance in the input and output markets of an economy.

The role of the financial sector in production and growth can be shown by the cash constraints faced in the input and output markets of the economy. Specifically, in the input market, the firms have to pay for the use of labour and capital before receiving revenue. Assume the price of labour and capital are *w* and *r* respectively. The cash needs of a firm to purchase the necessary inputs is given by

$$rK = F_k \tag{3.3}$$

$$wL = F_w \tag{3.4}$$

and

$$F_t = F_k + F_w \tag{3.5}$$

A firm needs funds to purchase capital and to pay for labour (as shown by equations 3.3 and 3.4 respectively). Let these be called fixed capital (F_k) and working capital (F_w) respectively. The sum of these gives the total cash requirements (F_t) of a firm (equation 3.5). As the output and its growth depend on the use of inputs over time, which in turn is determined by the availability of funds, the output supplied can be written as a function of the cash constraints as shown below:

$$Y^S = f(F_w, F_k) \tag{3.6}$$

The level and growth of technology used in production are important factors determining output and growth in an economy. One way to include this factor is to consider embedded technologies. This implies that technology is entrenched in capital. In this case, capital accumulation not only refers to its quantity but also its quality. As the quality of capital improves due to better use of technology, there is a corresponding need for a higher quality of human capital to manage it. Human capital can be improved through education, research and training. Thus there is a need to invest in the household sector to build human capital. Other than ensuring that institutions which provide education and training exist, there is a need for the availability of low cost funds that allow individuals to avail education and training. These facilities increase the knowledge and skill base in an economy and affect the productivity and efficiency of labour and thereby economic growth positively.

On the product market side, the output sold by firms can be constrained by the demand for goods. To understand the demand-side constraints, we define the budget constraint of the household sector. A household can spend less or more than its income I (= $wL+rK+\pi$; π being the profit) by saving (S) or borrowing funds for consumption (F_c) respectively. The cash constraint on the demand side indicates that the output purchased (Y^d) is a function of its income, savings and borrowings, as shown in the following equation:

$$Y^d = g(I - S + F_c) \tag{3.7}$$

Thus output produced in an economy can be constrained on the demand side by, among others, the cash available to the household sector in the form of credit (F_c).

The equilibrium output (Y^*) at a point in time in an economy is determined where quantity demand equals the quantity supplied (i.e., $Y^d = Y^s$). By using the supply- and demand-side cash constraints (from equations 3.6 and 3.7 respectively) we get the equilibrium output in terms of cash constraints as

$$Y^* = h(S, F_w, F_k, F_c) \tag{3.8}$$

Equation (3.8) shows that the quantity of real output produced and its growth in an economy will depend on the availability of different financial flows. We call these flows the *financial factors* of economic growth. As cash constraints can arise on the demand and supply sides of the product market, the short-side rule will determine the output produced in the economy: that is, if the supply (demand) is greater than demand (supply), then the latter determines the output produced in the economy.

To sum up, in a closed economy, the total resources mobilized (S) in the economy will be less than or equal to the total financing needs ($F_w + F_k + F_c$).[3] Note that there is a complementary relationship among the financial factors of growth. These factors must be financed in a balanced and proportional way to satisfy the needs of the firms and the household. For example, if a financial system can finance fixed capital (F_k) without difficulty but is unable to provide sufficient funds for working capital (F_w) due to lack of institutions or instruments, then growth will be hindered. Similarly, the household sector's inability to purchase durable goods on credit can dampen the aggregate demand and the growth in an economy. The role of the financial sector is to mobilize savings in the economy and allocate them efficiently among various heads.

From the simple model outlined above, we observe the financial sector's role in enabling growth as mobilization of saving in the economy and its allocation on the supply and demand sides of the product market. Though we have not explicitly discussed the government, this sector is an important player in the financial markets. Governments finance their expenditures from tax revenues and, in case of deficit, from borrowings. There can be two possible effects of government expenditure on investment and growth: expenditures by government can either increase the cost of capital and crowd out private investment, or stimulate private investment by acting as a complementary factor.[4] On the revenue side, governments use short- and long-term debt instruments (bills and bonds respectively) to finance their deficits. The funds mobilized through government borrowing also come from the resources generated by savings (S).[5]

Financial factors and their contribution to economic growth

Levine (1997, p. 689) identifies the functions of a financial system that relate to economic growth as 'the trading of risk, allocating capital, monitoring managers, mobilizing savings, and easing the trading of goods'.[6] He asserts that these functions of a financial system can enhance growth by increasing saving and promoting capital accumulation and technological innovation. Even though financial systems and structures may differ, these basic functions are common to all systems and induce growth in the economy. In providing the financial factors of growth, the financial sector performs various functions that facilitate economic growth. We briefly discuss below how each of the financial factors of growth (derived above) performs different functions that lead to growth.

Resource mobilization (s)

On the resource mobilization side, savers have different financial needs with regard to placing their funds in different institutions. Though people save for different reasons, the most important of these is to transfer resources across time for future use. Institutions in the financial sector provide the means to the public to store liquidity, a system for clearing and settling payments, and investment in various assets. After putting aside a part of income in liquid form to meet current and unexpected needs, the rest is put in assets/investments with different risk/return/maturity profiles. Whatever the format of savings, the financial institutions mobilize resources in the economy. By minimizing risk through diversification and other risk management practices and enabling capital accumulation, the financial sector not only encourages savings but also increases exchange in the input and output markets. All these factors stimulate economic growth.

Working capital (F_w)

As discussed above, working capital constitutes operational costs (such as paying wages to labour) and is needed for relatively shorter periods of time. Hamlin and Heartfield (1991) point out that one main difference between working and fixed capital is the way they are financed. Working capital requires short-term financing and is usually financed through debt. The financial sector allocates capital and enables exchange in the input market by providing working capital. In the process of financing, the financial institutions take the necessary measures to mitigate credit risk. One way this is done is by monitoring the operations of the firms, thereby inducing better governance. Thus the financial sector allocates funds for working capital, increases exchange in different markets, and improves the performance of firms affecting economic growth positively.

Fixed capital (F_k)

Fixed capital (F_k), being long-term investment, is typically financed through equity. As in the case of working capital, the financial sector efficiently allocates capital and enables exchange in the input markets by providing fixed capital. Equity financing improves governance in firms either through market discipline or by direct involvement of the shareholders in their management. In the process, they ensure that the risks involved in financing are minimized. Thus the financial sector induces economic growth by allocating capital efficiently, facilitating risk mitigation, improving corporate governance, and enabling exchange in the input markets.

Credit for the household sector (F_c)

Consumer credit is needed by the household sector in different situations. Credit can facilitate purchases when funds available to the household are lower than the expenditure in a given time period. Though people may sometimes need to borrow funds to purchase necessities, credit is mainly used to buy real estate and high-valued durable goods such as automobiles and other household items. The provision of consumer credit facilitates exchange in the product market and prevents a slowdown in economic growth induced from the demand side. In allocating credit, the financial institutions take all necessary steps to minimize the credit risks. Levine (1997) also recognizes the role of the financial sector in facilitating borrowing to improve skills and building human capital. Credit provided for education and training is usually of longer duration and is provided by public financial institutions.

The conventional financial system and financial factors of growth

A financial system can be analysed at four levels (Merton and Bodie, 1995, pp. 16–20). The first is at the system level: that is, a country's entire financial system. The second is at the institution level. At this level, different financial institutions in a financial system that provide various financial services are identified. The third level relates to the *activity* level in which the activities of financial institutions are elaborated. Activities would, for example, include lending, leasing, or equity financing. The fourth level concerns products where the financial products or instruments are identified and discussed. At this level the specific contracts used for financial transactions in different activities are studied.

A wide range of institutions and instruments are needed to provide different financial services to ensure growth in the economy. It is important to remember that rules, regulations and different governmental bodies play a very important role in determining the structure and scale of a financial system. It is the responsibility of these public institutions to establish the appropriate environment, legal and regulatory systems to facilitate financial intermediation and transactions. In order to appraise the role of Islamic financial system in facilitating growth in some perspective, we discuss the role of the conventional financial system in inducing growth. We do so by examining the contributions of conventional financial institutions towards various financial growth factors.

In conventional economies, two broad categories of financial systems have been identified (Hermes and Lensink, 2000). The first is the market-oriented financial system found in countries such as the USA, UK, and Ireland. This system is characterized by the dominance of the stock market with open corporations that have widely dispersed shareholders. These economies have well-developed and liquid financial markets in which ownership and control rights are frequently traded. Banks provide short-term and medium-term finance through credit, and usually do not have equity stakes in corporations. The second financial system (found in countries such as Germany and Japan) is the bank-dominated financial system, which is characterized by large banks and relatively illiquid capital markets. One special feature of this financial system is universal banking in which a bank can undertake multitude of activities. Banks not only provide credit, but also hold equity in corporations and get involved in their decision-making process.

Table 3.1 shows the main activities of different financial institutions and their contribution to various financial factors of growth. It does not provide

Table 3.1 Financial institutions, activities and growth factors

Institutions/instruments	*Activity type*	*Financial factors of growth*[a]			
		S	F_w	F_k	F_c
Private					
Commercial banks	Debt	x	x	x	x
Micro finance institutions	Debt	x	x	x	x
Corporate bonds market	Debt	x	x		
Near banks	Debt	x	x	x	x
Retailer credit	Debt				x
Real estate/leasing companies	Debt/Leasing	x		x	x
Mutual funds (stock market)	Equity	x			
Stock market	Equity	x		x	
Investment banks	Debt/Equity	x	x	x	
Private equity funds/venture capitalists	Equity/Debt	x	x	x	
Public government bills/ bonds market	Debt	x	x	x	
Educational loans	Debt				x
Development banks	Debt		x	x	

a: an x indicates that it has relevance to the financial functions.

an exhaustive list of all the financial institutions, but only the prominent ones that directly or indirectly affect growth in the real economy. Financial activity is divided into three categories: debt, equity and leasing. Note that the regulatory regime will determine, to a large extent, the size of different institutions and the activities that institutions can undertake in an economy. For example, while in a market-oriented financial system the stock markets will be relatively large, the banking sector will be dominant in a bank-dominated financial system. Similarly, in regimes where banks are allowed to undertake multiple activities (such as the universal banking system), commercial banks can get involved in all the activities and affect all the financial factors of growth.

Typically, large established firms use the stock market and investment banks to procure funds for long-term financing for fixed and working capital. In addition, such firms can borrow funds from the public by issuing bonds. Not all firms, however, can raise funds from the stock or bond markets. When a firm is new, it starts out as a small enterprise. The new entrepreneurs often do not have any track record or acceptable physical collateral to obtain funds from institutional sources such as commercial banks. The only source of finance for these firms is insider finance, where an individual or a group (family members, friends) uses savings to finance the setting-up of the project and bear the operating costs.In case of new start-up firms with innovative ideas, venture capitalists play an important role in providing funds for fixed and working capital. In some cases development banks may also invest in these ventures. As firms age, they develop a track record. Firms with high growth potentials can finance their expansion by using either venture capital or investment banks. Medium and large firms with long track records and acceptable physical collateral can get short-term and long-term credit from institutional sources such as commercial banks and near banks.

It may be noticed in Table 3.1 that near banks, investment banks and venture capitalists can provide all the financial factors (i.e., S, F_w, F_k, F_c) that facilitate growth. While commercial banks and near banks predominantly use debt as a mode of financing, investment banks and venture capitalists use equity. Fixed capital can be financed through the stock market, commercial and investment banks, development banks and venture capitalists. The main source of short-term credit for working capital is commercial banks. In the case of investment banks and venture capitalists, working capital can also be financed by using equity. As equity financing does not guarantee a fixed return, these financial institutions are actively involved in the management of the firms they invest in.

In the last two decades, micro finance institutions have evolved as specialized institutions and are playing an important role in serving the poorer sections of the population in many countries. The poverty-focused micro finance institutions provide financial support for the growth to the poorer sections of the population.They provide funds to the poor for micro enterprises and several saving programmes for the poor. Credit risk is mitigated by forming groups and using peer pressure to ensure repayments. Monitoring by the officials of the micro finance institutions and peer pressure improve the management of micro enterprises.Though most of their credit is short- to medium-term, these institutions also provide long-term loans for capital accumulation and asset-building (such as loans for building houses and tube wells).[7]

Other than retailer credit, the household sector's financial needs in a conventional economy are met by loans provided by commercial banks, near banks, leasing companies and micro finance institutions. The main function performed by retailer credit, mutual funds and real estate leasing funds is to enable exchange in the goods market, stock market and real estate market respectively. Stocks and bonds are means of raising funds from the financial markets using equity and debt instruments respectively. The firms can use these funds to cover their capital and labour costs. The prices of these instruments reflect the inherent risks involved. Financial institutions and investors allocate their funds among different stocks and bonds according to their risk/return preferences.

In addition to issuing government debt in the form of bills and bonds to finance both capital and operational needs, governments can also affect capital accumulation through specialized development banks. These development banks offer credit to prospective projects at concessionary interest rates. Similarly, educational loans given to the household sector affect both the quantity and quality of human capital. These funds, coming mainly from specialized public sources, enhance productivity and the efficiency of labour affecting economic growth positively.

The Islamic financial system and economic growth

In this section, we outline the main features of the Islamic financial sector and study its significance with respect to economic growth. To evaluate the Islamic financial sector in a comprehensive way, we examine it at the institution, activity and product or instrument levels. In doing this, we will identify the gaps at different levels that inhibit the financial sector's contribution to growth. Before relating the institutions to their activities and products, we briefly outline the main features of Islamic financial instruments.

Islamic financial instruments

Credit in an Islamic economy can be either interest free (*qarḍ ḥasan*) or loans that charge service costs only. These instruments, however, may not appeal to financial intermediaries as they cannot earn economic rates of return on their financing. While *qarḍ ḥasan* yields no return, loans that charge service costs cannot charge, in principle, anything in excess of the actual costs of providing funds. As no risk or maturity premiums can be charged on these loans, financial institutions may be reluctant to use them for financing purposes.

Other than loans, the principles of Islamic financing can be broadly classified as partnerships (*shirakāt*) and exchange contracts (*muʿāwaḍāt*).[8] Partnerships can be on the basis of profit-sharing or output-sharing. Profit-sharing again can take two forms, *mushārakah* and *muḍārabah*. Whereas in *mushārakah* more than one party can finance and participate in a project and distribute the profit at an agreed ratio, in *muḍārabah* one party supplies the funds and the other party carries out the project. They share the profit in agreed-upon proportions. One main difference between *mushārakah* and *muḍārabah* is that in the former the financier takes part in the management of the project, while in the latter he does not. From a financing point of view, financial intermediaries face various asymmetric information problems in using these instruments. In particular, the prevalence of the moral hazard problem may prevent financial intermediaries using profit-sharing modes of financing.[9]

Though there are different kinds of exchange contracts, the most important among them are contracts based on the deferred-trading principle. Deferred-trading contracts can be either price-deferred sales or object-deferred sales. In price-deferred sales (*bayʿ-muaʾjjal*) the object of sale is delivered at the time of the contract, but the price is paid later. The price can also be paid in the future in instalments. One type of financial transaction under this format is the mark-up sale (*murābaḥah*), in which a good or asset is sold to the client at a mark-up. The client pays for the good or asset at a future date in instalments. Note that *murābaḥah* contracts are usually of short- to medium-term duration.

Salam and *istiṣnāʿ* contracts fall under the category of object-deferred sales, the former being generally used for merchandise and agricultural goods and the latter for manufactured goods. In these contracts, the price of the good/asset is paid in advance and delivery taken at an agreed-upon time in future. A financier, however, may not be inclined to finance projects using this mode of financing unless there is a buyer for the good/asset that is being produced. *Ijārah* is a contract in which the client uses an asset by paying rent. One form of this arrangement can be a hire-purchase scheme or lease-purchase scheme (*ijārah wa iqtināʾ*), in which the instalment includes rent as well as a part of the price. When the instalments are completed, the ownership of the asset is transferred to the client.

Significance of the Islamic financial system for economic growth

A list of Islamic financial institutions, along with their primary activities and instruments used, is given in Table 3.2. Note that we have only included the institutions corresponding to the conventional ones.[10]

We notice in Table 3.2 that lending activity is replaced by sale contracts that create debt. The specific instruments that fall under sale contracts are *murābaḥah* and *salam/istiṣnāʿ*. The main activity of commercial banks, micro finance institutions, near banks and retailer creditors has taken the form of *murābaḥah*. The nature of bonds in an Islamic economy will also change, as these securities (corporate and government) must be backed by assets. While some bonds can be linked to assets through a leasing contract, others can be in the form of equities or *istiṣnāʿ/salam* contracts.[11] Investment banks and venture capitalists will use equity financing either in the form of *muḍārabah* or *musharakah* contracts. Mutual funds and stock markets enable individuals to invest directly or indirectly in secondary capital markets (stock exchanges). Real estate and leasing companies use *ijārah* contracts for financing. Loans can be only provided as *qarḍ ḥasan* or given on payment of service charges.

To analyse the role of the Islamic financial system in inducing economic growth, we will focus on the system's contribution to the financial factors of growth. To do so, we discuss the link between different Islamic financial instruments (along with the corresponding activity type) and the financial factors of growth. We also point out the institutions that use these instruments (and activities). The contribution of various Islamic financial instruments to each of the financial factors of growth is discussed next.

Resource mobilization (S)

All modes of financing can be used to attract savings and resource mobilization. Commercial banks use loans and *muḍārabah* modes to attract deposits

Table 3.2 Islamic financial institutions, instruments and activities

Institutions/markets	*Primary activity on the asset side*		*Other activities on the asset side*	
	Activity	*Instruments*	*Activity*	*Instruments*
Private				
Commercial banks	Sale (Debt)	*Murābaḥah*	Leasing/equity	*Ijārah/Muḍārabah*
Micro finance institutions	Sale (Debt)	*Murābaḥah*	Leasing/equity	*Ijārah/Muḍārabah*
Corporate bond market	Leasing	Asset-backed *ṣukūk*		
Near banks	Sale (Debt)	*Murābaḥah*	Leasing/equity	*Ijārah/Muḍārabah*
Retailer credit	Sale (Debt)	*Murābaḥah*		
Real estate/leasing companies	Leasing	*Ijārah*		
Mutual funds	Equity	*Muḍārabah/mushārakah*	Leasing/debt	*Ijārah/Murābaḥah/Salam*
Stock market	Equity	*Muḍārabah/mushārakah*		
Investment banks	Equity	*Muḍārabah/mushārakah*	Debt/leasing	*Murābaḥah/Ijārah*
Equity funds/venture capitalists	Equity	*Mushārakah*	Debt/leasing	*Murābaḥah/Ijārah*
Public				
Government bills/bonds market	Leasing	Leasing *ṣukūk*	Others: asset-backed bonds	*Equity/Istiṣnā*ʿ
Educational loans	Debt	Loans		
Development banks	Leasing	*Ijārah*	Equity	*Muḍārabah/Mushārakah*

(*qarḍ ḥasan* for current account deposits and the *muḍārabah* for investment deposits). Investment banks and venture capitalists can mobilize funds on a long-term *muḍārabah* basis. Mutual funds can attract financial resources through different instruments. For example, different sorts of funds exist, including *murābaḥah* funds, *salam* funds, leasing funds, and equity (*mushārakah*) funds. Similarly, asset-backed bonds can be based on *muḍārabah, salam* or *ijārah* modes.[12]

Working capital

As *murābaḥah* and *ijārah* are linked to goods or assets, these instruments cannot be used to finance variable inputs such as labour or working capital. Though *salam* is usually considered as a trade instrument, it can also be used for financing purposes. In these contracts, an advance payment is made for production and delivery of goods at a later date. In theory, the funds can be used for both fixed capital and working capital. If the financier, however, does not have a buyer for these goods, then the costs of liquidating these goods can increase substantially. While theoretically equity instruments (*muḍārabah* and *mushārakah*) can be used to finance working capital, the problem is to ascertain the rate of return on these investments. Moreover, there are no operational models available that enable the use of equity financing to finance working capital. Loans on service charges are a more practical way to finance working capital. This method, however, is not attractive for financial institutions, as they cannot charge in excess of the actual costs of providing the funds.

Fixed capital

In theory, almost all modes of financing can be used to finance fixed capital. *Ijārah*, in particular, appears to be an appropriate mode for financing fixed capital. Similarly, *murābaḥah*, whereby the financier sells fixed capital to the firm and the firm pays the price back in instalments, can be used. The problem of financing fixed capital with this instrument, however, may be that it is usually of short- to medium-term maturity, whereas fixed capital requires longer-term financing. In theory, loans can be provided with service charges and can be used to purchase fixed capital, but this method does not appeal to financiers, as pointed out earlier. Advance paid in a *salam* can also be used for fixed capital if there is a buyer for the good/asset being produced. Both modes of equity financing can be used to finance fixed capital. There are, however, difficulties in ascertaining the profit share and ensuring returns on investments.

Credit to the household sector

Other than loans on service charges, only fixed-income modes of financing, such as *murābaḥah* and *ijārah*, appear to be appropriate to finance household needs. However, due to the reasons already pointed out, the use of loans to finance the household sector will be limited in practice.

Table 3.3 Islamic financial instruments and financial factors of growth: theoretical models

Instruments	*Activity type*	*Theoretical models*[a]			
		S	F_w	F_k	F_c
Murābaḥah	Sale (Debt)	Y (=2)	N (=0)	Y (=2)	Y (=2)
Salam/istiṣnā'	Sale (Debt)	Y (=2)	Y (=2)	Y (=2)	N (=0)
Muḍārabah	Equity	Y (=2)	Y (=2)	Y (=2)	N (=0)
Mushārakah	Equity	Y (=2)	Y (=2)	Y (=2)	N (=0)
Ijārah	Leasing	Y (=2)	N (=0)	Y (=2)	Y (=2)
Qarḍ	Loan	Y (=2)	Y (=2)	Y (=2)	Y (=2)
Total		12	8	12	6
Index (%)		100	66.7	100	50

a: Y (= 2) indicates alternatives available; N (= 0) indicates no alternatives available.

The roles of different instruments in an Islamic financial system in providing for each of the financial factors of growth are summarized in Tables 3.3 and 3.4. After identifying the different instruments and their corresponding activities, these tables show the likelihood of their contribution to the different financial factors of growth. While Table 3.3 indicates the existence of theoretical models for different instruments that contribute to various financial factors of growth, Table 3.4 shows the availability of operational models for the same.

To have a quantitative notion of the role of the Islamic financial system, we derive an index showing the extent to which the system can contribute to each of the growth factors. To arrive at the index, we give a value of 2 when

Table 3.4 Islamic financial instruments and financial factors of growth: operational models

Instruments	*Activity type*	*Operational models*[a]			
		S	F_w	F_k	F_c
Murābaḥah	Sale (Debt)	Y (=2)	N (=0)	Y (=1)	Y (=2)
Salam/Istiṣnā'	Sale (Debt)	Y (=2)	L (=1)	L (=1)	N (=0)
Muḍārabah	Equity	Y (=2)	L (=1)	L (=1)	N (=0)
Mushārakah	Equity	Y (=2)	L (=1)	L (=1)	N (=0)
Ijārah	Leasing	Y (=2)	N (=0)	Y (=2)	Y (=2)
Qarḍ	Loan	Y (=2)	L (=1)	L (=1)	L (=1)
Total		12	4	7	5
Index (%)		100	33.3	58.3	41.7

a: Y indicates alternatives available; N indicates no alternatives available; L indicates limited use.

instruments can contribute to the financial factors with ease (i.e., alternatives are available, shown by Y in the tables). We give a value of 1 if instruments can contribute in a limited way (i.e., the alternatives are limited or constrained, indicated by L in the tables) and a value of 0 in cases when the instruments cannot contribute to the growth factors (i.e., no alternatives available, demonstrated by N in the tables). Given that there are six instruments (with four activity types), the maximum number showing the contribution to different financial factors of growth can be 12. The index for each financial factor is then derived as a percentage of this maximum number.

Table 3.3 shows that, at the theoretical level, there are no problems for the Islamic financial sector in resource mobilization (S) and financing fixed capital (F_k). All the Islamic instruments can be used for these financial factors of growth as indicated by the index of 100 per cent. As already indicated above, while *murābaḥah* and *ijārah* instruments cannot be used to finance working capital (F_w), theoretical models using other instruments (*salam/istiṣnā*ʿ, *muḍārabah*, *mushārakah* and *qarḍ*) can be used, giving it an index of 66.7 per cent. Similarly, the index for credit to the household sector (F_c) equals 50 per cent as theoretically only *murābaḥah*, *ijārah* and *qarḍ* can be used to finance this sector.

Table 3.4 indicates the availability of operational models in the Islamic financial system to satisfy the requirements of various financial factors of growth. There does not appear to be any significant problem in mobilizing resources (S) using any of the instruments, giving it an index of 100 per cent. The index for working capital (F_w) falls from 66.7 per cent in Table 3.3 to 33.3 per cent in Table 3.4, indicating operational problems in using these instruments. Though theoretical models of using *salam/istiṣnā*ʿ, *muḍārabah*, *mushārakah* and *qarḍ* exist, operational models for using these instruments are limited. *Salam/istiṣnā*ʿ are not appealing if there are no buyers for the good/asset that is being financed. Similarly, financial institutions do not use profit-sharing modes as incentive-compatible operational models that resolve the moral hazard problems in financing have not been developed yet. Similarly, the index for fixed capital (F_k) falls from 100 per cent in Table 3.3 to 58.3 per cent in Table 3.4. While the problems associated with instruments discussed under working capital are same in the case of fixed capital, the problem of using *murābaḥah* is the maturity mismatch. The corresponding index for household sector credit (F_c) falls to 41.7 per cent (from an index of 50 per cent in Table 3.3), reflecting the operational problem in using *qarḍ* to finance this factor.

* * *

It appears from the above discussion that there are operational problems in providing the different financial factors of growth in an Islamic financial system. While the system has problems of varying degrees in financing different factors of growth, the problem appears acute in financing working capital. Specifically, as *murābaḥah* and *ijārah* modes of financing are tied to goods and assets, these cannot be used for working capital. Furthermore, while theoretically equity modes of financing can be used for working capital, it is difficult to do so at the operational level. Similarly, unless the financier has a buyer to purchase the asset/good being financed, a *salam* contract may not be a feasible alternative for financing.

Towards a comprehensive Islamic financial system

Hermes and Lensink (2000) assert that a financial system's positive contribution to economic growth will be determined largely by the way the system is designed. Aspects of financial system design include not only the types of existing financial institutions and instruments, but also the establishment of a legal, regulatory and supervisory environment. To understand the Islamic financial sector's role in bringing about growth, we examine the different aspects of the financial system and suggest some policies and strategies that may help in developing it. Note that while in a narrow sense growth refers to an increase in the national output in an economy over time, an Islamic economy will also emphasize the distributive aspects along with growth.[13]

The role of the government and central bank/regulatory authorities in controlling and stabilizing the financial sector is very important. Other than establishing a congenial environment through laws, rules and regulations that encourage the Islamic financial sector, these organs must also ensure the stability of the financial system as a whole. The role of the regulators in formulating rules and standards is crucial for the development and stability of an Islamic financial system. The financial sector is prone to systemic risks that can spread instability throughout the financial system, affecting the economy and growth adversely.[14] The inherent instability of the financial institutions induces governments to intervene not only for the stability of the financial markets but also to protect different stakeholders. Establishing good governance practices and structures is important in bringing stability and efficiency to the banking sector.[15]

Levine, Loayza and Beck (1999) find that countries in which laws protect creditors' claims against firms, with legal systems that rigorously enforce contracts, and accounting systems and standards that produce high-quality standardized and comprehensive corporate financial statements, tend to have better developed financial intermediaries. This suggests that legal and accounting reforms which strengthen creditor rights, contract enforcement and accounting practices can promote the development of financial intermediaries and thereby accelerate economic growth. If contracts are not enforceable, there can be a disruption of the operations of financial institutions. The result would be under-investment, which in turn slows economic growth.

This is particularly true for an Islamic financial system, which emphasizes profit-sharing modes of financing. Other than the overall environment, different financial institutions and instruments have to be encouraged and developed to serve various needs of firms in the economy.

While an Islamic economy cannot have a 'pure profit-sharing' financial system, there is a need for a balanced mix between fixed income and profit-sharing modes of financing (Jarhi al-, 1999). Data on different Islamic financial institutions (banks and micro finance institutions), however, show that most of them use either debt or leasing contracts.[16] These instruments cannot be used to finance working capital. Another problem of using fixed income modes of financing is that these instruments are short term. An implication of shying away from long-term equity financing is that Islamic banks are not performing an important role in financial intermediation in capital markets that spurs economic growth. The solution to these problems is the development of operational models of instruments and institutions that can use equity financing.

The problem of financing different growth factors by using equity-based instruments may be tackled at different levels. At the instrument or activity level, equity financing can be increased if incentive-compatible profit-sharing contracts that Islamic financial institutions can use are developed. These contracts would have an incentive structure that would minimize, among others, the moral hazard problem.[17] At the institutional level, there is a need to establish more financial institutions that engage in equity financing. The institutions in this category are, among others, universal banks, venture capital firms and investment banks. Finally, at system level a legal system that enforces equity-based contracts and a regulatory regime that encourages their use need to be developed.

Until recently, the Islamic financial system had been dominated mainly by Islamic banks that are mostly involved in short-term and fixed return financing. The lack of development of other financial institutions can be problematic in an Islamic economy. It has been observed that finance from commercial banks overwhelmingly tends to go to larger firms. This may also be true for Islamic banks as they are modelled on conventional commercial banks. Since the Islamic economic system pays particular attention to income distribution, there must be a mechanism for smaller firms or micro enterprises to have access to finance. This can be done either by Islamic banks opening special schemes/windows for financing small firms and enterprises, or by establishing venture capital and micro finance institutions.[18]

An important factor that will determine growth and distributive equity in the economy is the development of the overall human capital. While governments have traditionally subsidized education, good quality higher and technical education is expensive. This prevents many people, particularly from the poorer sections of the population, accessing it. One way to resolve this problem is to make funds available to deserving individuals for education and training. As the financing of human capital has to be in the form of loans (either *qarḍ ḥasan* or based on service fees), this may not be provided by the private sector financial institutions. Specialized public institutions are required that can provide this essential service so that the most important resource in the economy (human capital) can be developed to enable economic growth.

Conclusion

This chapter studied the salient features of an Islamic financial system and evaluated its role in contributing to growth. We derived the financial factors of growth and evaluated the performance of the Islamic financial system with respect to its contribution to these factors. The chapter identified some gaps in the Islamic financial system that need to be addressed. Specifically, it was shown that there are operational problems related to the use of equity-based instruments (*muḍārabah* and *mushārakah*) to finance different financial growth factors, in particular working capital. In an Islamic environment, debt contracts such as *murābaḥah* and leasing contracts (*ijārah*) cannot be used to finance working capital. Furthermore, no operational models for using *muḍārabah* and *mushārakah* to finance working capital exist. While *salam/istiṣnāʿ* contracts and credit on service charges can be used, financiers may face certain problems in using them.

In order to make a meaningful contribution to growth of an economy, the Islamic financial system has to develop institutions and instruments that serve the current and future financial needs of the people in society. Given the complementarities among the financial factors of growth, the ability of the Islamic financial sector to bring about growth will be constrained by its inability to finance all these factors in a balanced way. To solve the problem of financing different growth factors and enhancing economic growth, equity-based instruments and institutions have to play a more active role in an Islamic economy. In this regard, there is a need to develop operational models of corporate finance in general, and workable equity-based instruments and institutions in particular.

With its emphasis on distributive equity along with growth, an Islamic financial system should have financial institutions and instruments that also serve small firms. If the market-oriented financial system is dominated by the stock market and well-developed financial markets, and the bank-dominated model is characterized by large banks, then an Islamic financial system will be one that is dominated by equity-based institutions such as private equity funds, venture capitalists and investment banks. Note, however, that an Islamic economy will also have debt instruments. The Islamic banks would be more in line with universal banks so that they can hold equity stakes in firms along with providing credit facilities.

Given that the Islamic financial system is in its infancy, research and institutional development of this system has, until recently, focused mainly on Islamic banks that were designed in line with conventional commercial banks. The chapter shows that the thrust of research in Islamic finance should be on operational aspects of equity-based institutions and instruments. At the instrument level, this can be done by first investigating the problems that financial institutions face in using profit-sharing modes of financing and then suggesting operational models that remove these constraints. At the institutional level, institutional structures that enable the use of the equity-based financing need to be developed. The development of institutions that reflect Islamic values and goals are indispensable for a comprehensive Islamic financial system that fulfils all the financial needs in the economy.[19]

Comment

Humayon Dar

This study provides a comprehensive account of how different Islamic modes of financing can potentially be used for resource mobilization in different sectors of an economy. It also highlights some important limitations of the contemporary practice of Islamic banking in stimulating economic growth. It substantiates the view of Honohan (2001) that the existing menu of Islamic financial instruments is more limited than is generally accepted by the proponents of Islamic finance. The author seems to accept the contention that there is a positive relationship between financial development and growth and that the causality runs from the former to the latter. The following three messages emerge from the study.

Provision of working capital is a major problem faced by Islamic banks: there is no real Islamic alternative for financing working capital

In the absence of a simple and otherwise effective instrument such as interest, the problem of financing working capital has haunted proponents of Islamic finance, which has so far failed to come up with a genuine Islamic alternative to financing the working capital requirements of clients. The author mentions that the existing Islamic modes of financing – *muḍārabah, mushārakah, ijārah* and mark-up based arrangements – have a limited role to play in financing working capital. This, at best, is only partly true. Working capital financing should not pose a significant problem to Islamic banks if they increase their investment portfolio in favour of equity financing. In fact, in an equity-based relationship between a bank and a business, working capital financing may not arise as a problem at all. Suppose a bank and a firm enter into an equity-based deal wherein the firm seeks funding for a venture capital over a period of three years. If total required funding is $3 million, the firm can always ask for a financing facility of $3.5 million over the same period. The firm can use the funds if and when it needs to access the excess facility of $0.5 million on a PLS basis, like the remaining of the money available to it. The working capital financing thus becomes a part of the overall deal and as such should not pose a significant problem.

In more general cases of working capital, a loan carrying service charges has a great potential to serve as an instrument for working capital financing. The banks tend to provide working capital financing to their clients when they have some history of doing business with them. The business houses operate their business (and current) accounts with specific banks from which they seek working capital financing when required. The banks can either use a 'loan carrying a service charge' variant of *qarḍ ḥasan* or what has for long been rebuffed by Islamic economists: the idea of a time multiple counter loan (TMCL). The idea is very simple. A loan is divided into its amount and its period, each multiple of which is defined as loan value.

Thus a deposit of $1,000 by a business in its current account for one month may be decomposed into $1,000 (the amount) and the period (30 days), giving us a total loan value of 30,000 dollar-days. Similarly, if a business maintains a current account for no less than $1,000 per month for a year, its total value of the current account deposits is $12,000 dollar-months or 365,000 dollar-days. A customer, having accumulated a certain value of loan over a period of time, may be eligible to get an interest-free TMCL. In the above example, the business may be entitled to get a TMCL of $12,000 for a month or $365,000 for a day. Some banks, including Barclays and HSBC in the UK, have shown their willingness to offer interest-free loans to some of their Muslim (business) clients who manage to maintain a certain level of balance in their current accounts (although they do not refer to it as a TMCL, the underlying idea is the same). If conventional banks are willing to adopt such structures, why not Islamic banks who claim to be more socially responsible than their conventional counterparts? Hence, the reason for the reluctance on the part of Islamic banks to use *qarḍ ḥasan* needs to be found somewhere other than its financial viability.

Equity-based financing is important for growth in line with Islamic emphasis on equitable growth

The author argues that Islamic banking faces the challenge of developing instruments that could easily be used by incumbent institutions offering Islamic financial services. As such institutions are relatively scarce even in Muslim countries, there is a need to develop new institutions that could operate on the principles of Islamic finance, and which emphasize equitable growth with an ultimate objective of poverty elimination. The author appears to advocate the structure of universal banking, which accommodates multi-dimensional activities that Islamic banks may have to undertake to internalize informational asymmetries, a major source of adverse selection and moral hazard in the lending process. Universal banking, being of German origin, may be a useful route to further development of Islamic banking, as there is an indication that countries with a German legal origin have better developed financial intermediaries (Levine, Loayza and Beck, 1999).

The author does not provide examples of new instruments, operational structures and suggestions for legal reforms in countries where Islamic banking has assumed mainstream relevance. There is some anecdotal evidence that most Muslims perceive Islamic banking and finance as a social enterprise and expect it to play a socially responsible role in development process. Hence, there is a need to develop a model of Islamic banking that combines the efficiency of modern banking with the passion of charity to provide financing for development. In Islamic history, institutions such as *waqf* and *zakāh* have played an important role in the development process. Some salient features of a model of Islamic banking that combines modern banking practices with the institutions of *waqf* and *zakāh* are briefly described here.

In Pakistan, the paid-up capital requirement for establishing a bank is Rs500 million. A registered banking *waqf* may raise this fund through *ijārah* bonds (*ṣukūk*), donations, equity (yielding social return as opposed to financial return) and any other permissible mode to sponsor a bank (call it *Waqf* Bank). A primary objective of *Waqf* Bank would be to finance *awqāf* (not-for-profit organizations) in different sectors, such as housing, education, health, agriculture, and small and medium-sized enterprises. Suppose a housing *waqf* seeks finances from the *Waqf* Bank for developing a housing complex. The housing *waqf* wishes to provide residential property to people, preferably in lower-income brackets, on a loan-carrying-a-service-charge basis. For financial sustainability, the housing *waqf* plans to run businesses and services in the housing complex on a commercial basis, which may include social services through hospitals, schools, shopping complexes, petrol filling stations, restaurants, and so on. The housing *waqf* does not necessarily have to provide all these services by itself; it can encourage other organizations (such as a health *waqf*, or an educational *waqf*, etc.), to build and run hospitals and schools. All these *awqāf* may be part of an umbrella organization sharing a common vision and philosophy. In this way, the bank can serve as a financial intermediary as well as an engine for growth. This is only a brief sketch of the structure of an Islamic bank established for promoting development and growth.

Such *waqf*-type structures already exist in Muslim countries, and there is a need to study their operations to explore the implications for the further development of Islamic banking. Most such organizations are non-financial firms, though. An example of such a structure is the Fauji Foundation in Pakistan, a not-for-profit organization primarily working for the welfare of retired military personnel. It runs the largest non-government welfare programme in the country, operating 250 health and educational institutions. It is also one of the largest industrial conglomerates, having 14 industrial and commercial enterprises. Organizational structures such as this must provide important lessons for the further growth of Islamic banking and finance as an engine of equitable growth.

A limited variety of financial institutions does not help the Islamic financial system to fulfil even some fundamental functions

The author rightly argues that the Islamic financial system in its present form lacks variety. The most common activity undertaken by Islamic banks has been trade financing, although now investment banking is also emerging as a significant activity for Islamic financial institutions. However, there still is a need to develop specialized institutions for resource mobilization in specific sectors. Pension funds provide just one example, although one can equally argue for housing, education and a number of other sectors that desperately need operational modes of Islamic finance.

Further research

A natural progression from this chapter is towards a time-series analysis of financial sector development and economic growth in the countries where Islamic banking has now existed for some time. The cross-sectional and panel data analysis now abound and it would be quite instructive to investigate the nature of the relationship between financial sector development and economic growth in the Islamic countries, and what effect Islamic banking and finance might have on this relationship. A more meaningful study may involve an assessment of Islamic financial institutions and their contribution to economic growth, as Islamic finance does not exist at a system level except in a couple of countries where financial reforms are at best in their infancy.

Comment

Sayyid Tahir

The stated objective of the chapter is 'to analyse and evaluate the role of the Islamic financial system in facilitating economic growth'. The author proceeds as follows.

First he identifies four financial factors for economic growth: saving (S), fixed capital financing (F_k), working capital financing (F_w) and household credit (F_c). In this respect, financial institutions are said to perform a positive role by (i) minimizing risk through diversification and other risk management practices, (ii) enabling capital accumulation, (iii) efficiently allocating capital, (iv) facilitating exchange in the input and product markets, and (v) improving corporate governance.

Next he gives an overview of the conventional financial system and how it facilitates the four financial factors mentioned above. He lists different financial institutions in a conventional economy and the activities they are engaged in, and examines their contribution to economic growth by providing different financial services. A total of ten institutions are listed in the private sector. Some of these are involved in purely debt activities, some in purely equity, some in both equity and debt, and one in debt and leasing. Their efficacy as regards the four financial factors of growth, as above, is also explained. These details serve as prelude to the author's own contribution.

The author starts his study of the growth-enhancing potential of the Islamic financial system by first listing the likely financial instruments. He then presumes that the financial institutions listed by him would also exist in the Islamic set-up. Table 3.2 lists the types of activities the said financial institutions might undertake, and the financial instruments they might use on their asset (or financing) side. The liability or resource mobilization side of these institutions is overlooked in this table, but a redress for this omission is made in the analysis of the contribution of the various Islamic financial instruments to each of the financial factors of growth. It is noteworthy that the analysis is not carried out by institution. The author also tries to give a quantitative notion of the role of the Islamic financial system. The basis for his conclusions is given in Tables 3.3 and 3.4. He gives his recommendations on establishing a comprehensive Islamic financial system in the penultimate section.

It is noteworthy that financial factors of growth are perceived at macro level, but the argument for derivation is cast at micro level This methodological slip is, however, not critical for the purpose of the analysis. The Islamic financial instruments noted by the author raise some questions. Individual money-lenders have never been allowed to advance loans on the basis of a 'service charge' throughout Islamic history. In the *Sharīʿah*, a thing prohibited at individual level is also prohibited for groups of individuals. Given this, it is difficult to see how the use of a 'loan on the basis of service charges' can be condoned for financial institutions that are group entities. Similar questions can be raised about *ijārah wa iqtinā'*. This transaction constitutes combining the acts of sale and leasing in a single transaction. 'Leasing' means 'not selling'. Having two mutually exclusive goals in the same transaction lacks *Sharī'ah* sanction. Other than this, one may note that in an Islamic milieu interest-free loans or *qarḍ ḥasan* will exist at a personal level. They should not be expected to be available to financial institutions established for economic reasons. This point is not missed by the author but, at several places, he gives conflicting signals in this regard.

In his analysis of the Islamic financial system and economic growth, the author presumes that the financial institutions in an Islamic milieu would largely be the same as those currently found in the conventional financial system. This proposition needs some review. The matrix of Islamic financial instruments implies that role function of financial institutions will change in an Islamic set-up. They would facilitate transactions at the grassroots level by coming into the picture as traders, lessors and partners (as economic agents). Thus, unlike interest-based financial institutions, Islamic financial institutions would no longer be pure financial intermediaries, collecting money with one hand and passing it on with the other without linking it to real economic activities. The implications of change in the role function for financial institutions can also be seen with reference to Table 3.2 in the chapter. The listed activities and instruments are the same for 'commercial banks', 'near banks' and 'investment banks', not to mention 'micro finance institutions'.[20] This is the conclusion that follows in the absence of any strong reason for limiting the use of the *mushārakah* option to investment banks only. The question arises: will economic factors not lead to blurring of the line of distinction between these institutions in the Islamic set-up?

One may also note that holding shares and providing financing on an equity basis are two separate things. When a party buys shares in an existing company, it is a trading – rather than a financing – act. This, together with the points raised by the author, begs a clear explanation of the 'Equity' entry in Table 3.2.

Another point noteworthy about Table 3.2 is that it pertains to financing matters. Unlike the approach followed for conventional financial system in Table 3.1, the author chooses to discuss separately matters related to mobilization of savings (*S*). He notes that:

> All modes of financing can be used to attract savings and resource mobilization. Commercial banks use loans and *muḍārabah* modes to attract deposits (*qarḍ ḥasan* for current account deposits and the *muḍārabah* for investment deposits). Investment banks and venture capitalists can mobilize funds on a long-term *muḍārabah* basis. Mutual funds can attract financial resources through different instruments. For example, different

sorts of funds exist, including *murābaḥah* funds, *salam* funds, leasing funds, and equity (*mushārakah*) funds. Similarly, asset-backed bonds can be based on *muḍārabah, salam*, or *ijārah* modes.

It seems that the author has lost control of his argument here. First, *muḍārabah* and *mushārakah* differ mainly in respect of who contributes to the capital. It is possible that banks can commit a part of their capital and invite depositors to provide funds on a participatory basis.[21] This would be *mushārakah* between banks and depositors.

Notwithstanding the purpose for which mutual funds, or for that matter any other financial institution, may mobilize funds, the transaction between them and the resource-owners/savers will continue to remain either *muḍārabah* or *mushārakah*. Therefore, there is a need to review the author's claim that 'All modes of financing can be used.'

Several other questions arise on this part of the chapter. For example, according to the author, 'While theoretically equity instruments (*muḍārabah* and *mushārakah*) can be used to finance working capital, the problem is to ascertain the rate of return on these investments.' On the contrary, I think the problem lies in designing the transaction.[22] His claim that there are no operational models that enable the use of equity financing to finance working capital is also not tenable. Last but not least, as noted above, lending – whether with or without service charges – will not be an option for Islamic financial institutions.

His derivation of an index for contribution of Islamic financial system to various financial factors of growth in Tables 3.3 and 3.4 is questionable on several counts. As noted above, the assignment of positive weights to *murābaḥah, salam/istiṣnāʿ* and *ijārah* towards mobilizing *S* is not correct. The same point applies to other non-zero weights in Table 3.3. The analysis in Table 3.4 raises questions of a different sort. As we know, the Islamic financial system does not exist in practice. He has not given sufficient grounds to justify the numerical weights reported in this table. This casts considerable doubts on the conclusions drawn by him.

Notes

1. On 24 June 2002 the *Sharīʿah* Appellate bench of the Supreme Court of Pakistan set aside its earlier judgment in which it had directed the government of Pakistan to eliminate *ribā* from the economy by 30 June 2002.
2. Empirical evidence suggests that the contributions of these sources differ for developed and developing countries. In most developing countries capital accumulation is the most important factor explaining growth, followed by labour, with technical progress having an even smaller effect. In developed countries, the most important source of growth is technological progress. The contribution of the factors of production, particularly capital, is less significant (see Maddison, 1970; Robinson, 1971; Lim, 1996; Young, 1996).

3. In an open economy, a part of the funds used in the economy can come from foreign sources. The inclusion of the foreign sector does not change the qualitative results of this chapter and is omitted to avoid complications.
4. See Ahmed and Miller (2000).
5. As pointed out, in an open economy another source of borrowing would be foreign sources.
6. Merton and Bodie (1995) identify six functions of financial system that are very similar to those outlined by Levine (1997). According to Merton and Bodie (1995) the functions provided by a financial system are clearing and settling payments (to facilitate trade), pooling of resources, transfer of economic resources, managing risk, providing price information, and dealing with incentive problems.
7. For an extensive study on micro finance, see Hulme and Mosley (1996a, 1996b), Kimenyi, Wieland and Pischke (1998), Otero and Rhyne (1994) and Schneider (1997).
8. Detailed expositions of the different principles of Islamic financing are found in Kahf and Khan (1992) and Ahmad (1993).
9. For a discussion on the problems that Islamic banks face in using profit-sharing modes of financing, see Ahmed (2002b), Aggarwal and Yousef (2000) and Khan (1995).
10. There are and can be some specialized institutions unique to the Islamic financial sector (such as *muḍārabah* companies, *ijārah* companies, etc.) that are not included.
11. For a list of Islamic bonds and securities, see Khan and Ahmed (2001, p. 148).
12. One of the commentators on this chapter has questioned the use of instruments (*murābaḥah, mushārakah*, etc.) for resource mobilization. As pointed out above, these are done through mutual funds. In these funds, the relationship between an investor and financial institution is that of *wakālah* (agency). In these contracts, the financial institution acts as an agent and invests in different funds on behalf of the investors.
13. Islamic economists have emphasized that both equity and distributive aspects are essential elements of an Islamic economy (Naqvi, 1981; Chapra, 1985, 1992; Sadeq, 1990).
14. The Asian crisis of the late 1990s shows how years of growth can be wiped out in a very short time due to financial crisis. For discussions on the impact of the Asian financial crises, see Wade (1998).
15. For a discussion on corporate governance in Islamic financial institutions, see Chapra and Ahmed (2002).
16. To see the dominance of fixed-income instruments in Islamic banks see Iqbal, Ahmad and Khan (1998) and for micro finance institutions see Ahmed (2002a).
17. For a discussion on incentive-compatible profit-sharing contracts that can be used in financing, see Ahmed (2002b) and Khan (1987).
18. Islamic Bank Bangladesh has a Rural Development Scheme (RDS) through which it finances micro enterprises. Ahmed (2001) shows that the scheme can be carried out by Islamic banks at no extra cost. For a discussion on financing micro enterprises by micro finance institutions, see Ahmed (2002a).
19. *Muḍārabah* companies and the RDS micro-finance programme of Islami Bank Bangladesh Ltd are a couple of examples of such institutions.
20. The activity entry in the 'Other activities' column reads 'Debt/Leasing' for investment banks. It should be 'Sale (Debt)/Leasing' in order to be consistent with other entries in this table.

21. See, for example, International Institute of Islamic Economics (IIIE, 1999), ch. 4, for details.
22. See IIIE (1999).

References

Aggarwal, Rajesh K. and Tarik Yousef (2000), 'Islamic Banks and Investment Financing', *Journal of Money, Credit, and Banking*, 32, 93–120.

Ahmad, Ausaf (1993), *Contemporary Practices of Islamic Financing Techniques*, Research Paper Number 20, Jeddah: Islamic Research and Training Institute, Islamic Development Bank.

Ahmed, Habib (2001), 'Frontiers of Islamic Banking: A Synthesis of Social Role and Micro-finance', manuscript.

Ahmed, Habib (2002a), 'Financing Micro-enterprises: An Analytical Study of Islamic Micro-finance Institutions', *Islamic Economic Studies*, 9 (2), 27–64.

Ahmed, Habib (2002b), 'Incentive Compatible Profit-Sharing Contracts: A Theoretical Treatment', in Munawar Iqbal and David Llewellyn (eds), *Islamic Banking and Finance: New Perspectives on Profit-Sharing and Risk*, Cheltenham: Edward Elgar.

Ahmed, Habib and Stephen M. Miller (2000), 'Crowding-out and Crowding-in Effects of the Components of Government Expenditure', *Contemporary Economic Policy*, 18, 124–33.

Chapra, M. Umer (1985), *Towards a Just Monetary System*, Leicester: The Islamic Foundation.

Chapra, M. Umer (1992), *Islam and the Economic Challenge*, Leicester: The Islamic Foundation.

Chapra, M. Umer and Habib Ahmed (2002), *Corporate Governance in Islamic Financial Institutions*, Occasional Paper Number 6, Jeddah: Islamic Research and Training Institute, Islamic Development Bank.

Hamlin, A. P. and D. F. Heartfield (1991), 'Competitive Management and Working Capital', *Management and Decision Economics*, 12, 207–17.

Hermes, Niels and Robert Lensink (2000), 'Financial System Development in Transition Economies', *Journal of Banking and Finance*, 24, 507–24.

Honohan, Patrick (2001), 'Islamic Financial Intermediation: Economic and Prudential Considerations', manuscript, Washington, DC: The World Bank.

Hulme, David and Paul Mosley (1996a), *Finance Against Poverty, Volume 1*, London: Routledge.

Hulme, David and Paul Mosley (1996b), *Finance Against Poverty, Volume 2*, London: Routledge.

Hussein, K. A. (2004), 'Operational Efficiency in Islamic Banking: The Sudanese Experience', *Research Paper Number 65*, Jeddah: Islamic Research and Training Institute, Islamic Development Bank.

International Institute of Islamic Economics (1999), *IIIE's Blueprint of Islamic Financial System*, Islamabad: International Institute of Islamic Economics.

Iqbal, Munawar, Ausaf Ahmad and Tariqullah Khan (1998), *Challenges Facing Islamic Banking*, Occasional Paper Number 1, Jeddah: Islamic Research and Training Institute, Islamic Development Bank.

Jarhi al-, Mabid A. (1999), 'Islamic Economics from Vantage Point', Keynote Lecture, International Conference on Islamic Economics Towards 21st Century, 9–12 August, Kuala Lumpur, Malaysia.

Kahf, Monzer and Tariqullah Khan (1992), *Principles of Islamic Financing*, Research Paper Number 16, Jeddah: Islamic Research and Training Institute, Islamic Development Bank.

Khan, Mohsin S. and Abdelhak S. Senhadji (2000), *Financial Development and Economic Growth: An Overview*, IMF Working Paper WP/00/209, Washington, DC: International Monetary Fund.

Khan, Tariqullah (1995), 'Demand and Supply of Mark-up and PLS Funds in Islamic Banking: Some Alternative Explanations', *Islamic Economic Studies*, 3 (1), 39–78.
Khan, Tariqullah and Habib Ahmed (2001), *Risk Management: An Analysis of Issues in Islamic Financial Industry*, Occasional Paper Number 5, Jeddah: Islamic Research and Training Institute, Islamic Development Bank.
Khan, Waqar Masood (1987), 'Towards an Interest-Free Islamic Economic System', in Mohsin S. Khan and Abbas Mirakhor (eds), *Theoretical Studies in Islamic Banking and Finance*, Houston, TX: The Institute for Research and Islamic Studies.
Kimenyi, Mwangi S., Robert C. Wieland and J. D. V. Pischke (eds) (1998), *Strategic Issues in Micro-finance*, Aldershot: Ashgate.
King, R. and R. Levine (1993a), 'Finance and Growth: Schumpeter Might be Right', *Quarterly Journal of Economics*, 108, 707–37.
King, R. and R. Levine (1993b), 'Finance Entrepreneurship and Growth: Theory and Evidence', *Journal of Monetary Economics*, 32, 513–42.
Kireyev, A. (2001), *Financial Reforms in Sudan: Streamlining Bank Intermediation*, IMF Working Paper No. 53, Washington, DC: International Monetary Fund.
Levine, Ross (1997), 'Financial Development and Economic Growth: Views and Agenda', *Journal of Economic Literature*, 35, 688–726.
Levine, Ross, Norman Loayza and Thorsten Beck (1999), *Financial Intermediation and Growth: Causality and Causes*, Policy Research Working Paper 2059, Washington, DC: The World Bank.
Lim, D. (1996), *Explaining Economic Growth: A New Analytical Framework*, Cheltenham: Edward Elgar.
Maddison, A. (1970), *Economic Progress and Policy in Developing Countries*, London: Allen & Unwin.
McKinnon, R. I. (1973), *Money and Capital in Economic Development*, Washington, DC: Brookings Institute.
Merton, Robert C. and Zvi Bodie (1995), 'A Conceptual Framework for Analyzing the Financial Environment', in Global Financial System Project, *The Global Financial System: A Functional Perspective*, Boston, MA: Harvard Business School Press.
Naqvi, Syed Nawab Haider (1981), *Ethics and Economics: An Islamic Synthesis*, Leicester: The Islamic Foundation.
Otero, Maria and Elisabeth Rhyne (eds) (1994), *The New World of Microenterprise Finance*, West Hartford, CT: Kumarian Press.
Robinson, S. (1971), 'The Sources of Growth in Less Developed Countries: A Cross-Section Study', *Quarterly Journal of Economics*, 85, 391–408.
Sadeq, Abulhasan Muhammad (1990), *Economic Development in Islam*, Selangor, Darul Ehsan: Pelanduk.
Schneider, Hartmut (ed.) (1997), *Micro-finance for the Poor*, Paris: Development Centre of the Organization for Economic Cooperation and Development.
Shaw, E. S. (1973), *Financial Deepening in Economic Development*, New York: Oxford University Press.
Tsuru, Kotaro (2000), 'Finance and Growth: Some Theoretical Considerations and a Review of the Empirical Literature', *Working Paper Number 228*, Paris: Economics Department, OECD.
Wade, Robert (1998), 'The Asian Debt and Development Crises of 1997: Causes and Consequences', *World Development*, 26, 1,535–53.
Young, Alwyn (1996), 'Lessons from the East Asian NICs: A Contrarian View', *European Economic Review*, 38, 964–73.

4

The Role of Islamic Financial Institutions in Sustainable Development

Abul Hassan and Abdelkader Chachi

Sustainable development is an economic issue, but there is an ethical standpoint that lies behind it. In the light of the need for sustainable development and the call of Agenda 21, the United Nations Environment Programme (UNEP) recognized the importance of financial institutions. Islamic financial institutions may interact with the environmental issues in various ways: as investors, innovators, valuers and as powerful stakeholders. In this chapter, a transactional model of Islamic financial markets is used to indicate how it is possible to influence economic and financial transactions.

Introduction

In its 1987 report entitled *Our Common Future*, the World Commission on Environment and Development defined sustainable development as: 'development, which meets the needs of the present without compromising the ability of future generations to meet their own needs'.[1] Although the idea is simple, the task is substantial. It means meeting four objectives simultaneously, throughout the whole world:

(a) social progress which recognizes the needs of everyone;
(b) effective protection of the environment;
(c) prudent use of natural resources;
(d) maintaining high and stable levels of economic growth and employment.

Many governments and non-governmental organizations (NGOs) have long feared that sustainability and development might be incompatible. In particular, they fear that the existing economic trends and the fallout from international agreements could freeze global economic and political inequalities in the name of sustainability, and that this would stifle progress and movement towards socio-economic parity in the developing countries. As a result, financing development has always been the main priority for the southern countries in international negotiations. At the United Nations Conference on Environment and Development (UNCED), popularly known as the Rio Earth Summit, held in 1992, financing and technology transfer were the two 'cross-cutting issues' passed by the South. A decade later, in 2002, these two issues continued to provide central themes at the Johannesburg World Summit on Sustainable Development (WSSD). The UN Conference on Financing for Development (FfD) held in 2002 in Monterrey also repeatedly focused on development financing mechanisms at the behest of the developing countries.

Notwithstanding the persistence of the issue, the trend since 1992 has been disappointing. At the Rio Summit, the UNCED Secretariat estimated the financing needs of Agenda 21 to be close to US$600 billion per year, including $125 billion per year as grants or concessional financing. In practice, despite growing economic prosperity in the North and repeated commitments to 'new and additional financing', there was a net decline, even in existing official development assistance (Banuri and Spanger-Siegfried, 2001). In 2000, official development assistance (ODA) fell to its lowest level ever, declining to $53 billion from $56 billion per year (IIED, 2002).[2] The aid level in 2000 represents only 0.22 per cent of the GNP of the developed and advanced countries (DAC), less than a third of the UN target of 0.7 per cent. Even this low volume of aid is not spent primarily in countries whose population is in absolute poverty or on measures that directly benefit the most disadvantaged groups.

In the light of the need for sustainable development and the call of Agenda 21, the UNEP recognized the importance of financial institutions by stating that 'financial institutions which assume the risk of companies and plants can exercise considerable influence – in some cases control – over investment and management decisions which could be brought into play for the benefit of the environment'. The Islamic financial markets can present an opportunity for environmental policy, which may be particularly useful in view of the need for a wider range of policy instruments. The aim of this chapter is to examine and explore to what extent the Islamic financial institutions (IFIs) can encourage the corporate sector and directly participate in sustainable development.

The next section discusses Islamic perspectives on sustainable development, while the third section gives an overview of different models for understanding corporate responsibility in sustainable development. The fourth section focuses on the role of the Islamic financial institutions (Islamic banks, investment companies, insurance companies) in sustainable development. A transactional model of the Islamic financial markets is used to indicate how it is possible to influence financial transactions. The following section discusses the relationship between the companies, investors and environment, and the final section offers some conclusions and recommendations.

Sustainable development from an Islamic perspective

One does not find a formal Islamic theory of sustainable development in the current literature. However, its absence from the current literature on Islamic economics does not mean that such a theory cannot be built. Asad (1987) argued[3]: 'in an ideology like the Islamic one, there can be no dividing line between the "spiritual" and the "worldly" spheres – and therefore also no dividing line between man's faith and his practical life'. The *Qur'ānic* portrayal of nature, as found in numerous verses, is multi-faceted. God creates nature, the *Qur'ān* emphatically declares.[4] Whereas God is characterized by Unity (*tawḥīd*), nature is characterized by duality,[5] in the sense of complementarity or diversity as denoted by the Arabic word *zawj*. Another characteristic of nature in the *Qur'ān* is order or balance.[6] The idea of a divinely arranged order in nature which is found in the Qur'ān could be said to refer to the idea that nature is the purposive creation of an omnipotent and omniscient God and is therefore perfectly ordered and structured.[7] Evil human forces should not be allowed to disrupt the order of nature. In this regard, the Qur'ān states: 'Do not spread corruption on earth after it has been so well ordered'[8] (*Qur'ān* 7:56).

According to Asad (1984), Islamic doctrine asserts that: 'Man is an animal in the sense of organically belonging to that group of living beings which are endowed with the faculties of sensation, perception and movement, as well as in the sense of being dependent on physiological needs and functions more or less resembling those of other animal beings.'[9] Man's distinction lies in trusting reason, and volition whereby man has been given the ability to exercise choice between good and evil. This rational consciousness gives man the 'ability to form concepts and to bring them together in countless combinations by means of mental processes which can be guided and directed by his will'.[10] Consequently, whereas other animals adapt themselves to the environment (or else suffer the fatal consequences), man has become increasingly skilful in adapting his environment, through the use of science and technology, to suit his own ends. Islam endorses these activities and thus environmental transformation is, from the Islamic perspective, an inevitable component of life.[11] But, according to Islam, man should not carry out these activities arbitrarily. The *Qur'ān* sets up a vision of nature in relation to God and man. It also sets out an ethical code to guide man. Waste is abhorred,[12] as is haughtiness and all its expressions in boastful displays of wealth. Instead, Islam exhorts moderation and distributive justice.[13] There is also in existence a body of Islamic resource law, dating from the time of the Prophet (peace be upon him), which prohibits private ownership of common property resources such as pasture, woodland, wildlife and water, which must be managed for the common good. Wildlife and forests are safeguarded in *ḥimā* or reserves, which are established solely for conservation purposes (Sardar, 1988). Islamic jurisdiction rules can be applied to the management of natural resources.

Chapra (2000) argues that in all matters, including economic, a Muslim's faith has to be placed first because it provides the worldview which influences the whole human personality, behaviour, life-style, tastes, preferences and attitudes towards human beings, resources and the environment. It tries to promote a balance between the material and the spiritual urges of the human self, foster peace of mind in the individual, enhance family and social solidarity and prevent the development of animosity. A Muslim's faith provides the moral filter which tries to keep self-interest within the bounds of social interest by changing individual preferences in accordance with social priorities and eliminating or minimizing the use of resources for purposes that frustrate the realization of the social vision.[14] These are the components which fulfil the objectives of the *Sharīʿah.*

There are two commandments of major importance in the *Sharīʿah*, which have an immense bearing on the sustainable development issue. These two are the command to pay *zakāh* and the prohibition of usury (*ribā*). We shall briefly discuss each of these in the light of the definition of sustainable development to highlight the relationship between them.

Zakāh, or obligatory alms giving, is one of the 'Five Pillars of Islam'. It is a tax on personal wealth that is paid on, or more properly taken from, three forms of wealth: crops, livestock and money. It is an obligation based on clear *Qur'ānic* instructions, 'Establish the prayer and pay the *zakāh*.'[15] The seriousness of the obligation to pay *zakāh* is indicated by the fact that it can, in certain circumstances, be collected by force, even if that implies waging a war against those who refuse to pay it.[16] The economic institution of *zakāh* thus presupposes the political institution of *Khilafah* both for its execution and enforcement.

The acquisition and accumulation of wealth is permitted if it is pursued through lawful means: that is, if the individual meets all the attendant obligations (including payment of *zakāh* and other voluntary taxes), and if it does not distract one from the remembrance of God. The principle of mutual interest is used in such cases to establish social optimality in the distribution of resource and wealth. So, *zakāh* and *ṣadaqah* (voluntary charity) are part of an effective social apparatus to ensure distributive equity and social justice. The act of giving is so important that generosity and charity have been declared 'an occupation without a loss'. Islam views social justice as a vital objective of social policy, which is evident from the fact that it repeatedly urges Muslims not to seek salvation through self-alienation or the monastic life, as this could entail one's withdrawal from the active promotion of society's well being.[17] Thus the pursuit of social justice as a component of sustainable development has a well recognized place in Islamic theology.

Ribā (usury) is traditionally defined as 'any unjustified increment between the value of the goods given and the counter value of the goods received'.[18] The seriousness of the prohibition against usury is indicated by many verses.[19] In simple terms, *ribā* can be understood as lending money on interest, including any transaction in which money, or what acts as money, is effectively bought for a time. It is not out of place to mention here that gold and silver are commodities with their own market value, which can be, and are, bought and sold in their own right. But the excessive circulation of paper monies brings two main dangers to any economy: inflation and stagnation. The direct causal link between usury and inflation is very clear from the credit creation of the central banks. It proves that the more 'money' there is in circulation to pay for the same amount of goods (as is inevitable under the present system), the more prices go up. So abolishing usury – which is what the Muslims are called upon to do – would mean reducing inflation.

Most of the day-to-day transactions now taking place involve usury in some form or other. Since usury is forbidden in Islam, it brings with it trouble. This is so because, from the Muslim point of view, every permitted act brings with it a blessing from Allah, while every prohibited act brings with it the opposite. With usury so prevalent, it is not surprising that there is such an extent of degradation and despoliation associated with it today.

The basic ethical standpoint of the Muslims is belief in God and acceptance of His laws, which include economic laws. The primary obligation in Islam is to pay *zakāh*, while the primary economic prohibition is to avoid any kind of *ribā*. However, neither of these is possible without *Khalīfah*, that is, the political authority of a *Khalīfah* or an *Amīr* within a group which accepts his leadership and which, as a group, can put these commandments into practice. Sustainable development is thus not so much a question of managing land, water (and so on) as managing the people who could take care of economic development. The *Qur'ān* supports this argument: 'God does not change what is with a people until they change what is in themselves' (13:11).

Islam also does not offer an elaborate formal model for the enhancement of well being in the ecological sense; instead, it presents principles that can be used for the development of appropriate models. Therefore sustainable development, in the sense of maintaining ecological balance, also needs to be understood within this implicit but potentially formal framework. Islam is a monotheistic religion that has a holistic view of the world.[20] According to Islam, the true ownership of all resources resides with God. In sharing this ownership, humanity is God's supreme creation and its role is to serve as God's vicegerent (*Khalīfah*) on the earth. While superior human intelligence means power and control over all other things on Earth, this is not absolute.

Nobody can violate the basic premise of trusteeship while using it to his advantage.[21] Since the environment and ecology are part of God's creation, their misuse may be interpreted in two ways: as a transgression of the absolute authority of God, and as harming both the violator and the person who is injured. Thus any misuse of the environment that involves waste and destruction is a sinful act in both senses.

Ahmad (1976) argues that the development process may be directed through *tazkiyah* (purification and growth) in order to improve the quality of life and welfare of human beings in this world and hereafter. The quality of life and welfare of human beings are determined by many elements. Development is concerned not only with economic development but also with human development. The foundation blocks of the Islamic approach to development include: *tawḥīd, rabūbiyyah, Khilāfah and tazkiyah.* The Islamic concept of development should be derived from its concept of *tazkiyah,* as it addresses the problem of human development in all its dimensions and is concerned with growth and expansion towards perfection though purification of attitudes and relationships. Sustainable development is thus clearly a familiar term to many people and is on the political agendas of governments of the Islamic countries as well as countries throughout the world. 'Sustainable development' can be covered under the definition of 'balanced development', a term used by Ahmad (1976, pp. 171–90).

Understanding corporate responsibility in sustainable development

The struggle to define the boundaries of corporate responsibility for social and environmental matters has deep roots in the history of business. From the beginning of the Industrial Revolution, those within and outside the business world have battled over the very notion and extent of corporate responsibility. Different models have emerged, all of which exist in the Islamic world today. We give only a brief description of the following four models.

Ethical model

We find many informal models in Islamic history. With inspiration from the *Qur'ān* and the sayings of the Prophet Muhammad (peace be upon him), many Muslim businessmen have played an active role in promoting socio-economic development in Islamic countries. The history of Muslim philanthropy has encompassed donations in cash or in kind, community investment, and provisions of essential services such as *madāris* (schools for religious education), schools, infirmaries, and so on. Many Muslim firms, particularly 'family run businesses', continue to support such Islamic philanthropic initiatives. But the first formal ethical model of corporate responsibility can be seen in the pioneering efforts of nineteenth-century corporate philanthropists such as the Cadbury brothers in England.[22]

Static model

A second model of corporate responsibility emerged during the time of *Khalīfah* Umar Ibn al-Khattab (d.644CE). The office of consumer protection and market supervision, the *muḥtasib*, was instituted. Cartels, monopolies, hoarding and any other methods of artificially interfering with market prices were banned in Islamic law. The means of making a profit was made generally beneficial to the community.[23] The boundaries between the state and society were clearly defined for state enterprises. Elements of corporate responsibility, especially those relating to community and worker relationships, were enshrined in Islamic law and management principles.

Liberal model

Indeed, a third model of corporate responsibility underpins the worldwide trend towards privatization and deregulation, by which companies are solely responsible to their owners. This approach was encapsulated by the American economist Milton Friedman[24] (1958), who challenged the very notion of corporate responsibility for anything other than the economic bottom line.

'If anything is certain to destroy our free society, to undermine its very foundation, it would be a widespread acceptance by management of social responsibilities in some sense other than to make as much money as possible. This is a fundamentally subversive doctrine' (Friedman, 1958, p. 23). Many in the corporate world and elsewhere would agree with this concept, arguing that it is sufficient for business to obey the law and generate wealth which, through taxation and private charitable choices, can be directed to social ends.

Stakeholder model

The rise of globalization has brought with it a growing realization that, with increasing economic rights, business also has a growing range of social obligations. Citizen campaigns against irresponsible corporate behaviour along with consumer action and increasing shareholders' pressure on corporate policies have given rise to the 'stakeholder model' of corporate responsibility. This view is often associated with R. Edward Freeman,[25] whose seminal analysis of the stakeholder approach to strategic management in 1984 brought the concept of stakeholding into the mainstream of management literature (Freeman, 1984). According to Freeman, 'a stakeholder in an organization is any group or individual who can affect or is affected by the achievement of the organization's objectives'.

The experience of the past decade has served to reinforce this viewpoint. With companies facing increasing scrutiny in the global economy, the corporate responsibility agenda now encompasses a wide range of issues including provision of quality, safe products at fair prices, ethical business practices, fair employment policies, and environmental protection. Companies are increasingly expected to perform according to a 'triple bottom line'[26] of economic, social and environmental elements. In addition, increasing focus is being placed on the growth of corporate power and the need for greater accountability and transparency to society (for example, through reportage and stakeholder dialogue). Indeed, there is an emerging consensus throughout the world that companies need to go beyond their traditional 'economic' roles.

* * *

Each of the four models of corporate responsibility described above is prevalent to some extent in Islamic countries. What is noticeable today is the dynamic nature of corporate responsibility in Agenda 21 of the United Nations[27] Action Programme for Sustainable Development, and the need to clarify the implication for corporate practice. One of the weaknesses of the current situation is the tendency for the agenda to be set up at a global level, largely by institutions located in the industrialized world, with little understanding of the diversity of approaches and their track record in other parts of the world. For example, a 20-country public opinion survey on corporate social responsibility carried out by the Toronto-based 'Environics International' in July 2001 concluded that some Third World countries (including Bangladesh, Indonesia and Pakistan) rank very low in terms of the level of social responsibility demanded from companies.

To clarify the implication of corporate responsibility within the entire corporate sector is beyond the scope of this study. The present study will examine and explore the extent to which the IFIs can motivate, encourage, and finance the corporate sector to participate in sustainable development in accordance with the approach of the stakeholders' model.

Role of the Islamic financial institutions

The World Commission on Environment and Development (WCED), also known as the Brundtland Commission, recognizes the importance of financial institutions. It emphasized that financial institutions, which assume the risk of companies and plants, can exercise considerable influence, and in some cases, control, over investment and management decisions, which could be brought into play for the benefit of the environment. So far, the role of the Islamic financial institutions has not been explored in detail at the Islamic world level. The IFIs may interact with the environment in a number of ways including:

(a) as investors, supplying the investment needed to achieve sustainable development;
(b) as innovators, developing new financial products to encourage sustainable development (e.g., in energy efficiency);
(c) as valuers, pricing risks and estimating returns for companies, projects and others;
(d) as powerful stakeholders (as shareholders and lenders they can exercise considerable influence over the management of companies);
(e) as polluters – whilst not being dirty industries, financial institutions do consume considerable resources.

In view of the indirect nature of many of the interactions above, policies are likely to be most effective if they aim to complement and work with existing financial activity.

The stakeholders in the corporate sector of the Islamic countries have tended to play down their potential role in moving towards sustainable development, believing that such matters are primarily the role of governments. However, their view has often tended towards dismissing environmental concerns as being of marginal importance to their business and, at first sight, the short-term expediencies of the financial markets and the altruistic, long-term concerns behind sustainable development might appear to have little in common.

In order to achieve sustainable development, it will require substantial investment in environmental technology, in new energy systems, in an environmentally sensitive infrastructure and in information technology (Zeinelabdin, 1993, pp. 61–75). This may require financial innovation to develop mechanisms for the new Islamic markets that sustainable development will create. It may also involve working with the policy makers of Islamic countries to ensure that the most appropriate structures are established to enable ready financing. IFIs can respond quickly to new opportunities, particularly when the potential is presented to them in a clear and consistent manner and, although large, the financing needs of sustainable development in Islamic countries are well within the scope of the financial markets of Islamic countries. However, inconsistent or ineffective policy development may send a negative signal to the market, and can result in adverse market sentiments against environmental projects.

The financial institutions of Islamic countries exercise considerable influence over most areas of economic activity, from the individuals struggling to make mortgage repayments, to the directors of multinational companies facing investors and analysts at the company Annual General Meeting. Of all the stakeholders of a company, financial institutions are usually the most powerful, yet have frequently been ignored from the perspective of achieving environmental change. Thus it is not surprising that, to date, the financial institutions have rarely used their influence for environmental matters. From the perspective of environmental policy makers, this situation represents a potential opportunity, particularly useful in view of the fact that the Organization of the Islamic Conference/United Nations Cooperation Committee has recognized the need for a wider range of policy instruments, especially the use of market-based tools (Zeinelabdin, 1993). Ideally, environmental policy makers in Islamic countries would like to see the IFIs complementing and reinforcing the signals that policy makers are trying to establish, including financially 'rewarding' environmentally superior behaviour (for example, with a lower cost of capital or a higher share price) and penalizing the bad.

Like conventional financial institutions, the IFIs also create some direct environmental impacts from their own operations, such as power usage, paper use and business travel. While not thought of as major polluters, there is scope to reduce this impact, and often to do so without incurring financial costs. The service sector is becoming increasingly important within the economies of Islamic countries, and as a whole its environmental impact is significant. Given their influence, the IFIs are well placed to play a leadership role within the sector in demonstrating environmental responsibility.

In order to achieve this change, the policy makers may have a number of options. Existing environmental legislation may be modified or interpreted in ways to make it more relevant to the Islamic financial markets. New environmental legislation may be evolved to encourage or coerce the financial markets to consider environmental issues. Financial instruments can be used to persuade the financial sector to get involved. Finally, the Islamic financial markets themselves are highly regulated and subject to legislation, and there may be scope here to adapt legislation to incorporate environmental aspects.

Transaction model of the Islamic financial markets

Islamic markets will only use their influence for the benefit of the environment if they see that it is in their interest, which means that it will help them to generate profits either directly or indirectly (by improving the quality of their business or their reputation). The indirect considerations are particularly important in the investment performance through better advice or management.

While this is straightforward, to apply it is rather more difficult. It can be very difficult to know beforehand whether a particular activity will be profitable or will enhance investment returns. Before considering any new activity, Islamic financial institutions will want to consider what they are letting themselves in for very carefully. As a result, it is useful to understand how the Islamic financial markets work in supplying capital. Figure 4.1 provides a model of the Islamic financial markets' operations in this matter.

Analysis is the key part of the process and will be largely driven by the objective of making profitable investment decisions. A pivotal factor in

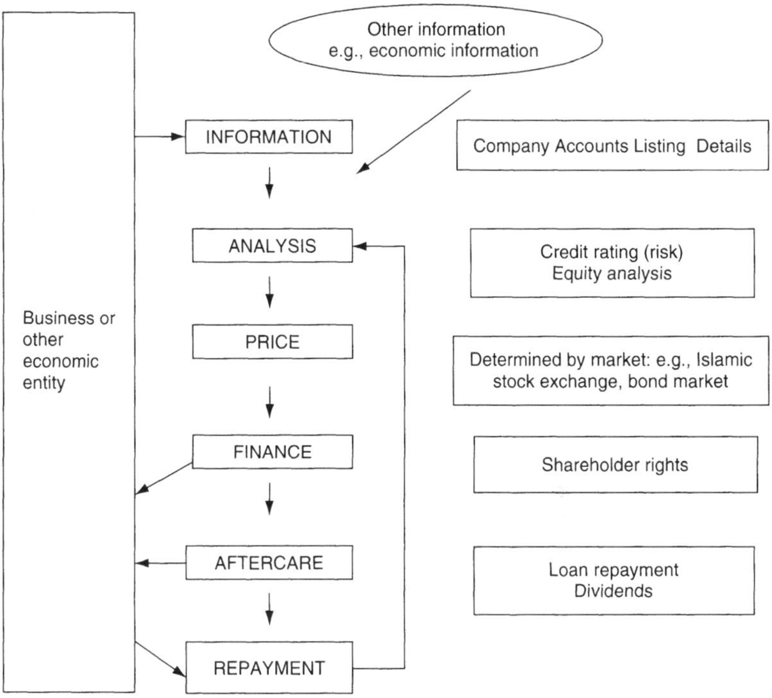

Figure 4.1 Transaction model of Islamic financial markets

analysis will be the estimation of the actual and perceived risks involved. One important aspect of analysis is that it involves costs which can be quite substantial. Thus an initial estimation is often made of the likely outcome of the analysis, with many propositions being rejected at an early stage (Gazni and Tamer, 1997). The price is primarily determined by the market, and is largely dependent on the type of finance and the risk once it is known. Aftercare refers to the fact that most financing lasts for a period of time and the Islamic financial institutions have a valid interest in supporting their investments once finance has been provided, which can be done through shareholder actions, through covenants on loans or through general provision of services which enhance the business.

This model applies both to individual financial transactions and to the development of new business lines, although the latter can be far less quantitative, and will be expected to offer the potential to recoup the initial costs several times over. This model highlights the fact that for a financial activity or modification to an activity to make sense to an Islamic financial institution, not only does it have to make sense in simple financial terms (to offer a fair return/be correctly priced), but it also has to be broadly viable and relevant to business, including covering the various costs involved in going through the steps above.

Like conventional financial systems, if the Islamic financial institutions are to integrate environmental considerations into their decision making, they need to be convinced that not only are they profitable in the narrow sense, but also that the arguments are sufficiently strong to make the environment a key issue for the IFIs, facing challenges and competition both internally and externally. Practically, the model suggests that information and analysis present key obstacles for the environment as, historically, obtaining good environmental data is a challenge. This will increase the costs and reduce the reliability of analysis and makes it more difficult for Islamic financial institutions to justify many environmental actions. That said, there is often considerable latitude in decision making in Islamic financial institutions; rarely are decisions black and white. Thus, in terms of individual transactions, environmental factors may play a significant role in marginal financing decisions, even if information is incomplete.[28] At the company level, while it may be difficult to justify new environmentally related activities in narrow business terms, they may offer benefits to an Islamic financial institution such as good publicity, and appear a good proposition in overall terms. Possible strategies are outlined below.

'Niche' strategies

The IFIs could see the environment as offering the potential for profitable lines of business, such as:

(a) building expertise in providing finance for key environmental sectors, including environmental technology, renewable energy, water and waste;
(b) developing financial products to assist in the use of environmental services such as energy efficiency;
(c) developing 'green' products in compliance with the *Sharīʿah* for clients and customers.

If the above-mentioned businesses are to offer attractive opportunities to the IFIs, they will require the existence of growing, profitable market segments. The extent to which such opportunities exist is clearly open to debate, but there is some evidence to suggest that substantial unexploited opportunities exist.[29] These opportunities represent a 'niche' approach in terms of an Islamic bank's business, although some of the niches could be quite substantial. The present impact of financing on the environment will depend on the extent to which finance is mobilized towards key sectors.

General strategies

Apart from the above, the IFIs could see the environment as an opportunity to improve the overall quality of their business, for instance by:

(a) improving the quality of their loan book by managing risks such as environmental liability;
(b) improving the quality of their investment decisions by including environmental factors;
(c) improving the quality of advice offered to clients e.g., in investment research.

All these opportunities represent a 'broad' approach, cutting across sectors, which could in theory have far-reaching consequences for many industrial sectors. However, the immediate impact on the environment is harder to quantify as it will depend on the extent to which such actions change the behaviour of the businesses and other economic entities involved. Initially, the effect is to remove an obstacle to environmentally responsible behaviour by companies, who appear to find the financial markets ignorant of, and possibly unsympathetic to, the actions many progressive companies are taking. In the long run, as companies see that the financial markets are prepared to recognize and reward environmentally superior behaviour, the effects could be substantial.[30] A key factor in this approach is whether environmentally responsible behaviour does contribute to superior financial performance (such as corporate profitability, investment returns, etc.), and is thus a matter worthy of the attention of Islamic financial institutions.

Sectors and clients

The Islamic financial markets cover a wide range of different functions and products and serve a wide range of different clients. The Islamic financial sector may be divided into Islamic banks, Islamic asset management companies and Islamic insurance companies (*takāful*). Islamic banks and asset management companies will trade off risk against potential return and may be interested in upside potential; insurers actively aim to adopt risk and offset it internally.[31] These different attitudes to risk can clearly result in differing attitudes in each sector towards environmental issues. Similarly, different IFIs have differing customer groups such as small and large industries, individuals, the public sector, and NGOs, and have different levels of influence over them. This will also affect where and how Islamic financial institutions can have an environmental impact and where they can best develop environmental practice. The main customer groups are reviewed below.

Large companies

Islamic banks are substantial lenders to large companies in the Muslim countries, and also provide a variety of other financial services, such as transaction processing and treasury management. Their ability to influence larger corporations is relatively limited, as competition is strong and these services are rarely central to large corporations. The greater influence on larger corporations will come from the investment sector and is discussed later. Some companies may be more subject to Islamic bank influence, such as private (unlisted) companies or those with tightly held shares, smaller listed companies more dependent on banks, and companies in financial difficulties. However, in certain sectors Islamic banks can have a greater influence, particularly where high levels of lending are normal. These include property (real estate), lending and project finance (*mushārakah*), and lending for stand-alone infrastructure projects: this can be relevant for the environmental sector. In this field, the Islamic banks can impose a variety of conditions relating to the construction and operation of the facility, through conditions and covenants on lending. These can include environmental considerations. While many Islamic banks will conduct an environmental risk review as part of the credit assessment this tends to be retrospective, and few can appear actively to impose and enforce environmental conditions. Environmental impact assessments can be a useful tool with such projects for identifying environmental project risks and suggesting risk management procedures. Liability regimes will also have an impact on the risk assessment of such financing.

Small and medium enterprises

Islamic banks are the most significant source of external finance to small and medium enterprises (SMEs) and can exert considerable influence on them since most of the SMEs have a banking relationship. The Islamic banks can send the following powerful signals to the SMEs.

Influence management through lending arrangements. When lending to SMEs, the Islamic banks may consider the quality of management and other risks, which can include environmental factors. The Islamic banks, when deciding whether to extend funds, can explicitly include environmental considerations in the conditions they impose on lending and in the terms of business they offer.

Supporting companies with information. The IFIs are a major source of information for companies, particularly SMEs in the Islamic countries, and there is potential for Islamic financial institutions to act as a conduit of information in the environmental area.

Specialist environmental financial services. There is some scope for Islamic banks to develop Islamic financial products, which contribute to the environment, such as energy efficiency loans or the leasing of environmental technology.

Specialist support for environmental companies. Most emerging sectors can face difficulty getting recognition from the financial markets because they are new, the risks are unknown, the technology unfamiliar and the markets uncertain. The environmental business sector certainly faces these difficulties. By actively trying to understand the sector and the issues it faces, the IFIs may at least try to reduce some of the obstacles the emerging businesses face, although one cannot expect them to forgo normal financial judgement. Interestingly, while several Islamic banks are actively involved in areas such as renewable energy financing, often neither their environment nor their publicity departments seem to be aware of such activities.

Households and individuals. Individuals have a major impact on the environment through their activities and consumption of goods and services, and in some cases their impact proves more intractable than commercial impacts. The IFIs can have a major impact on the activities of individuals through the provision of suitable financial arrangements: for instance, access to interest-free mortgage finance is a prerequisite to widespread home ownership, and car ownership may be increased by the availability of car loans and hire purchase. In the absence of suitable financing arrangements, products or goods may struggle to achieve sales, particularly if they have high capital costs and long life spans (in economic language, most consumers have a marginal discount rate far higher than the financial market norms).[32] This may often apply to environmental goods and services, which involve an up-front capital cost. The obvious example is energy efficiency, which in theory offers very attractive financial returns, but is impeded by the fact that individuals are unwilling to fund such investments and the Islamic financial markets have largely failed to provide suitable financing vehicles.

The public sector. The public sector comprises a major part of the economy of most Islamic countries, and thus will contribute directly to a large part of the environmental impact of the country, particularly if sectors such as water, waste, energy and transport are in state hands. Islamic financial institutions are also suppliers of capital to governments and public sector organizations and thus theoretically could have some influence over how that capital is provided and used. However, in most cases, public sector funding carries an explicit or implicit sovereign guarantee and thus there is little scope for individual public sector activities to be assessed on either their environmental or financial impacts by financing organizations. In extreme cases, it could be argued that if environmental mismanagement at a national level threatens the productive capacity of a country, then this should be reflected in the overall credit rating of the country. If public sector financing is provided at a more local level, without recourse to the central authorities, then environmental impacts might possibly be significant enough to merit the attention of the Islamic financial markets.

Non-governmental organizations. Non-governmental organizations include organizations such as charities, cooperatives, academic institutions, micro finance institutions, and so on. While having both modest needs for finance and low environmental impact, they can be important at the margin, as they can be working in critical areas or in an area actively seeking to apply financial innovation to the solution of key environmental problems; thus they can play a role in financing the environmental sector. Environmental economists and social activists have repeatedly emphasized that the financing in sustainable development should begin by investing in people (e.g., by investing in education, by refinancing the micro financing and by promoting social responsibility). As Harran al- (1999) argues, the availability of even modest amounts of capital can encourage entrepreneurial activity and create employment. While it is true that many micro finance organizations do not have a direct environmental focus, the activities of the Islamic banks supporting the micro finance organizations certainly help to address the social aspects of sustainable development.

Islamic banks

Unlike their conventional counterparts, Islamic bankers do not expect to advance money and receive a predetermined sum on a fixed date in the future. Under the *Sharīʿah*, they are instead responsible for ensuring that money is invested in viable projects, with reliable borrowers. If the project succeeds the banker shares in the profit. If it fails, the banker suffers losses.

The *Sharīʿah*, which dictates the activities of the Islamic banks as well as forming the basis of the daily lives of all Muslims, requires that reward comes from risk sharing. Profit must be justified through the creation of value that the banker brings to complement the value of the borrower's efforts and skills. Against a background of rapid growth in the economies of Islamic countries over the last 25 years or so, and an increasing desire to compete internationally, Islamic banks have begun to change and develop to provide a range of alternative financial products firmly based on Islamic principles.[33] Islamic financial techniques have been employed successfully in a growing number of major projects in the West. Islamic banks, such as the Al Barakah Group, Al Rajhi, National Commercial Bank, Faisal Islamic Banks Group, Bank Islam Malaysia Berhad, Dubai Islamic Bank and the Islamic Bank Bangladesh Ltd, amongst others, have completed project deals using the *ijārah* (lease financing technique) and many industrial projects, including the building of power stations, refineries and schools, by using *istiṣnāʿ*. The Islamic Development Bank has also financed many projects which are directly linked to sustainable development.

Spread across the Islamic world and beyond, there are more than 200 Islamic financial institutions: banks, mutual funds, mortgage companies, insurance companies; in short, an entire parallel economy in which the Islamic *Sharīʿah* has the final say. Industry growth has averaged 10–15 per cent a year. Sniffing opportunity, conventional banks such as Citibank and HSBC have opened Islamic 'windows' in the Gulf. The industry's market share is modest, at about 10 per cent (Useem, 2002). Islamic banks in Muslim and non-Muslim countries have total assets of over $200 billion. Thus they have sufficient influence on the economy of the Islamic world and its environmental impact. Islamic banks' services cover a wide range, including: deposits and lending in the modes of *muḍārabah, mushārakah* and *murābaḥah,* providing cheques and other transaction processing, and selling financial products and services. In principle, investment on a long-term basis (*mushārakah*) is the most important activity in the Islamic banking system. A key factor in determining the influence of Islamic banks on the environment will be the nature of the clients. Thus, it is worth looking at the key client groups individually, including large companies, SMEs and individuals. There is, however, scope for Islamic banks to influence consumer behaviour through the financial products they offer. Now Islamic banks have focused on two areas: some have made considerable progress in developing internal environmental management systems to reduce their own environmental impact, and others now include environmental analysis in their credit assessment process.[34] One particularly encouraging area of activity is providing practical support to small businesses on how to manage their environmental impact, through information packs and other support.[35] Where Islamic banks have been less progressive is in developing new financial products with an environmental perspective for both business and individuals, such as energy efficiency loans, and encouraging the development of such products appears desirable. It has been observed that developing environmental management systems (EMS) is growing in popularity, and there is an improvement in reporting within Islamic banks.[36]

The investment sector

The potential of the investment sector lies primarily in the signals about the advantages of environmentally sound behaviour which it can send to investors.[37] These signals will depend on who is seeking finance. It is observed that the influence of investors over the public sector is limited, and largely confined to monetary macroeconomics. The most significant influence of the Islamic investor community is therefore on industry, particularly on large companies. The investment community can send the following powerful signals to the industry.

Pricing ratings of new capital for companies. When a company first obtains a listing or seeks to raise new capital, the process of due diligence provides an opportunity to examine a company's overall strategy and management, including environmental issues. Full consideration of environmental factors could influence the amount and price of capital available to companies, rewarding good companies with cheaper debt (due to lower environmental risk) or access to equity at better ratings. Conversely, investors may avoid companies with too great an environmental risk.

Share ratings and company valuations by equity markets. If investors were to reward companies with a superior environmental track record with higher share prices, this would send a powerful signal about the merits of good environmental behaviour to the industry. For this to be effective, investors should anticipate the results of good environmental initiatives, rather than wait for the results to become evident. Financial markets need to be convinced that such behaviour leads to superior financial performance. At present, this has been a source of much contention and analysis, but evidence is emerging to support this hypothesis. Financial markets need to be convinced of the significance and validity of the findings.

Ownership of companies via their share capital. The IFIs control the majority of the share capital of most public companies, either directly or on behalf of their investors (fund managers), and are the most powerful of all stakeholders. In theory, they have the power to direct companies to take account of the environment in their management strategy. In practice, action has been limited: shareholdings are normally diffused, making majorities difficult to achieve; and institutions are reluctant to become active if financial benefits are uncertain. Other stakeholders thus enjoy more influence on the management of major companies. But if Islamic financial institutions are persuaded of the financial benefits of superior environmental performance, they can encourage such action.

As a whole, investors are probably less interested in the environment than bankers. However, a number of pressures are emerging on the investment sector (as illustrated in Figure 4.2).

Industry. Leading companies have become increasingly frustrated by the failure of the investment community to recognize and reward the environmental progress they have made. In particular, the international business organization, World Business Council for Sustainable Development (WBCSD), has been active in this area, developing the concept of eco-efficiency and encouraging its use among investors.

Investors. There is growing interest from individual investors in environmentally responsible investment, and this has led to the development of some progressive environmental investment funds in the conventional sector.[38] Institutional investors[39] have also started to explore this area,

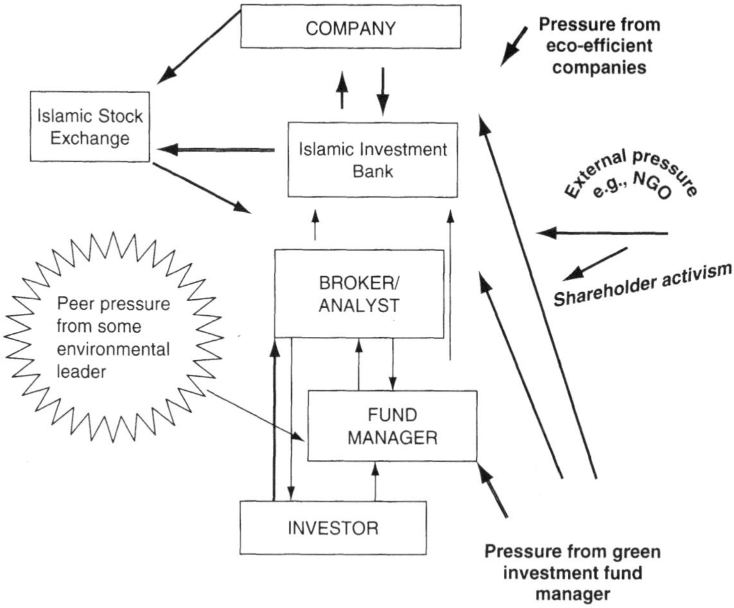

Figure 4.2 The environmental pressures on the investment sector

reassured by the good investment performance of such funds. As a 'green' product with no price or quality premium, the potential market for such products is likely to be substantial. Another avenue that some investors have pursued is shareholder activism. They have become frustrated by the indifference of investing institutions and are taking their concerns directly to large companies. This has proved effective in the USA, but is more limited in the Islamic countries where shareholders' rights are less developed, and there may be scope to develop it in Islamic countries.

NGOs. Environmental NGOs have also started to target fund managers and investment banks over their investments and involvement with environmentally damaging companies. To date, they have not had any major success, but have started to influence the sector.

Within the investment industry. A few organizations among the investment sector have started to take environmental issues more seriously and may be creating some peer pressure for change.

One of the major concerns for the investment sector is the relationship between environmental performance and investment performance.[40] The evidence from the conventional investment sector on balance suggests that environmental performance does contribute to good financial performance. However, many in the investment sector remain unconvinced, and action is needed both to persuade doubters and to reinforce signals, such as through the development of environmental taxation. In order to encourage the investment sector to incorporate environmental issues, a number of obstacles need to be overcome. Two key obstacles are market inertia in investment practices, and the balance between long-term and short-term analysis. However, the most important issue is probably the difficulty of obtaining good quality information in ways that the sector can understand and use. Methods need to be found to provide relevant information to the sector.

The insurance sector

The Islamic insurance sector in the Islamic world is still in its infancy. The potential of this sector to achieve sustainable development lies in its ability to price various types of environmental risk and to help pay for environmental damage. Potential environmental issues can affect risks in a number of areas, and the conventional insurance industry has taken an issue-based approach by:[41]

(a) building on a greater understanding of the interaction between the environment and Islamic insurance companies, where there is some potential for practical action and business opportunities;
(b) using sustainable development as a risk management tool; companies that are acting unsustainably are likely to present greater risks than those that are not (the precautionary principle would appear to be fundamentally about risk reduction);
(c) looking at the potential for industry-wide actions to reduce environmental risk, such as by developing standards, lobbying, and so on;
(d) looking at the opportunities for the development of new insurance products to address environmental challenges;
(e) considering the insurance of new risk categories, such as technology risk;
(f) developing products for the environmental sector, such as insurance against weather problems for the renewable energy sector.

Companies, investors and the environment

Companies increasingly see environmental issues as being relevant to their business development, yet financial markets in general, particularly investors, are not interested. Companies are increasingly aware of the environmental pressures they are under and have developed a range of practical tools to address them.[42] Understanding the financial implications of the environment on companies involves:

(a) identifying how the environment affects companies (this rarely happens directly);
(b) knowing how company management can respond, using tools such as environmental management systems, eco-efficiency and risk management;
(c) communicating relevant information;
(d) understanding the financial implications of their environmental impact and the management response.

Figure 4.3 illustrates this relationship. Figure 4.3 also helps to identify where information is likely to be useful to the financial markets.

Information on the company's approach to environmental issues is desirable, including strategy, management systems, and so on. Such information is often qualitative but financial analysts are used to assessing management quality from such information. Environmentally relevant

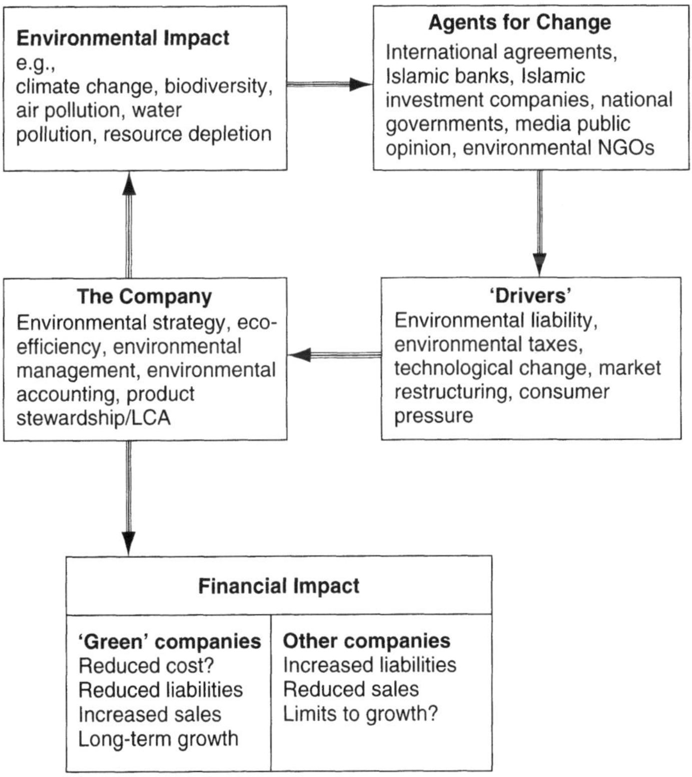

Figure 4.3 The relationship of companies, investors and the environment

financial information on costs and liabilities is likely to be useful. However, such information will only cover certain areas and may not provide a guide to future financial performance and risk.

Company environmental information will be useful both as an indicator of the pressures it experiences, and the risks it runs. While the feedback process in the model is imperfect, companies having a larger environmental impact will come under pressure to change. The WBCSD and others have argued that environmental performance may also be an indicator of the effectiveness of the management of the company. Responsible analysts should also keep track of the pressures or 'environmental drivers' that companies face directly. Companies cannot report on this sort of information themselves as it is outside their control.

Environmental reporting and rating agency

Information is the key to financial evaluation, but there is limited useful information on environmental performance and management. The main existing sources of information are not geared to financial audiences:[43]

(a) environmental reporting targets multiple audiences and many companies do not report;
(b) the potential with annual reports is erratically exploited and lacks standardization;
(c) publicly available information faces substantial practical obstacles.

In order to address this, there is the possibility of developing standardized and financially useful environmental reports, potentially as part of the annual reports, encompassing Islamic financial information, environmental performance data and qualitative information on environmental policy and management. An alternative approach is through the development of environmental rating agencies that can provide a summary analysis geared to the needs of the financial markets.[44] At present, such services have limited appeal, but they offer long-term potential. An effective way of encouraging the development of these services would improve the quality of information made available through the public regulators.

Environmental business sector

The environmental business sector consists of businesses ranging from traditional environmental businesses, such as waste management, to emerging 'green' pioneers, such as renewable energy and eco-tourism. They have a critical role to play in achieving sustainable development, and thus ensuring they have access to private sector finance is crucial. Despite apparently good prospects, with rapidly growing markets, the financial performance of the sector has been disappointing. Indeed, the poor performance of many high profile companies has been a major factor in creating a negative impression about the environment amongst Islamic financial institutions.

In response to the challenges faced by environmental sector companies, a number of innovative approaches and specialist organizations have developed in the conventional sector, such as project finance, venture capital, leasing, environmental and ethical banks, specialist environmental financiers, and environmental funds. These products can easily be replicated Islamically, and Islamic financial institutions should come forward with a positive approach. To encourage the Islamic financial markets and in order to support the sector, there is a need for measures at both the macro level, such as clear policy and dissemination, and at the micro level, such as training on Islamic financial markets for environmental entrepreneurs. There is scope to support innovation in Islamic finance to the sector.

Conclusions and recommendations

This study has found a wide range of activities which leading IFIs may undertake to encourage sustainable development and environmentally responsible behaviour. Bringing Islamic financial markets into the realm of environmental sustainability is an activity which needs to be undertaken carefully and with sensitivity towards the dynamics of the Islamic financial markets. The Islamic financial markets' function is to carry out the services their clients require. Innovation is only worthwhile when it is seen to pay. Thus there is limited demand from industrial clients for environmental financial services, other than a few specific areas of concern. Environmental companies are too small and diffused to offer a major financing opportunity for the market as a whole, yet there is scope to work within these limitations. The potential for environment factors to be relevant to Islamic financing and investment decisions is greatly limited by the lack of usable information on these issues. The demand for environmentally oriented funds should be substantially increased if obstacles to their sales are overcome. Supporting niche activities more directly, such as the development of innovative Islamic financing approaches, should help encourage their development.

The following policy options are recommended for consideration by the Islamic Development Bank (IDB), the IFIs and the Organization of the Islamic Conference (OIC). The options have been chosen on the basis of their potential to have a major long-term environmental benefit. In addition, many of the policy options chosen do not involve spending huge public funds or imposing major burdens on industries. Indeed, one of their key aspects is that they are likely to improve the functioning of existing policy measures.

The Islamic Development Bank should establish an institute, an Islamic Institute for Sustainable Developmental Research, within the structure of the Islamic Development Bank in order to conduct research, disseminate information and encourage Islamic financial institutions to undertake the environment seriously.

IDB/OIC may take a lead role in improving the flow of environmental information relevant to the financial markets. This could be done through the standardization and improvement of information collection and through the development of environmental reporting standards targeted at the Islamic financial markets.

IDB/IFIs should also consider taking action to increase the demand for environmentally responsible investment. Such action would create substantial demand-based incentives for Islamic financial institutions to develop environmental expertise and products. Actions include (as part of its involvement in consumer investment protection) requiring Islamic financial institutions to ask investors if they are concerned about how their money is invested in the environment and in development, and (as part of its eco-labelling scheme) a label for environmentally responsible investments.

IDB/IFIs should consider ways to encourage the development of environmental Islamic financial products for business and consumers. One cost-effective mechanism for IDB/IFIs would be to support rewards for innovation in environmental finance. This would provide an incentive for companies and would facilitate publicity and dissemination.

IDB/IFIs are also advised to consider ways to improve their existing support of the environmental business sector by investing in the potential role for the public sector, by persuading investment banks to take the lead in encouraging private sector finance to support the sector, and by involving the Islamic financial markets more closely in the supportive activities. This ensures that the recipients are aware of broader financing issues, and that the Islamic financial sector is able to step in as public sector support ends.

The overall consequence of the suggested policy actions would be to make Islamic financial institutions a positive force to participate in the sustainable development programmes. Such a programme of action would provide a major complement to, and reinforcement of, other more conventional environmental policy actions and would help to achieve the objectives of sustainable development.

Comment

Abulhasan M. Sadeq

The very nature and principles of Islamic finance as used by IFIs involves investment and partnership in economic activities rather than working merely as financial intermediaries, as is the case with conventional financial institutions (CFIs). Thus the financial operations of IFIs tend naturally to have positive implications for sustainable development (SD), which may not be as true for their conventional counterparts.

The chapter deals with the role of IFIs in SD. It is rightly mentioned that a formal Islamic theory of SD is not available; which does not, however, imply that such a theory cannot be developed. A number of ideas and concepts, such as *tawḥīd*, duality (*zawj*), balance, rational consciousness, *zakāh, ribā*, the environment, and so on are discussed. However, the entire chapter seems to be more or less centred on the environment and its role in SD. Even the role of IFIs in SD has been confined mainly to policy suggestions as to how to make IFIs environment-friendly financial institutions, rather than how IFIs can contribute to SD due to their methods of financing which are different from those of their conventional counterparts, although the title of the chapter tends to lead one to expect the latter instead of the former. While reference to the environment is important in the context of SD, it would be useful to consider other variables including education, poverty, production and consumption patterns, health, science, agriculture, industry, business and energy,[45] all of which are important for SD as well.

The issue of corporate responsibility in the context of SD is discussed with respect to different models. No doubt corporate responsibility in SD is an important area that needs emphasis, but its relevance to the present discussion seems to be less than appropriate, unless a linkage is established between corporate responsibility and SD through IFIs. The authors have discussed several models of corporate responsibility such as the ethical model, the static model and the liberal model. According to the authors, 'the first formal ethical model of corporate responsibility can be seen in the pioneering efforts of nineteenth-century corporate philanthropists such as the Cadbury brothers in England'. In the absence of elaboration,[46] a reader may have certain questions on his mind, such as the following.

What are the 'pioneering efforts' that provide 'the first' ethical models of corporate responsibility in the nineteenth-century, such as that of the Cadbury brothers? If it is the philanthropic effort of the Cadbury brothers,[47] such efforts must exist in Islamic history long before the nineteenth century: for example, in the form of *waqf*, both at the individual and corporate levels. So, in what sense do such nineteenth-century efforts provide 'the first' ethical models of corporate responsibility? Even the authors have referred to many Muslim firms doing this, some of whom existed before the nineteenth century. Furthermore, what is the meaning of the first ethical 'formal' model of corporate responsibility? It seems to be an action on the part of some philanthropists rather than a 'formal' model, theoretical or otherwise. How can such ethical responsibility be linked to IFIs or SD? Some elaboration from the authors would have clarified such queries in the minds of some readers.

In the 'static model', the authors have referred to the office of consumer protection, the *muḥtasib* (the institution of *ḥisbah*). In this context, it would be useful to provide the linkage between the institution of *ḥisbah* and SD, and to elaborate why it has been described as a static model. In the liberal model, the authors refer to the Friedmanian free economy model in which the corporate sector does not assume any social responsibility other than pure economic motives. It is not very clear in what sense it is a liberal model of corporate responsibility, or in what sense it is related to IFIs or SD.

In the section on the role of the Islamic financial institutions, the authors have dealt with three matters: (i) a transaction model of Islamic financial markets, (ii) strategies to motivate the Islamic financial sector, and (iii) the role of Islamic banks, the investment sector, and the insurance sector. The transaction model of Islamic financial markets is based on the assumption that Islamic markets will be motivated solely by their economic interests, or profits; and environmental considerations will be taken into account only if these are in the interest of the IFIs and/or firms. This presents a model of the Islamic economy that is a true replica of capitalism, which is absolutely based on self-interest, at least in a theoretical sense of pure capitalism. This notion is not in conformity with Islamic norms of business and economic activities. The Islamic concepts of *lā ḍarara wa lā dirār* (do not hurt others and do not get hurt) and that of social interest, along with individual interest (including the matters of externalities) combined with the social imperatives built into the concept of *infāq* (spending for the sake of Allah) for public welfare, require Islamic markets to go beyond the considerations of self-interest.

The above assumption of self-interest has been reflected in the model itself. It is not clear how it is a transaction model of an Islamic financial market, or how is it different from a conventional model. Decision making in any conventional financing also depends on relevant business information, and an analysis of the perceived risks and profitability, involving different factors such as market price, finance, aftercare, repayments and so on.

The chapter deals with both 'niche' and 'general' strategies that will motivate or facilitate environmentally-friendly undertakings. The factors leading to SD have again been limited to the environment, which seems to be a partial view of the phenomenon. The suggested strategies favourable for SD are not the ones that are built into the Islamic system and thus normally adopted by IFIs, but rather those which, according to the authors, should be adopted by the IFIs. Thus, these are not the usual advantages of the IFIs to indicate that the IFIs are superior over CFIs with respect to SD; rather, these are mere suggestions.

These suggestions are in no way specific to IFIs; indeed, all of them may equally be applicable to the CFIs. Only one strategy, 'developing green products in compliance with *Sharīʿah* for clients and customers', may be specific to Islamic finance. But even this may be adopted by the CFIs as well, since many CFIs in Muslim countries presently possess Islamic windows. In any case, this is really a suggestion to develop appropriate *Sharīʿah* approved products.

It has been observed in the chapter that some Islamic banks 'have made considerable progress in developing internal environmental management systems to reduce their own environmental impact'. Also, some Islamic banks 'include some environmental analysis in their credit assessment process'. Further, '[i]t has been observed that developing environmental management systems (EMS) is growing in popularity, and there is an improvement in reporting within Islamic banks'. This is encouraging. It would be useful, however, to elaborate these matters and to relate how these would contribute to SD.

An important observation on the discussion of the role of IFIs in the context of Islamic banks is that the Islamic banks, due to the nature of their operations which have been developed in accordance with the Islamic system, have not been found or shown to be superior to conventional banks with respect to SD, but rather policy suggestions have been made regarding environmental considerations during their financing. Similar suggestions can be made for conventional banks as well, and hence IFIs do not have any comparative advantage over CFIs in SD due to their being Islamic banks.

In investment, IFIs have been advised to send signals to companies about adopting environment-friendly strategies to help them obtain financial capital, share ratings and company valuations by equity markets, and so on. These are again policy suggestions for making IFIs environmentally-aware financiers, which may equally be valid for CFIs, and hence IFIs do not seem to have any advantage over CFIs with respect to SD.

With respect to the role of Islamic insurance in SD, the approach taken seems to be to discuss strategies to face the challenges of environmental risks on the part of the Islamic insurance institutions in providing insurance coverage, rather than how Islamic insurance can contribute to SD due to the nature of its finance, which is different from that of conventional insurance companies, or how Islamic insurance can be made environmentally friendly.

As we know, some modes of financing in the case of IFIs, especially Islamic banks, are distinctively different from those of CFIs, which are favourable for sustainable development. Arguably, the most important and desirable modes are *muḍārabah* and *mushārakah*, which provide a relationship of industrial partnership between IFIs and the clients, instead of IFIs being mere financial intermediaries. This partnership on the part of IFIs will contribute to industrial and economic progress. Excess liquidity often emerges as a serious problem in financial institutions, which breaks the continuity in the pace of fund use and development and, in turn, in SD. The application of *muḍārabah* and *mushārakah* modes of financing can help solve this problem by facilitating full utilization of funds, *ceteris paribus*.

An example may clarify this matter, which can be demonstrated by a hypothetical case.[48] In order to do this, let us make some assumptions. First, the pre-decided profit ratio between a *muḍārabah* entrepreneur and the contributor of capital is 60:40; if the money is borrowed from a conventional bank, the interest rate is $10 for $1,000 per project period. Second, the project life is three months (meant for trading). The example is presented in Table 4.1. In this example, an entrepreneur can invest up to $9,000, since the marginal efficiency of capital equals interest payments at this level of investment: that is, when the entrepreneur adds $1,000 to a previous investment of $8,000, he earns $10 as a profit, which he has to pay entirely to the financier leaving nothing for himself. His total profit after interest payments is $505 ($595 – $90) when $9,000 is invested. If he invests $8,000 instead, he still earns $505 ($585 – $80). Therefore, it will be less risky for the entrepreneur to invest $8,000 instead of $9,000.

An entrepreneur under an Islamic financial system can continue investment profitably beyond $9,000, since he keeps on receiving positive profits up to an investment of $13,000. He may even increase his investment up to $14,000 without risk, since risk is borne by the contributors of capital, although the net gain from the additional investment will be zero.

Table 4.1 Full utilization of funds by Islamic banks

Total investment	*Total profits*	*Marginal efficiency of capital*	*Distribution of profits under Islamic financial system (muḍārabah)*	
			Share of the entrepreneur	*Share of the contributor of capital*
5,000	520		312.0	208.0
6,000	550	30	330.0	220.0
7,000	570	20	342.0	228.0
8,000	585	15	351.0	234.0
9,000	595	10	357.0	238.0
10,000	603	8	361.8	241.2
11,000	608	5	364.8	243.2
12,000	611	3	366.6	244.4
13,000	613	2	367.8	245.2
14,000	613	0	367.8	245.2

It is obvious from the above hypothetical example that investment (and thus employment and output) is expected to be higher in an Islamic financial system, and that there is, at least theoretically, a potential of full utilization of bank funds with an obvious positive effect on economic growth, which is an essential ingredient of sustainable development.

Savings are not expected to be adversely affected by the elimination of interest in the case of IFIs. Instead, the savings potentiality of an Islamic economy is higher.[49] If this potential is fully tapped by IFIs and utilized due to its investment-friendly modes of financing, the growth rate of the economy concerned is expected to be higher than that of a CFI-based economy. This will contribute to SD.

Sustainable development involves many issues and factors. Such issues and factors include the environment, education, poverty, production and consumption patterns, health, science, agriculture, industry, business, and energy.[50] Any discussion of SD without these issues appears to be incomplete.

Comment

Victor Murinde

The chapter discusses the role of Islamic financial institutions (IFIs) in sustainable development programmes. Some policy issues are considered and plausible recommendations are proposed. However, there is no attempt to present case studies of IFIs or particular economies, and there is no econometric work on sustainable development (e.g., trends and projections/simulations).

The chapter mentions models of corporate responsibility in sustainable development. In this context, it may be pointed out that the four main models mentioned in the chapter do not exist in absolute form; rather, in the living corporate world, corporate structures are hybrid models. The implication of this observation is that IFIs are likely to mimic a hybrid model of corporate responsibility rather than the absolute form of any one model.

Among the key roles of financial institutions all over the world, in the context of sustainable development in Islamic as well as non-Islamic environments, is that financial institutions should reduce transaction costs and engender lower financial risk for all economic agents. Importantly, financial institutions should reduce agency problems through monitoring mechanisms which minimize information asymmetry. Lower agency problems reduce the possibility of moral hazard and adverse selection problems. However, it appears that the current operational practices of Islamic banks present a departure from the convention. For example, Al-Deehani, Karim and Murinde (1999) find that, given the contractual obligation binding Islamic banks' shareholders and investment account holders to share profits from investments, an increase in investment accounts financing enables Islamic banks to increase both their market value and their shareholders' rates of return *at no extra financial risk to the bank*. Investment account holders are, therefore, fully exposed to financial risk. This finding has serious implications for sustainable development as well as for corporate social responsibility. Central banks, with oversight of Islamic banks, have a duty to internalize this aspect into their regulatory policies for Islamic financial institutions.

The conclusions and policy recommendations are plausible; however, there are a number of important issues which are not addressed. First, the role of central banks which oversee the operations of IFIs is important. Very relevant here is the nature of the regulatory regimes for IFIs at the national as well as international level. The existing regulatory machinery for banks is seriously constrained in the face of financial globalization. Second, it should be pointed out that sustainable development requires the maintenance of the very socio-economic institutions which generate development. How is this possible in the age of globalization, as for example under the World Trade Organization and the General Agreement on Trade and Services? I believe that it is very important to take up these two issues.

It is regrettable that there is no attempt to present case studies of IFIs or particular economies and no econometric work on sustainable development (e.g., trends, projections or simulations). Surely there have been many good case studies on Islamic banks, as well as good econometric studies on sustainable development in economies with Islamic banks! Let us think of a number of questions in sequence.

Question 1: Can we evaluate the financial, developmental and technological developmental role of IFIs in the economic development of host economies? I suppose we can do this, albeit with some limitations, if we follow Murinde and Kariisa-Kasa (1997).

Question 2: Can we quantitatively measure the contribution of IFIs to economic development, in the sense of the incremental capital–output ratio (ICOR)? I suppose we can in the context of Lifumba and Murinde (2003).

Question 3: Can we quantitatively measure and then forecast the contribution of IFIs to *sustainable* economic development in the host economies? I suppose we can do this if we combine elements of Questions 1 and 2, and if we devise surrogate measures of *sustainable* economic development.

Notes

1. WCED (1987).
2. Financing for Sustainable Development (2002), pp. 2–29.
3. Asad (1987), p. 133.
4. *Qur'ān* (3:191; 38:27; 46:3).
5. *Qur'ān* (13:3; 31:10; 36:36; 53:45).
6. *Qur'ān* (7:56; 14:33; 15:19; 16:10–15; 54:49; 55:3–13; 67:3).
7. Baker (1998), p. 80.
8. *Qur'ān* (7:56).
9. Asad (1984), p. 144.
10. Asad (1984), p. 146. In order to avoid giving a truncated version of Asad's conception of man, the following passage should also be quoted:

    > The *Qur'ān* makes it clear that our comprehension of reality can certainly be deepened and widened by what we describe as 'mystical experience', in other words, through an intuitive, spiritual contact with the Divine and, hence, with those truths which are neither open to our self-perception nor can be fully grasped by analytical thinking.

11. Baker (1998), p. 83.
12. *Qur'ān* (7:31).
13. *Qur'ān* (9:60; 59:7).
14. Chapra (2000), p. 119.
15. *Qur'ān* (2.43).
16. Khan (1979).

17. Ansari (1994).
18. Vadillo (1991), p. 15.
19. Such as *Qur'ān* (2:275–9).
20. Siddiqi (1995).
21. Ansari (1994), pp. 394–401.
22. John and Benjamin, the Cadbury Brothers of Birmingham, pioneered the development of chocolate around 1847. Detailed history available at www.cadbury-schweppes.com/company_information//company_history/200_ year_history.html
23. Harfiyah (1998), p. 8.
24. Recipient of the 1976 Nobel Prize for economic science, Milton Friedman is widely regarded as the leader of the Chicago school of monetary economics.
25. Pioneer of the stakeholder and 'business ethics' concept in the context of corporate responsibilities. Freeman developed a framework for identifying and managing the critical relationships of the modern corporation.
26. At its narrowest, the term 'triple bottom line' is used as a framework for measuring and reporting corporate performance against economic, social and environmental parameters. At its broadest, it captures the whole set of values, issues and processes that companies must address to minimize any harm resulting from their activities and to create economic, social and environmental value. It is signified as three lines representing society, economy and environment.
27. See UNCED (1992).
28. Samulders (1998), pp. 30–65.
29. Holland (1995).
30. Gentry, Durante and Fernandez (1995), p. 18.
31. It should also be noted that as a result of these differences, the precise interpretation and use of the concept of risk varies between the financial sectors.
32. Klynveld, Peat, Marwick & Goerdeler (1997).
33. Iqbal (1997).
34. Sources of information: Annual Reports of some of the large Islamic banks.
35. For example, see Annual Report (2000) of Islami Bank Bangladesh Ltd.
36. Various reports from the Accounting and Auditing Organisation for the Islamic Financial Institutions, Bahrain. Please see in detail Serafy el- (1996), pp. 87–107.
37. While the investment sector does have some direct environmental impacts, these are relatively modest. Generally the same issues arise as for Islamic banks, although conventional investment companies are probably less active in this area (although not oblivious to its implications: the publishing of the Halifax Building Society prospectus for its flotation was one of the largest printing runs in the UK, and the society did promise to plant sufficient trees to repair the damage).
38. Most investors who seek to invest in 'green' companies do so through some form of collective investment fund (e.g., ethically managed funds, environmental sector funds, green managed funds, etc.).
39. For example, ihilal – an Islamic Mutual Fund Company.
40. For more details, please see ESD (1995).
41. For more details, see ISO (1995).
42. Please see European Commission (1995).
43. ACBE (1997).
44. UNEP (1994), pp. 3–16.
45. For a list of SD issues, see UNCED (2002).
46. No further elaboration has been provided on the model beyond the quoted sentence, except for a website reference in the footnote.

47. Since it should not be the development of Cadbury chocolate by the Cadbury brothers.
48. This example is taken from Sadeq (1990), pp. 22–3.
49. For a reasonably detailed discussion on this, see Sadeq (1992).
50. For a list of SD issues, see UNCED (2002).

References

ACBE (1997), 'Environmental Reporting and Financial Sector: An Approach to Good Practice', *Advisory Committee on Business and Environment*, London: Department of Environment.

Ahmad, Khurshid (1976), 'Economic Development in an Islamic Framework', in Khurshid Ahmad (ed.), *Studies in Islamic Economics*, Jeddah: Center for Research in Islamic Economics, King Abdulaziz University and Leicester: The Islamic Foundation.

Albaraka Islamic Investment Bank (1998, 1999, 2000), *Annual Reports*.

Ansari, M. I. (1994), 'Islamic Perspective on Sustainable Development', *American Journal of Islamic Social Sciences*, 11 (3), 394–401.

Ansoff, H. I. (ed.) (1969), *Business Strategy: Selected Readings*, Harmondsworth: Penguin.

Asad, Muhammad (1984), *The Message of the Qur'ān*, Gibraltar: Dar Al-Andalus.

Asad, Muhammad (1987), *This Law of Ours*, Gibraltar: Dar Al-Andalus.

Baker, Ilyas (1998), 'Flight of Time, Ecology and Islam', in Harfia Abdel Haleem (ed.), *Islam and Environment*, London: Ta-Ha.

Banuri, T. and E. Spanger-Siegfried (2001), *Strengthening Demand: A Framework for Financing Sustainable Development*, London: IIED and Ring.

Chapra, M. Umer (2000), *The Future of Economics: An Islamic Perspective*, Leicester: The Islamic Foundation.

Deehani al-, T., R. A. A. Karim and V. Murinde (1999), 'The Capital Structure of Islamic Banks under the Contractual Obligation of Profit Sharing', *International Journal of Theoretical and Applied Finance*, 2 (3), 243–83.

Dubai Islamic Bank (1997, 1998, 2000), *Annual Reports*.

Environics International (2001), *eFlash Report, Corporate Social Responsibility (CSR) Index*, Toronto: Environics International, July.

ESD (1995), 'Effective Financing of Sustainable Development', *Environmentally Sustainable Development*, Report No. 10, Washington, DC: The World Bank.

European Commission (1995), *Financial Investment for the Environment Sustainability*, London: European Commission.

Faisal Islamic Bank of Egypt (1984, 1989, 1991, 1993, 1995), *Annual Reports*.

Financing for Sustainable Development (2002), *A Report on WSSD FfD UN Summit*, London: International Institute for Environment and Development.

Freeman, R. E. (1984), *Strategic Management: A Stakeholder Approach*, Boston, MA: Pitman.

Friedman, Milton (1958), 'Three Major Factors in Business Management: Leadership, Decision Making and Social Responsibility', Speech delivered at the Eighth Social Science Seminar, 19 March 1958, as cited in Ansoff (1969).

Gazni, J. and J. Tanner (1997), 'Global Survey on Environmental Policies and Practices of the Financial Services Industry: The Private Sector', Washington, DC: National Wildlife Federation (http://www.nwf.org/finance/survey.html).

Gentry, B., G. Durante and L. Fernandez (1995), *Private Sector Flows and the Environment: Defining the Opportunities and Issues*, New Haven, CT: UNEP/Yale Centre for Environmental Law and Policy, p. 18.

Harfiyah, Abdel Haleem (ed.) (1998), *Islam and Environment*, London: Ta-Ha.

Harran al-, Saad (1999), 'Introduction: Cases in Islamic Finance', *Arab Law Quarterly*, 14 (3), 193–202.

Holland, J. (1995), 'The Corporate Governance: Role of the Financial Institution in their Investment Companies', *Association of Chartered Certified Accountants Research Report 46*, London: Association of the Chartered Certified Accountants (ACCA).

International Institute for Environment and Development (2002), *Financing for Sustainable Development*, a report on the World Summit on Sustainable Development, London: International Institute of Environment and Development, pp. 2–29.

Iqbal, Munawar (1997), 'Islamic Banking in Theory and Practice', a paper presented at the 5th Intensive Orientation Course on Islamic Economic, Banking and Finance organized by the Islamic Foundation, UK, IDB, Jeddah, and Loughborough University, UK, from 25 to 28 September 1997 at the Markfield Conference Centre, Leicester, UK.

Islami Bank Bangladesh (2000), *Annual Report*, Dhaka: Islami Bank Bangladesh.

Islamic Cooperative Development Bank, Sudan (1986–87, 1987–88), *Annual Reports*.

ISO (1995), *Insurance Service, Superfund and the Insurance Issues Surrounding Abandoned Hazardous Waste Sites*, New York: Insurance Service Office.

Khan, Muhammad Muhsin (1979), *Ṣaḥīḥ Bukhārī* (Translation), Lahore: Kazi, IX, pp. 286–7.

Klynveld, Peat, Marwick & Goerdeler (1997), *KPMG Survey: The Environmental Challenge and Small and Medium Sized Enterprises in Europe*, The Hague: KPMG Millieu.

Lifumba, C. and V. Murinde (2003), 'Assessing the role of the African Development Bank in the economic development of borrower member countries', Mimeo, African Development Bank, Abidjan.

Murinde, V. and J. Kariisa-Kasa (1997), 'The Financial Performance of the East African Development Bank: A Retrospective Analysis', *Accounting, Business and Financial History*, 7 (1), 81–104.

Our Common Future (The Brundtland Report) (1987) *Report of the 1987 World Commission on Environment and Development*, Oxford: Oxford University Press.

Sadeq, Abulhasan M. (1990), *Economic Development in Islam*, Kuala Lumpur: Pelanduk, pp. 22–3.

Sadeq, Abulhasan M. (ed.) (1992), 'Development Finance in an Islamic Economy: Domestic Sources', *Financing Economic Development: Islamic and Mainstream Approaches*, Kuala Lumpur: Longman, pp. 11–24.

Samulders, Sjak (1998), 'Technology Change, Economic Growth and Sustainability', in Vanden Berg Joren and Hofkes (1998), pp. 30–65.

Sardar, Ziauddin (1988), *Islamic Futures: The Shape of Ideas to Come*, Kuala Lumpur: Pelanduk.

Serafy el-, Saleh (1996), 'The Environmental Accounting for Sustainable Development: Conceptual and Theoretical Issues Relating to the System of Integrated Environmental and Accounting (SEEA)', *Journal of Economic Cooperation Among the Islamic Countries*, 17 (1–2), 87–107.

Siddiqi, M. N. (1995), 'Towards Regeneration: Shifting Priorities in Islamic Movements', *Encounters*, Leicester: The Islamic Foundation, pp. 3–29.

United Nations Conference on Environment and Development (1992), *Agenda 21: United Nations Conference on Environment and Development* (UNCED), New York: United Nations.

United Nations Environmental Programme (1994), 'Company Environmental Reporting: A Measure of the Progress of Business and Industry Towards Sustainable Development', *UNEP/IE Technical Reporting No. 24*, Paris: UNEP, pp. 3–16.

Useem, Jerry (2002), 'Islamic Finance, Banking on Allah: Devout Muslims Don't Pay or Receive Interest. So How Can Their Financial System Work?', *Fortune Magazine*, 10 June, 7–11.

Vadillo, Umar (1991), *Fatāwā on Paper-Money*, Granada: Madinah Press.

Vanden Berg Joren, C. J. M and M. W. Hofkes (eds) (1998), *Theory and Implementation of Economics for Sustainable Development*, London: Kluwer Academic.

World Commission on Environment and Development (1987), *Our Common Future*, Oxford: Oxford University Press.

Zeinelabdin, Abdelrahaman (1993), 'Technology, Sustainable Development and Environment: OIC/UN Cooperation', *Journal of Economic Cooperation among Islamic Countries*, 14 (2), 61–75.

5

Efficiency of Islamic Banks in Malaysia

Mariani Abdul Majid, Nor Ghani Mohammed Nor and Fatin Faezah Said

In recent years, Malaysian Islamic banks have been facing an increasingly competitive environment. This trend is expected to continue as the competition from conventional banks picks up not only in response to the Association of South East Asian Nations (ASEAN) Free Trade Agreement (AFTA), but also as a consequence of the general globalization of markets. How Islamic banks will be affected by the increased competitive pressures depends in part on how efficiently they are run. This chapter examines the productive efficiency of Malaysian Islamic as compared to conventional banks over the 1993–2000 period. Using the stochastic cost frontier function approach, efficiency scores have been determined for each bank to determine their relative positions on the efficiency ladder. An inefficiency model is estimated to link the inefficiency of input use to output. The results show that the efficiency level of Islamic banks is not statistically different from conventional banks. In addition, there is no evidence to suggest that bank efficiency is a function of ownership status (i.e., public or private), or nationality (foreign or local).

Introduction

During the early years after independence, foreign banks dominated the Malaysian banking scene. For instance, two years after independence (1959), there were only eight local banks out of the 26 commercial banks in operation. Twenty years later, the role played by the local banks improved considerably. In 1982, the number of commercial banks increased to 38 with 22 domestic banks and 16 foreign banks. However, the number shrank significantly (although the split between local and foreign banks is still maintained) in the 1990s following a spate of 'mergers and takeovers' as banks tried to secure particular niches and economies of scale in order to stay competitive. By August 2001, there were 27 commercial banks in all, including two Islamic banks.

Alongside the conventional banking system, the Islamic banking system has steadily evolved to become a major player on the Malaysian financial landscape. Its birth could be traced back to the establishment of the Pilgrimage Fund and Management Council in 1969, although its function was then limited to mobilizing savings for Muslims who wish to perform Hajj. The establishment of Bank Islam Malaysia Berhad (BIMB) in 1983 marked the beginning of a new era in Islamic banking in Malaysia. The year witnessed the creation of a fully-fledged Islamic banking institution offering financial services in accordance with Islamic jurisprudence. The Islamic banking system received a further boost when a scheme called the Interest-free Banking Scheme, whereby conventional banks can open windows for Islamic banking products, was launched in 1993. Another important event for Islamic banking in Malaysia occurred in October 1999 when a second Islamic bank, Bank Muammalat Malaysia Berhad (BMMB) opened its doors to the public. By the end of 2001, there were 36 conventional banking institutions offering Islamic banking products in Malaysia (14 commercial banks, 10 finance companies, five merchant banks and seven discount houses) in addition to the two fully-fledged Islamic banks (Bank Negara Malaysia, 2001).

Despite its growth, the market share of the Islamic banking system in Malaysia is relatively small.[1] This is one of the reasons for assessing the efficiency of Islamic banks relative to their conventional counterparts. Efficient operation will not only ensure banks' survival through growth but will also demonstrate practically that the Islamic financial system is a viable alternative to the conventional system.

The gale of economic liberalization currently sweeping across the globe provides another reason for looking into the efficiency of Islamic banks since it poses a further competitive challenge to the Islamic banking institutions. It is expected that by the year 2007, trade liberalization will require Malaysian domestic banks to compete with other global players on an equal footing. Such a change implies that local Islamic banking institutions will have to be efficient, innovative, competitive and resilient. This is particularly important since foreign banks that are arguably more efficient may also offer Islamic banking products to take advantage of the high demand for Islamic banking products.

The policy relevance of this study can be seen by looking at the target set by the Malaysian central bank (Bank Negara Malaysia) for the Islamic banking institutions to command a 20 per cent market share by 2010, as outlined in its financial sector master plan. How the increased competition expected in the future would affect Islamic banks will partly depend on how efficiently the banks operate in the new competitive environment. Efficient banks will gain competitive advantage while the inefficient ones may be driven out of the market. Islamic banks are placed at a disadvantage since they are said to be operating currently in a restricted environment.

The opportunity set available to the managers of Islamic banks is smaller in the sense that conventional banks can adopt any business strategy available to Islamic banks but not vice versa. Of course, this may not necessarily mean that the Islamic banks are going to be less efficient but it does open up the possibility of such a state of affairs. Despite its importance, a study of bank efficiency, particularly Islamic banks, in Malaysia is presently lacking in the literature.

This chapter aims to determine the efficiency of Islamic banks relative to other commercial banks in Malaysia, using the stochastic cost frontier approach. The chapter proceeds as follows. The next section reviews some efficiency studies on banking services, while the following section describes the model, estimation technique and the efficiency indicators used. The penultimate section presents the empirical results. The chapter ends with some concluding remarks.

Efficiency studies in banking services

There are numerous empirical studies that try to look into the relative efficiency of financial institutions operating within a country (and in some cases among countries). Generally, these studies differ in the specific methodology used, variables considered and the type of banks included in the sample. Some of these studies are reviewed below by dividing them into works on bank efficiency in general and comparative efficiency between Islamic and conventional banks.

Using stochastic cost frontier methodology, Mendes and Rebelo (1999) study the performance of 221 Portuguese banks in the 1990–5 period. They found that increased competition faced by banks during the period under study did not lead to an improvement in the overall cost efficiency. The study also found no clear evidence on the existence of a predictable association between size and cost efficiency, and banks could in fact remain competitive by exerting firm control over costs. In a similar study, Zaim (1995) found that the financial reform introduced in Turkey in the mid-1980s had succeeded in pushing commercial banks into taking positive measures to enhance technical as well as allocative efficiencies. By comparing performance between the pre- and post liberalization eras, the study concluded that banks in Turkey recorded some improvement in efficiency during 1980–90. Lovell and Grifell-Tatje (1997) used Spanish banking data over 1986–93 to show that savings banks reacted to banking deregulation by engaging in efficiency-enhancing merger activities. During the same period, the commercial banks instead chose to adjust their loan and deposit interest rates as a way of fending off increased competition from savings banks. Savings banks were also found to have a more efficient form of organizational structure compared to the commercial banks. Chang, Hasan and Hunter (1998) found that foreign-owned multinational banks operating in the US were significantly less efficient than their local counterparts. The study used 1984–9 banking data and trans-log formulation of the stochastic cost frontier method to estimate the cost inefficiency scores. In another study, Mester (1993) used the stochastic econometric cost frontier approach to investigate efficiency of banks operating in the Third Federal Reserve District in the USA using 1991–92 data. Findings from the study suggests that there is less to be gained in terms of cost savings from changing output size or mix than from using inputs more cost efficiently.

Kwan and Eisenbeis (1996) used semi-annual data for a sample of 254 bank holding companies from 1986 to 1991 in order to find the relationship between scale and efficiency. The banks were grouped into size-based quartiles to allow for different production technologies for each size class. Separate cost functions were estimated for each size quartile using the method of maximum likelihood. After controlling for other factors, on average, smaller banking firms were found to be less efficient than larger banking firms. They also tended to exhibit greater variations in inefficiencies than the larger firms. These findings suggest that, on average, large banking firms operate closer to their respective efficient frontier than the small banking firms. Average inefficiency appears to have declined over the period 1986 to the mid-1990s, apparently responding to the increased competition in banking brought about by market and regulatory changes. The persistence of inefficiency rankings suggests that relatively efficient (inefficient) banking firms tend to stay relatively efficient (inefficient) over a fairly long period.

In a cross-border efficiency study, Abd Karim (2001) found that larger banks tend to be more cost efficient compared to their smaller rivals, although the degree of advantage obtained from scale economies decreases for some ASEAN countries (Indonesia, Malaysia, the Philippines and Thailand). The study employed the stochastic cost frontier approach.

In a study on the risk of failure faced by the inefficient banks Cebenoyan, Cooperman and Register (1993) found that banks and S&Ls (Savings and Loans Associations) in the USA with low efficiency estimates face failure at greater rates compared to those with higher efficiency estimates. Similarly, in a study of bank failures during the 1920s, Wheelock and Wilson (1995) found that the less technically efficient a bank was, the greater the likelihood of its failure. Similar findings are also reported by Berger and Humprey (1997) in a survey of financial institutions' efficiency literature where many studies find that most bank failures are directly related to poor management quality, a low capital position, a large number of problem loans and a weak or negative cash flow.

A number of studies on Islamic banks' relative efficiency or productivity are also found in the literature. Unlike the current study, these studies tend to use general comparisons of accounting ratios as a method of analysis. Hamid (1999) evaluates the performance of one of the five Islamic banks in Bangladesh, the Islami Bank Bangladesh Limited (IBBL) in comparison with two comparable conventional banks using accounting ratios. IBBL is found to be more productive in terms of total income compared to the other two conventional banks. However, one of the two conventional banks studied is better than the Islamic bank in terms of labour productivity. He reasoned that the comparatively new Islamic bank incurred higher costs because of its strategy of hiring experienced bankers from conventional banks. In another study (Samad and Hassan, 1999), the profitability performance of an Islamic bank in Malaysia, BIMB, was compared to eight conventional banks using financial ratios. The study found that the average profit of BIMB is significantly lower than the conventional banks. The authors argued that this is to be expected since the investment opportunities for BIMB in stocks and securities are smaller due to religious constraints. Sarker (1999) did a study on all the Islamic banks based in Pakistan by developing the so-called Banking Efficiency Model. Efficiency measures on productivity, operation, allocation, distribution and stability were computed as financial ratios. The study concluded that Islamic banks could not achieve maximum efficiency under the conventional banking framework because of the constraints that they faced. Metwally (1997) compared the performance of 15 conventional banks and 15 *ribā*-free or interest-free banks from all over the world. The study tested for structural difference between the two groups of banks in terms of liquidity, leverage, credit risk, profit and efficiency. The study found that *ribā*-free banks face more difficulties in attracting deposits compared to the conventional banks. Second, *ribā*-free banks tend to be more conservative in utilizing funds for lending and are disadvantaged in terms of investment opportunities. As a result, these banks have higher cash to deposits ratios than conventional banks. However, statistical results suggest that profitability and efficiency differences are not statistically significant between the two types of banks.

Methodology and data

In estimating cost frontiers, two general approaches can be found in the literature, namely non-parametric and parametric methods. The non-parametric data envelopment analysis (DEA) approach determines which bank in the sample produces a particular output combination at the given input prices at least cost. This defines the best practice bank for that output/input combination. A bank's relative efficiency is measured by the ratio of its own cost to the cost of the 'best practice' bank that faces the same input prices and produces the same output bundle. The advantage of using the DEA is that it does not require an assumption on the distribution of the error terms. The disadvantage of using DEA is that it attributes any unfavourable influence, even those that are beyond a bank's control, to inefficiency.

An alternative method, the one used in this study, is the parametric stochastic frontier approach developed by Aigner, Lovell and Schmidt (1977) and Meusen and Broeck (1977). This method postulates a two-component error structure: a controllable factor and a random uncontrollable factor. Consider the following cost function of a firm:

$$C_i = f(y_j, w_k) + \epsilon_i \quad i = 1, \ldots n \tag{5.1}$$

where C_i represents the total cost of the firm; y_j represents various products or services produced by the firm; w_k represents the prices of inputs used by the firm in the production of the products and services; and ϵ represents the random disturbance term, which allows the cost function to vary stochastically. The uncertainty being captured by the ϵ in the cost function can further be decomposed as follows.

$$\epsilon_i = v_i + u_i \tag{5.2}$$

where v represents random uncontrollable factors that affect the total cost (such as machine performance, weather and luck). They are identically distributed as normal variates and the value of the error term in the cost relationship is, on average, equal to zero. On the other hand, the u represents individual firm cost deviations or errors that are due to factors that are under the control of the firm, such as technical and allocative efficiency.

The stochastic frontier model postulates that a firm's observed cost will deviate from the cost frontier because of random noise (uncontrollable component), v_i, and possible inefficiency (controllable component), $u_{i.}$. The controllable inefficiencies are one-sided since they can only increase costs above the frontier or best practice levels, while the random fluctuation can either increase or decrease cost. Since uncontrollable factors are assumed to be symmetrically distributed, the cost frontier, $f(y_j, w_k) + \epsilon$, is therefore stochastic. Thus, when estimating a cost function with a composite error term, it is assumed that the sum of two-sided error represents random fluctuations in cost and a one-sided positive error represents inefficiency (see Mester, 1996, for details).

In this chapter the trans-log cost function is chosen since this is the most frequently used functional form in banking efficiency studies (Abd Karim, 2001). The trans-log stochastic cost frontier can be written as follows.

$$\begin{aligned} \mathrm{Ln}C_{it} = {} & B_o + \sum_{j=1}^{n} B_j \ln y_{it} + \sum_{k=1}^{m} B_k \ln w_{kit} + 1/2 \sum_{j}^{n} \sum_{l}^{m} B_{jl} \ln y_j \ln y_l \\ & + 1/2 \sum_{k}^{m} \sum_{p}^{m} B_{kp} \ln w_{kit} \ln w_{pit} + 1/2 \sum_{j}^{n} \sum_{k}^{m} B_{jk} \ln y_{jit} \ln w_{kit} \\ & + B_q t + u_{it} + v_{it} \end{aligned} \tag{5.3}$$

In w_{kit} = natural logarithm of the *k*th input price ($k=1, 2, \ldots m$);
t = year of observation; and
*B*s are the coefficients to be estimated.

The v_{it} s are random variables due to measurement errors in the input variable or the effect of unspecified explanatory variables in the model, and the u_{it} s are non-negative random variables, associated with inefficiency of input used, given the levels of outputs and the inputs. Most studies on inefficiency use what has now come to be known as the intermediation approach in measuring a flow of bank services. Under this approach output is measured in terms of the dollar value of loans. Deposits are treated as inputs and loans as outputs (Sealey and Lindley, 1977). It is a popular approach partly because of the ease of acquiring required data. The intermediation approach includes both operating and interest expense (or income distributed to the depositors in the case of an Islamic bank). In equation (5.3), total cost (*C*) is defined to include all labour and capital expenses and interest expenses (or income distributed to depositors for an Islamic bank: see Habshi al-, 1999 for further discussion). The outputs are Ringgit amounts of loans, advances and financing; Ringgit amounts of deposits, placement with other financial institutions and cash and short-term funds; and Ringgit amounts of securities and investments. Input prices include staff expenses per employee, expenses on land, building and equipment per Ringgit of assets, and expenses on interest or income distributed to depositors per Ringgit of deposits.

Following Jondrow *et al.* (1982), a measure of a firm's inefficiency can be written as;

$$U_i = [\sigma\lambda/(1+\lambda^2)]\ [-\ \phi(\epsilon_i\ \lambda/\sigma)/\phi(\epsilon_i\ \lambda/\sigma) + (\epsilon_i\ \lambda/\sigma)] \qquad (5.4)$$

where

$\sigma = [\sigma^2{}_v + \sigma^2{}_u]$
ϕ = the standard normal density function;
ϕ = the cumulative normal density function; and
$\lambda = \sigma^2{}_u/\sigma^2$

This measure of controllable inefficiency for the *i*th firm (i.e., U_i), can then be used to examine the inefficiency effects (Chang, Hasan and Hunter, 1998). The cost inefficiency effects are assumed to be defined by:

$$U_{it} = \gamma_0 + \sum_{i=1}^{n} \gamma_j D_{jit} + \sum_{i=1}^{m} \gamma_j Z_{jit} \qquad (5.5)$$

where

D_1 is the dummy variable for public/private ownership: $D_1 = 1$ if an observation involves a government-owned bank, zero otherwise;

D_2 is the dummy variable for Islamic bank: $D_2 = 1$ if an observation involves an Islamic bank, zero otherwise;
D_3 is dummy variable for foreign/local ownership: $D_3 = 1$ if an observation involves a foreign owned bank, zero otherwise;
Z_1 = logarithm of the size of bank;
Z_2 = square of logarithm of the size of bank;
Z_3 = interaction between bank size and public/private ownership;
Z_4 = interaction between bank size and foreign/local ownership;
Z_5 = year of observation.

Equation (5.5) above implies that besides considering the effect of inefficiency in the use of input for producing the output, variations in the inefficiency effects are also influenced by other variables. This study allows for variations in the inefficiency effect to be different for bank ownership type (public/private as well as foreign/local), type of bank (Islamic/conventional), bank size and year of observation.

The data set is created using information obtained from banks' annual reports and the Bankers' Directory of the Association of Banks in Malaysia (ABM). The latter information source is used since some annual reports do not provide information on the number of employees. All monetary amounts are in Malaysian Ringgit (RM). Banks with incomplete data were excluded from the sample. The eventual data set contains complete data for 34 banks (24 local and 10 foreign) from a total of 55 commercial banks in operation during the period under study (1993 to 2000).

Empirical results

Before discussing the results of estimated cost frontier and inefficiency model, it may be worthwhile to first look at some descriptive statistics (Table 5.1) for the inefficiency measures computed for several pertinent bank categories/classifications.

Table 5.1 Descriptive statistics for inefficiency measures for various bank categories

	Mean	*Std dev.*	*Minimum*	*Maximum*
Conventional	0.302	0.240	0.030	1.230
Islamic	0.280	0.162	0.090	0.600
Local	0.321	0.248	0.050	1.230
Foreign	0.254	0.199	0.030	1.080
Asset size > RM12 billion	0.319	0.209	0.110	0.860
Asset size RM6–12 billion	0.290	0.269	0.090	1.200
Asset size RM3–6 billion	0.409	0.338	0.120	1.230
Asset size < RM3 billion	0.226	0.206	0.030	0.810

Std dev. = standard deviation.

Notice that Islamic banks do marginally better than conventional banks in terms of efficiency although both produce at a cost that is 30.2 per cent and 28 per cent respectively higher than necessary. The slight edge achieved by the Islamic banks over conventional banks is not, however, statistically significant. This observation provides no evidence that Islamic banks may be less efficient compared to their conventional counterparts due to a more restrictive business environment.

It is also interesting to note that foreign banks are generally more efficient than local banks. Further tests suggest that the difference is statistically significant at the 5 per cent level. This finding has important implications for the prospects of local Islamic (and conventional) banks when the banking market is opened to more foreign bank participation.

No clear conclusion can be derived from Table 5.1 regarding the effect of size on inefficiency. There is no clear observable pattern linking these two variables, although the smallest bank appears to be the most efficient. However, as is the case for any bivariate relationship (including those discussed above) that fails to control for the effects of other relevant variables, this does not imply that no relationship exists between the variables. Indeed, results of the inefficiency model as displayed in Table 5.3 provide a more reliable representation of the relationship between inefficiency and several structural variables.

The stochastic cost frontier (equation 5.3) was estimated using the maximum likelihood method and the results of the estimation are given in Table 5.2. Results of the inefficiency model are reported in Table 5.3.

To the extent that there is an overriding interest in the empirically estimated inefficiency model, much of this section is devoted to a discussion of the results presented in Table 5.3.

The coefficient of the dummy variable used for the Islamic bank is positive but not statistically significant, suggesting that Islamic banks are no less efficient than their conventional counterparts. This finding is comforting to proponents of Islamic banking since it implies that Islamic banks are equally cost efficient even when the business environment is in some sense more restrictive.

Both bank size coefficients (BankSize and BankSize^2) are statistically significant. Not only does bank size influence inefficiency, it also does so in a non-linear fashion. Taken together, with the negative coefficient for BankSize and the positive one for $\text{BankSize},^2$ it appears that increasing size initially provides some scale economies before diseconomies of scale set in after a critical size is reached. Such a relationship between size and inefficiency provides some evidence for a U-shaped average cost function.

Ownership status (public versus private) appears to make no difference in terms of inefficiency since the coefficients on Private and Private interacted with BankSize variables are not statistically significant. This finding strengthens the consensus in the literature about the relative efficiency of

Table 5.2 Maximum likelihood estimates for the trans-log stochastic cost frontier model

	Coefficient	*t-ratio*
Constant	–19.9081	–3.75
Deposits	0.4492	0.93
Investment	–0.2797	–0.24
Loan	3.9513	2.57
Price Capital	0.8922	1.56
Price Labour	–3.1278	–2.99
Price Borrowed Fund	–1.8497	–1.41
Deposits2	–0.0263	–1.13
Loan2	–0.0640	–0.54
Investment2	0.0747	0.86
PriceCapital2	0.0061	0.40
PriceLabour2	0.0625	1.77
PriceBorrowedFund2	–0.2568	–2.72
Deposits X Loan	–0.0469	–0.72
Deposits X Investment	0.0359	0.53
Loan X Investment	–0.0932	–0.45
Deposits X Price Capital	–0.0158	–0.36
Deposits X Price Labour	0.0640	0.87
Deposits X Price Borrowed Fund	–0.1095	–1.08
Loan X Price Capital	–0.0881	–0.87
Loan X Price Labour	0.0416	0.22
Loan X Price Borrowed Fund	–0.0414	–0.18
Investment X Price Capital	0.0490	0.59
Investment X Price Labour	0.0835	0.54
Investment X Price Borrowed Fund	0.2736	1.46
Price Capital X Price Labour	0.0755	0.86
Price Capital X Price Borrowed Fund	0.0903	0.87
Price Labour X Price Borrowed Fund	–0.0699	–0.35
Lambda	3.0157	3.99
Sigma	0.4193	11.54

Table 5.3 Ordinary least square estimates of the inefficiency model

	Coefficient	*t-ratio*
Constant	–16.7311	0.14
Islamic bank	0.1241	1.36
BankSize	–2.3763	–6.77
BankSize^2	0.0802	7.55
Private	0.3247	0.39
Private X Bank Size	–0.0172	–0.33
Foreign	0.6610	1.31
Foreign X Bank Size	–0.0404	–1.23
Year	0.1241	0.01

private and public firms, which is that there is no clear superiority of one form of organization over another when it comes to efficiency.

The Foreign and Foreign X Bank Size interaction variables are also not statistically significant, suggesting that foreign banks are no more efficient than local banks. This finding augurs well for the future prospects of locally owned banks when the market is fully liberalized. However, such optimism must be seasoned with caution since it is not known whether foreign banks may become more efficient once the existing restrictions on foreign banks are lifted (e.g., limits on the number of branches).

Conclusion

This study attempts to determine the efficiency of Islamic banks relative to other commercial banks in Malaysia by employing the stochastic cost frontier approach. An inefficiency model is estimated to link the inefficiency of input use to produce output to factors such as whether a bank is Islamic or otherwise. The study finds that there is no statistically significant difference in the level of efficiency between Islamic and conventional banks operating in Malaysia based on data for the period 1993–2000. There is also no evidence to suggest that bank efficiency is a function of ownership status (public/private or foreign/local). The study does, however, find that inefficiency is related to bank size and in a non-linear fashion. Increasing size initially provides some scale economies before diseconomies of scale set in once a critical size is reached, thus suggesting a U-shaped average cost function.

Comment

Zubair Hasan

Islamic banking and finance is poised to make rapid progress in Malaysia. From 8 per cent of the assets of the local banking industry at present, it is expected to capture 20 per cent by 2010. This is not a tall order considering the increasing state support that Islamic banking has received over more than two decades of its existence in the country. An important feature of this growth has been the success of Islamic banks despite competition from the interest-based institutions. The envisaged expansion would require an orderly development of financial services. The country has plans for the erection of a sound structure of governance, product diversification, and marketing.

In view of the imminent takeoff of Islamic banking in Malaysia, the work of the authors of this chapter on the efficiency of Islamic banking in Malaysia is timely and welcome. The authors rightly foresee an increasingly competitive challenge which the Islamic banks will have to counter in years ahead because of the recently concluded Free Trade Agreement of the ASEAN countries, and the unabated march of globalization. Of course, improving the operational performance of Islamic banks is imperative if they are to meet this challenge.

On the basis of the results they obtained, the authors claim that 'the efficiency level of Islamic banks is not statistically different from conventional banks'. Likewise, they find 'no evidence to suggest that bank efficiency is a function of ownership status'. These conclusions are important, and have serious policy implications. It is difficult to accept them at their face value as some recent studies in the area provide evidence to the contrary. The work calls for a closer examination.

Measuring technological change and efficiency

Technological change and improvements in efficiency are important elements of production growth in any country. Technological change is measured as a shift in the frontier production function, while efficiency improvement has two components, technical and allocative. Both are generally defined as a relative distance (or inefficiency) from a norm, designated as the frontier. Technical inefficiency, for example, exists when the actual or observed output of a firm from a given input mix is less than the maximum possible. In the same way, allocative inefficiency arises when the input mix is not consistent with cost minimization (i.e., when a firm does not equate marginal returns of inputs with true factor prices in the market).

The two concepts of technological change and efficiency are illustrated in Figure 5.1, assuming that a firm i produces a single product Y, using two inputs X_1 and X_2. The two equal-product curves Q_1 and Q_2 represent production frontiers for the same physical output at two points of time, T_1 and T_2.

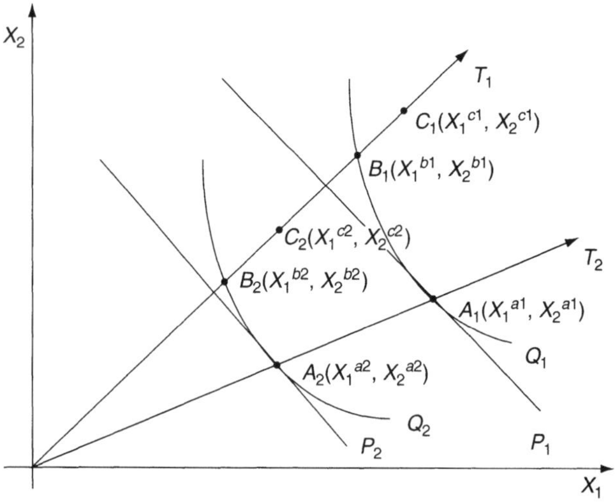

Figure 5.1 Impact of technological change and efficiency improvement on output

The functions are based on the best technologies used by the firms in the industry. However, firm *i* may not reach the frontier because of technical inefficiencies. Of the points shown in the figure A_1, B_1, A_2 and B_2 are *technically efficient*, but C_1 and C_2, being off the frontiers, are not.

In the cost function framework, we can measure technological change, technical efficiency, allocative efficiency, and economic efficiency respectively under:

$$\text{Technological change} = [C\ (X_1^{a2}, X_2^{a2}) - C\ (X_1^{a1}, X_2^{a1})] / [C\ (X_1^{a1}, X_2^{a1})] \tag{5.6}$$

$$\text{Technical efficiency at time } T_1 = C\ (X_1^{b1}, X_2^{b1}) / C\ (X_1^{c1}\ X_2^{c1}) \tag{5.7}$$

$$\text{Technical efficiency at time } T_2 = C\ (X_1^{b2}, X_2^{b2}) / C\ (X_1^{c2}\ X_2^{c2}) \tag{5.8}$$

$$\text{Allocative efficiency at time } T_1 = C\ (X_1^{a1}, X_2^{a1}) / C\ (X_1^{b1}, X_2^{b1}) \tag{5.9}$$

$$\text{Allocative efficiency at time } T_2 = C\ (X_1^{a2}, X_2^{a2}) / C\ (X_1^{b2}, X_2^{b2}) \tag{5.10}$$

$$\text{Economic efficiency} = \text{Technical Efficiency} \times \text{Allocative Efficiency} \tag{5.11}$$

Solving equation (5.11), we get the following measures of economic efficiency:

$$\text{Economic efficiency at time } T_1 = C\ (X_1^{a1}, X_2^{a1}) / C\ (X_1^{c1}, X_2^{c1}) \tag{5.12}$$

$$\text{Economic efficiency at time } T_2 = C\ (X_1^{a2}, X_2^{a2}) / C\ (X_1^{c2}, X_2^{c2}) \tag{5.13}$$

These ratios give in each case the level of efficiency reached. We have to deduct each from one to measure the degree of inefficiency or deviation from the norm of efficient performance. Table 5.1 provides an illustration.

The measurement of efficiency in its various versions has become increasingly commonplace with the development of the frontier production function approach. The approach is deterministic in the sense that all deviations from the frontier attributable to inefficiency are stochastic and it is possible to alienate from the error term the purely random disturbance factor. The applications of the approach have been numerous and extremely varied. The literature on the subject is voluminous and growing. Even in the area of banking, where the study under review falls, there is no dearth of academic writings on this subject. In view of that, the authors' review of the literature may appear scanty in coverage and comment.

Model and data

Estimation of any sort of efficiency from the above list requires the specification of a functional form. The trans-log form of cost frontier is usually considered appropriate for studying the efficiency issues related in the area of commercial banking. This is a very general and flexible functional form that encompasses other approaches such as those based on the Cobb–Douglas production function. It imposes on the frontier the conditions of linear homogeneity and symmetry (i.e., the assumption of constant returns to scale). It looks at the question of efficiency in terms of cost minimization for a given output rather than output maximization from given inputs. These conditions can be varied to suit the purpose of the model.

The authors adopt this approach focusing on technical efficiency. They express the general form of the model in equation (5.1) as follows: the inefficiency term U_i is made an explicit function of k variables z_k ($k = 1 \ldots 5$ in the present case). The U_is are independently, but not identically, distributed as non-negative transactions of the normal distribution of the form:

$$U_{it} \sim N\left[\delta_0 + \sum_{k=1}^{M} \delta_0 z_{k,\,it}, \sigma^2\right] \qquad (5.14)$$

The specification of the model for the inefficiency effects, given the level of output, is:

$$U_{it} = \delta_0 \sum_{j=1}^{m} \delta_0 D_{jit} + \sum_{j=1}^{m} \delta_j z_{jit} \qquad (5.15)$$

Here m is the number of bank categories identified for the model. Instead of using m and n as superscripts in their equivalent equation (5.2), it might have been better if the authors had given the specific numbers – probably 4 as in their Table 5.1 – for reasons of clarity.

As noted earlier, the technical efficiency of a firm, *i*, is defined as the ratio of the frontier input cost to the corresponding observed cost of the inputs given the level of output the firm produces. The technical efficiency of the firm *i* at time *t* in the context of the stochastic production function can be expressed in terms of the errors as under:

$$TE_{it} = E[\exp(-U_{it})/(V_{it} + U_{it})] \tag{5.16}$$

which is the expectation of the exponential technical inefficiencies dependent on the error term ϵ_{it}. Since U_{it} is a non-negative random variable these technical efficiencies lie between zero and unity where unity indicates that the firm is technically efficient. The authors employ the usual maximum likelihood method in their work. The method estimates the unknown parameters of the stochastic frontier and the inefficiency effects from the data simultaneously. Tables 5.2 and 5.3 present the results of the exercise. Table 5.2 contains 28 parameters including the constant, but no explanation is provided.

The real issue in any application of the trans-log cost frontier function is the selection of variables included in the set of inputs and outputs of a firm, and specifying the constraints imposed on the model to isolate the unwanted influences affecting the results. Here the authors' work in this chapter is quite murky.

In the first place, one finds no background discussion of the development, present structure, and policies concerning banking institutions in Malaysia. Some crucial changes affecting the efficiency of banks (such as their enlargement in size and the reduction in their number in a restructuring exercise) took place after the 1997–98 financial turmoil. The banks are also very different from other production units in the economy, manufacturing in particular, in terms of explaining the input–output concept or measurement.

The study covers a fairly long period, 1993–2000, but the results have no time dimension: obviously the authors have used panel modelling for their work. Since the total number of banks they cover (34) is quite large, one wonders if the post-crisis data, with their greater homogeneity and ease of handling, would not have served the authors' purpose better. Or the data could have been used for a dynamic study of inefficiency (i.e., changes over time).

Again, only two Islamic banks appear in the sample and the results do not highlight their comparison with mainstream banks as planned. This makes the title of the chapter somewhat misleading. Also, what about the Islamic windows operating in the conventional banks? How have the authors dealt with the impact of this phenomenon on the efficiency of banking in the country, Islamic or otherwise? This is a difficult question, yet those measuring efficiency of banks in Malaysia can hardly afford to bypass it. One should at least discuss it as a limitation of the study.

The data set for 34 banks – 24 local and 10 foreign – is created using the banks' annual reports and the ABM Bankers' Directory to fill gaps in information on the number of employees in some cases. The banks have been identified for purposes of analysis as local and foreign, Islamic and conventional, private and public, and as large and small. Of course, the categorization used in the study is not unique as many categories overlap.

The study does not reveal the component details of the outputs or inputs selected for modelling. One finds a somewhat general discussion on the issue in the chapter. It is hinted that total cost (*C*) includes all labour and capital expenses plus interest. In the case of Islamic banks, interest is replaced with income distributed to the depositors. What is included in labour expense, or how capital expense is estimated, is not clear. The authors refer to a paper by Habshi al- (1999) for details. The paper is not readily available, and neither does it contain the needed explanations. Ideally, an explanation of this crucial point should have been included in the chapter. The authors mention three outputs: loans, advances, and financing. Again no details on their nature or content are provided, and inter-bank differences, at least with respect to mainstream interest-based banks and Islamic banks, should have been discussed. Financing in particular is a dubious category unless clearly explained.

The corresponding input prices include (i) staff expenses per employee, (ii) expenses on land, building and equipment per Ringgit of assets, and (iii) expenses on interest or income distributed per Ringgit of deposits. Here also the chapter has no explanatory discussion. For example, in (i) for averaging expenses of labour, all employees cannot be treated on the same footing; the proportion of officers to support staff is not the same in all banks. In foreign banks particularly, it is found to be generally loaded in favour of officers as opposed to support staff. Also, foreign banks earn a significantly larger share of their revenue from non-interest sources, through activities such as derivatives trading, consumer credit and merchant banking. Such matters are not given weight in the condensed data the work uses. Likewise, in (ii) historical and current costs differences between items and banks may have considerably distorted the aggregation.

Even the number of inputs and outputs used is not explicitly mentioned in the chapter. One way to know the number of outputs and inputs underlying a model is to look at the superscripts used in the specification.

The authors use in their model (equation 5.3) general superscripts n and m, not the numerals. I think the authors should have tested the appropriateness of the trans-log model form they have used compared to the linear construct as in Turati (2001). Possibly, the results would have been different.

Results and their discussion

Let us have a closer look at the details of the results obtained by the study. It may be recalled that the authors promised to provide the ranking of the banks in their sample on an efficiency ladder. Surprisingly, the section does not contain any such list. The results are based on three tables. Table 5.1 provides descriptive statistics for inefficiency measures for various bank *categories*. As the sample size helps in interpreting the results, it would have been better if the table had also provided the number of banks in each category.

The first conclusion of the authors is that Islamic banks have a slight edge over the conventional banks in matters of efficiency. The difference is not statistically significant, the authors admit, but it does lead them to conclude that Islamic banks in Malaysia are at least no less efficient than the conventional ones. The conclusion needs caution. The number of Islamic banks operating in Malaysia and included in the study is no more than two. In the aggregate, their transactions' value is not more than a drop in the ocean. And to reiterate, the authors do not mention how they have treated the Islamic windows operating in the conventional banks.

This, in fact, reopens the issue of defining the variables alluded to earlier. For example, how have dividends paid on equity capital been treated? Is the money included in the cost of capital? Likewise, what about retained earnings? Do they appear in the cost of capital calculations for Islamic banks? They cannot be treated at par with interest paid in the case of conventional banks. Interest payments are obligatory, but the amount distributed in Islamic banks is discretionary: retained earnings *ipso facto* belong to the depositors. Failure to recognize the distinction may have led *inter alia* to an underestimation of capital costs for Islamic banks, thus showing them to be more efficient than they in fact might be. Again, the authors have taken absolute amount of loans as a variable, but in the context of measuring bank efficiency, the *ratio* of loans to deposits has been found more appropriate.

Tables 5.2 and 5.3 provide the maximum likelihood method and Ordinary Least Squares results. The addition of relevant correlation coefficients to them might have been enlightening.

Comment

Shamim Ahmad Siddiqui

This chapter measures and compares the efficiency of two Islamic banks in Malaysia to those of the conventional commercial banks in that country. The authors have used the parametric stochastic frontier approach (commonly applied to measure the relative efficiency of a firm's production and cost levels) to estimate the parameters of banks' cost functions and then used the results to compute the levels of their relative inefficiencies. Taking these levels of inefficiencies as the dependent variable, another regression exercise is then carried out to investigate the causes of these inefficiencies. The results thus obtained are interesting and shed some light on the state of the two Islamic banks in Malaysia.

What follows here is an attempt to provide some suggestions for further research in this important area.

First, the review of literature surveys a reasonable number of studies for the purposes of the chapter. I would like to draw the attention of researchers to a couple of recent studies. A study of local and foreign banks in Switzerland by Rime and Stiroh (2003) applies an up-to-date method to a parametric approach. Another study, of Sri Lankan banks by Jankee (2002), uses an appropriate technique for panel data.

Second, Islamic banks have been established with a particular purpose and have to work in a particular way. The nature of their depositors and users of funds are inherently different from those of the conventional banks. While conventional banks must ensure the return of principals and any accrued interest on demand, the Islamic banks would violate their basic principles if they were to do the same. Similarly, the rules for both the use of funds and the users of funds are supposed to be different for Islamic banks. If this point is accepted, it may then be emphasized that any comparison of Islamic banks with those of the conventional banks must be carried out with reservations. As a matter of fact, the performance criteria for measuring the efficiency of Islamic banks should be somewhat different.[2]

An Islamic bank that is attempting to implement an Islamically preferable mode of banking may encounter relatively higher costs (especially in its infancy) than its conventional counterpart. This possibly higher cost may or may not be matched by a relatively higher return, particularly in its infancy. However, as the rules for Islamic banks are different, any comparison between them and the conventional banks must be qualified.

Third, in their literature review the authors mention, 'Sarker (1999) did a study on all the Islamic banks based in Pakistan... The study concluded that Islamic banks could not achieve maximum efficiency under the conventional banking framework because of the constraints that they faced.' This gives an impression that there are several Islamic banks in Pakistan which face competition from the conventional banks. In fact, the only Islamic bank in Pakistan is the recently established Al-Meezan bank. The central bank of Pakistan appears now to be taking some serious steps to establish a dual banking system by adopting a gradual approach.[3]

Fourth, while analysing banking efficiency, a detailed discussion on the non-parametric data envelope analysis, as well as the stochastic frontier approach, can be instructive. The DEA appears to be the most commonly used approach and definitely qualifies for better treatment. Almost every paper on bank efficiency discusses the advantages and disadvantages of the alternative approaches in some detail.[4] Resti (1997) utilized both techniques and found little difference in the results. Regarding technical debate for estimating efficiency, it is worth quoting Rizvi (2002) who notes that:

> There are, however, a few benefits and limitations of both techniques. [The] Former [parametric frontier technique] is based on the assumption that some maximising behaviour is present that can be estimated through some functional form (like cost, profit and production etc.). But there is no *a priori* ground for making such assumption, and therefore, non-parametric approach may be preferred (Button and Weyman-Jones, 1992). Moreover, till now there is no agreed functional form.[5] Therefore, one remains in doubt about the true efficiency estimate as results may be mudded with mis-specification of econometric model. Lastly, it is also difficult to use stochastic frontier technique when one is dealing with multiple inputs and multiple outputs. The benefit of using stochastic frontier techniques is that they address econometric issues by incorporating noise in the model, thus allowing noise to be isolated from inefficiencies. Also, the stochastic frontier technique can be used to measure allocative inefficiency, when price data is available.

Finally, It is important to see if cost minimization is actually the main goal of a bank. Revenue or profit maximization may be the over-riding objective of a commercial bank.[6] This aspect is normally the main focus of the ratio analysis approach to scrutiny of bank performance. Unlike the conventional banks, where bank shareholders are the only ones who are primarily concerned about banks' levels of profits, the depositors of Islamic banks also have a share in banks' profits. It would be quite interesting to see a brief comparison of profitability among Islamic banks, local conventional banks and their foreign counterparts in Malaysia and elsewhere.

Notes

1. By the end of October 2001, the total assets of RM59.0 billion belonging to Islamic banking institutions represented only 8.2 per cent of the total banking assets (RM717 billion). Similarly, the role of Islamic banks in financing activities is still small compared to the conventional banks where it accounted for a mere 6.5 per cent (RM28 billion) of a total of RM432 billion for the whole banking system. Total deposits in the Islamic banking system amounted to RM47 billion

(9.5 per cent) compared to RM495 billion total deposits in the entire system (Abdul Kader, 2002).

2. For example, an Islamic bank using preferred Islamic modes of finance could be regarded as successful even though its profit per share and returns to depositors are relatively lower than other Islamic banks (not using the preferred modes of finance) or conventional banks. One should also keep in mind that many Muslim depositors and shareholders of Islamic banks are not only mindful of the permissibility/legality of their earnings but also genuinely concerned about its *purity*.
3. A significant Islamic financial institution in Pakistan is the *muḍārabahs* who have been working since the mid-1980s. They have some unique features and their performance has been mixed. For a detailed discussion on *muḍārabahs* please see Siddiqui (1998).
4. For example, please see Rizvi (2002) and Rime and Stiroh (2003).
5. See, for example, McAllister and McManus (1993) for evidence to show that trans-log and Box-Cox functional forms do not perform well in estimating scale and scope efficiencies. Berger and Mester (1997) conclude that Fourier Flexible is superior in estimating efficiencies when compared to the distribution free approach and trans-log. Also see Altunba and Chakravarty (2001), who find that Fourier Flexible is not good at predicting efficiency/inefficiency.
6. See Jankee (2002).

References

Abd Karim, M. Z. (2001), 'Comparative Bank Efficiency across Select ASEAN Countries', *ASEAN Economic Bulletin*, 18 (3), 289–304.

Abdul Kader, M. R. (2002), 'The Operation of Islamic Banking Master Plan', Experts Meeting on Towards 20 per cent Market Share, Bank Negara Malaysia Strategy, Kuala Lumpur.

Aigner, D. J., C. A. K. Lovell and P. Schmidt (1977), 'Formulation and Estimation of Stochastic Frontier Production Function Models', *Journal of Econometrics*, 6, 21–37.

Altunba, Y. and S. P. Chakravarty (2001), 'Frontier Cost Functions and Bank Efficiency', *Economics Letters*, 72 (2), 233–40.

Association of Banks in Malaysia (Various issues), *ABM Bankers' Directory*, Kuala Lumpur.

Bank Negara Malaysia (2001), *Annual Report*, Kuala Lumpur.

Berger, A. N. and D. B. Humprey (1997), *Efficiency of Financial Institutions: International Survey and Directions for Future Research*, Philadelphia, PA: Wharton Financial Institutions Centre, The Wharton School, University of Pennsylvania.

Berger, Allen N. and Loretta J. Mester (1997), 'Inside the Black Box: What Explains Differences in the Efficiencies of Financial Institutions?', *Journal of Banking and Finance*, 21 (7), 895–947.

Button, K. J. and T. G. Weyman-Jones (1992), 'Ownership Structure, Institutional Organization and Measured X-inefficiency', *American Economic Review*, 6 (2), 429–44.

Cebenoyan, A. S., E. S. Cooperman and C. A. Register (1993), 'Firm Efficiency and the Regulatory Closure of S & Ls: An Empirical Investigation', *Review of Economics and Statistics*, 75, 540–5.

Chang, C. E., I. Hasan and W. C. Hunter (1998), 'Efficiency of Multinational Banks: An Empirical Investigation', *Applied Financial Economics*, 8, 689–96.

Federal Reserve Bank of New York (2001), *Evidence from Switzerland* (draft), 7 May.

Habshi, S. M. al-, (1999), 'Financial Performance Measurement and Distribution Policy of Islamic Financial Institutions', Paper presented to the International Conference on Islamic Economics Towards 21st Century, 9–12 August, Kuala Lumpur, Malaysia.

Hamid, M. A. (1999), 'Islamic Banking in Bangladesh Expectations and Realities', Paper presented to the International Conference on Islamic Economics Towards 21st Century, 9–12 August, Kuala Lumpur, Malaysia.

Jankee K. (2002), 'Impact of Interest Rate Deregulation on X-efficiency in the Banking Sector: A Case Study of Mauritius', Paper presented at South and South East Asian Econometrics Conference held at Lahore University of Management Sciences, Lahore, Pakistan, 28–30 December.

Jondrow, J., C. A. K. Lovell, I. S. Materov and P. Schmidt (1982), 'On the Estimation of Technical Efficiency in the Stochastic Frontier Production Function Model', *Journal of Econometrics*, 19, 233–8.

Kwan, Simon H. and Robert A. Eisenbeis (1996), 'An Analysis of Inefficiencies in Banking: A Stochastic Cost Frontier Approach', *Economic Review, Federal Reserve Bank San Francisco*, 2, 16–26.

Lovell, C. A. K. and E. Grifell-Tatje (1997), 'The Sources of Productivity Change in Spanish Banking', *European Journal of Operational Research*, 98, 364–80.

McAllister, P. H. and D. McManus (1993), 'Resolving the Scale Efficiency Puzzle in Banking', *Journal of Banking and Finance*, 17 (2–3), 389–405.

Mendes, V. and J. Rebelo (1999), 'Productive Efficiency, Technological Change and Productivity in Portuguese Banking', *Applied Financial Economics*, 9, 513–21.

Mester, L. J. (1993), *Efficiency of Banks in the Third Federal Reserve District*, Philadelphia, PA: Wharton Financial Institutions Centre, The Wharton School, University of Pennsylvania.

Mester, L. J. (1996), 'A Study of Bank Efficiency Taking into Account Risk-Preference', *Journal of Banking and Finance*, 20, 1,025–45.

Metwally, M. M. (1997), 'Differences Between the Financial Characteristics of Interest-free Banks and Conventional Banks', *European Business Review*, 97 (2), 92.

Meusen, W. and V. D. Broeck (1977), 'Efficiency Estimation from Cobb–Douglas Production Functions with Composed Error', *International Economic Review*, 18 (2), 435–44.

Resti, Andrea (1997), 'Evaluating the Cost-efficiency of the Italian Banking System: What can be Learned from the Joint Application of Parametric and non-parametric Techniques', *Journal of Banking and Finance*, 21 (2), 221–50.

Rime, Bertrand and Kevin J. Stiroh (2003), 'The Performance of Universal Banks', *Journal of Banking and Finance*, 27 (11), 2,121–50.

Rizvi, Syed Fawad Ali (2002), 'Post Financial Liberalization Efficiency and Productivity of Banking in Pakistan', *Pakistan Development Review*, 41 (4), Part II, 605–32.

Samad, A. and M. K. Hassan (1999), 'The Performance of Malaysian Islamic Bank during 1984–1997: An Exploratory Study', *International Journal of Islamic Financial Services*, 1 (3), http://islamic-finance.net/journal.html.

Sarker, M. A. A. (1999), 'Islamic Banking in Bangladesh: Performance, Problems and Prospects', *International Journal of Islamic Financial Services*, 1 (3), http://islamic-finance.net/journal.html.

Sealey, C. W. and J. T. Lindley (1977), 'Inputs, Outputs, and a Theory of Production and Cost at Depository Financial Institutions', *The Journal of Finance*, XXXII (4), 1,251–66.

Siddiqui, Shamim A. (1998), 'A Critical Study of Bacha's Model and *Muḍārabahs* of Pakistan', *Journal of Accounting, Commerce and Finance: Islamic Perspective*, 2 (3), 1–36.

Turati, Gilberto (2001), 'Cost Efficiency and Profitability in European Commercial Banking', 7th European Workshop on Efficiency and Productivity Analysis, Oviedo, Spain.

Wheelock, D. C. and P. W. Wilson (1995), 'Evaluating the Efficiency of Commercial Banks: Does Our View of What Banks Do Matter?', *Federal Reserve Bank of Saint Louis Review*, 77 (4), 39–52.

Zaim, O. (1995), 'The Effect of Financial Liberalization on the Efficiency of Turkish Commercial Banks', *Applied Financial Economics*, 5, 257–64.

6

An Analysis of the Relationship between the Interest-free Financing System and Sustainable Development: The Case of Iran

Yadollah Dadgar

This chapter investigates the relationship between the interest-free financing system and sustainable development as it affects the Islamic Republic of Iran. The first section deals with the conceptual framework. The second section studies the consistency (or inconsistency) between Islamic teachings and sustainable development (SD). The third section reviews the performance of Iran's interest-free financing system in relation to SD. The last section provides some concluding remarks and policy implications.

Introduction

In this chapter we make some claims which will be examined later in the chapter: these are as follows.

First, the interest-free financial system is consistent with SD. Second, there are many points of contact between Islamic teachings and SD. Third, potentially speaking, interest-free financial elements in Iran can provide considerable support to SD. Fourth, the inefficiencies of current financial system in Iran stem from factors which are outside the interest-free system. Typically, complicated nature of laws and non-transparency of policy makers' behaviour, administrative and executive circumstances and even some ultra-economic factors are responsible for inefficiencies in Iran's monetary system. Finally, even though the current interest-free system in Iran suffers from some serious shortcomings, it embodies some successes, too. If Islamic economics is going to be successful, all its elements should be coordinated, on the one hand, and it should also be coordinated as a whole with other sub-systems (social, political, cultural), on the other. So if, for example, the banking system is acting on an interest-free basis, but the ownership of capital or the allocation system does not follow the Islamic laws, we will not get the expected results.[1]

Sustainable development embodies significant dimensions and covers important subjects. In an SD framework, a kind of development is maintained that meets the needs of the present without compromising the ability of the future generations.[2] Up to now, Iran and some other Muslim countries have been financing their expenditures (related to the present generation) through exploiting their natural resources (especially non-renewable ones such as gas and petroleum). By so doing, they are depleting those resources and, consequently, reducing the benefits for the future generations. Thus discovering alternative financial devices will help to maintain natural resources and SD. Implementation of the interest-free financial system (if done properly) is a plausible substitute. A profit and loss sharing (PLS) mechanism, *muḍārabah*, interest-free loans and direct investment are among other financial instruments which are used in Iran's banking system. Also, along with these monetary and banking devices, there are some fiscal instruments such as *zakāh* (and *khums*) and other *Sharī'ah* payments that can be used (to supplant or supplement other financing devices).

In 1983, the UN created the World Commission on Environment and Development, called the Brundtland Commission (after its Chairman, Gro Harlem Bruntland) to examine global environmental and development problems. In its 1987 report, *Our Common Future*, the Commission outlined a broad agenda for integrating economic development and environmental policies. It stressed the view that growth cannot continue at the present rate of environmental degradation. It introduced the concept of SD which was defined as 'development that meets the present without compromising the ability of future generations to meet their needs'. Robert Solow, who received the Nobel prize in 1987, has recently proposed a somewhat more precise definition of sustainability: 'a sustainable path for the national economy is one that allows every generation the option of being as well off as its predecessors'.[3] Clearly, natural resources are important to achieving SD. The concept of SD stresses the role of the environment as capital that, if exhausted, cannot be replaced.

According to the Commission, governments need to expand their role in the collection and dissemination of information and, where possible, should produce an annual account for each nation, environment and resource base 'to complement the traditional annual fiscal budget and economic development plans'. The idea is that the environment is part of our capital and, when we degrade it, we reduce our ability to generate real income in the future. Some of the Brundtland Commission's recommendations require government involvement in economies in order to produce and enforce environmental regulations. The Commission also feels that there are limits to the ability of competitive industry to reduce waste voluntarily: regulations and the imposition of uniform performance standards are essential to ensure that industry makes the investment necessary to reduce waste.

Recommendations are made for reforming international organizations, in which an extensive institutional capacity exists that could be redirected towards SD. The efficacy of existing institutions is reduced by their fragmented nature and weak coordination. A general consensus has emerged that one of the most important goals of national states and international organizations must be the pursuit of sustainable development. One question in this regard is: how do nation-states create wealth for today's generations without leaving a depleted environment for future generations? Some economic thinkers define SD as a development process in which natural resources are not depleted, and safe water, shelter and enough food and nutrition are available. Other scientists define it as achieving a desirable growth of per capita income, without destroying environmental resources. Also, some other writers explain SD as a stage of development during which present and future generations have equal opportunities.[4]

Historically speaking, the World Commission on Environment and Development focused on environmental problems in 1987. During the Earth Summit in 1992, it was stipulated that achieving development without considering a kind of safe environment is not possible. Not very surprisingly, the majority of the experts in SD emphasize that it does have multi–dimensional aspects. For example, Todaro (2000) first stressed that sustainability must be strengthened as a guiding principle of development. Then he added: 'In order to maintain SD, damage to soils, water supplies, and forests should be prevented.' Also, Pearce (1992) stipulated that: 'For economists, a development path is sustainable if and only if the stock of overall capital assets remains constant or rises over time. He adds that overall capital assets include not only manufactured, but also human, capital.[5]

Reducing foreign debts, controlling domestic consumption, establishing equitable distribution of income and wealth, maintaining ecological consistency, protecting cultural heritage, combating poverty and considering environmental ethics may also be mentioned as some other dimensions of SD.[6] All of these find support from Islamic theology. In the case of Iran, potentially speaking, there are some instruments that can be substituted for petrol/gas and other resources. Some of these are renewable resources, and among them are manufacturing and agricultural products, and tourism. Some others are fiscal devices, such as an interest-free banking system, *zakāh* and *khums*.[7]

In the case of Iran, gas and petroleum cover at least 90 per cent of initial energy requirements. They also represent more than 80 per cent of government revenues, so the country tends to deplete natural resources. In order to maintain SD, the country should develop substitutes for natural resources (especially non-renewable ones) for financing public expenditure. Efficient use of energy is one of the recommendations related to SD.

Consistency between Islamic teachings and sustainable development

Islamic teachings do pay attention to the above-mentioned elements. The *Qur'ān*, *ḥadīth* and the behaviour of the Prophet (peace be upon him) and his successors contain some obvious lessons regarding the protection of nature. We mention some of them here. The Holy *Qur'ān* stipulates that: 'He [God] brought you forth from the earth and settled you therein' (*Qur'ān*, 11:61). Encouraging people to keep to an ordinary and balanced consumption pattern is another *Qur'ānic* recommendation: 'And those who, when they spend, are neither extravagant nor niggardly, but hold a medium [way] between those [extremes]' (*Qur'ān*, 25:67). In addition, encouraging people to plant and cultivate trees and discourage their felling, making the killing of animals illegal, encouraging people to improve barren lands, emphasizing the significance of water and its role in daily life and so forth, are among the numerous orders and recommendations which are conclusive regarding SD: 'Eat good and lawful things and commit no oppression therein' (*Qur'ān*, 20:81), and 'Is not He who created the heavens and earth and sends down for you water' (*Qur'ān*, 27:60).

In *ḥadīth* we also have many directions that would promote SD. For example, the Prophet (peace be upon him) stressed, 'do not cut trees, otherwise you will be punished by God'. There are some orders about the protection of animals. People who harass animals are compared with 'Satan' (*Qur'ān*, 6:140). According to the Prophet (peace be upon him) anyone who plants and cultivates a tree gets a reward. Regarding social justice, which is a significant component in the SD literature, the *Qur'ān* emphasizes that: 'verily God enjoins justice' (*Qur'ān*, 16:90); that is, He orders it as an obligatory element in individual and social behaviour. In this connection, a special type of government intervention in Islam is also recommended. First, both public and private sectors are trustees with regard to property (the real owner and allocater is God). Second, government can intervene in all necessary matters where the private sector cannot work efficiently. So the Prophet (peace be upon him) stresses that: 'I will be responsible to resolve the difficulties of poor people and other market failure oriented problems.'

There are many other texts which hint at other dimensions of SD. People are invited by the *Qur'ān* to think deeply about nature, interpreting the environmental elements as *āyah* (sign), and even to swear to natural elements by Allah; these are some of the signals which show the importance of the environment. Also, emphasizing some legal economic activities and forbidding others could be thought of as indications of alternatives to natural resource exploitation. Paraphrasing the *Qur'ān*, the swearing of Allah as 'by the time' (*Qur'ān*, 103:1), 'by the steeds that run' (*Qur'ān*, 100:1), 'by the fig and the olive' (*Qur'ān*, 95:1), 'by the mount Sinai' (*Qur'ān*, 96:2), 'by the city of peace' (*Qur'ān*, 95:3), 'by the sun and its brightness' (*Qur'ān*, 91:1), 'by the moon', 'by the heaven and earth' (*Qur'ān*, 91:5–6), and also statements such as 'whatsoever is in the heavens and earth glorifies Allah' (*Qur'ān*, 62:1), are clear references to take care of, and benefit from, nature.

The interest-free system in Iran

The relationship between monetary and fiscal systems and SD is two-fold. On the one hand, strong and responsible fiscal devices can act as alternatives to natural resources in financing expenditure and consequently in supporting SD. On the other hand, some devices can be used to finance expenditure in order to rebuild the depleted environment because of unsustainable development. We argue and show that if we can lay the groundwork of establishing interest-free fiscal devices in a proper manner, the system can fulfil some of the above-mentioned functions.

Historical note

Some banks in Muslim countries have been carrying out financial activities based on interest-free systems since 1970. Some of them have been successful and others not. The Iranian experience is a special case because from 1984 its total banking system was based on interest-free instruments.[8] It is worth noting that during the 1930s, the followers of Gesell's theory found opportunities to initiate an interest-free money project. There were endeavours to introduce free money in Austria, France, Germany, Spain, Switzerland and the United States. One of the most successful interest-free systems was created in Austria. Dieter Suhr presents a report on the US stamp scrip movement by Hans R. L. Cohressen who, together with Irving Fisher, an economist, tried to introduce Gesell's concept of cost-bearing money into the USA (in 1933).[9] Keynes addressed some points about the efficiency of usury laws in the 1930s.[10] Muslim countries in the 1960s and 1970s increased their efforts to introduce an Islamic financial system. During the 1980s and 1990s, the IMF, World Bank and the IDB initiated some projects in this connection. Recently, some German thinkers have started researching ways to reform their monetary system towards some kind of interest-free mechanism.[11] Marvin Goodfriend, Vice Chancellor of the Federal Reserve, is suggesting the analysis of 'zero-interest' policy making.

Law of interest-free activities

The Islamic Parliament (in Iran) approved the law of interest-free activities in 1983. It contains 5 chapters, 27 articles and 4 notes. Chapter 1 involves the goals and duties of the banking system, which contains two articles. Article 1 describes the banking system goals which are making facilities, extending interest-free loans, and mobilizing these to finance employment and investment. Article 2 describes the duties of the banking system, such as issuing coins and currencies, regulating money and credits, supervising gold and other exchange transactions, applying monetary policy and activities related to bonds and bills, and opening different kinds of account (interest-free loans, saving, investments and demand deposits). Chapter 2, which contains Articles 3–6, deals with the provision of monetary resources. Through these articles, various kinds of deposits and the allocation of benefits are explained. Chapter 3, setting out Articles 7–17, discusses facilities granted by banks. In these articles, financing *mushārakah*, direct investment, *muḍārabah*, instalment selling, *muzāra'ah* and interest-free loans are developed. Chapter 4 contains Articles 18, 19 and 20, which involve applying monetary policy, determining the highest and lowest levels of profit and so forth. Finally, Chapter 5 contains Articles 21–27, which deal with some miscellaneous activities.

Empirical evidence

To analyse the performance of the interest-free system, we should review its activities quantitatively. First, we show the current Iranian banking pattern, and next we study the factors behind it. We look at profit taken from facilities granted, profit paid to deposits, the amount of banking assets, and their changing patterns and other banking activities. Table 6.1 shows the expected profit rate of granted facilities. We can see that although the

Table 6.1 Expected profit rate for facilities granted in Iranian Islamic banks (%)

Year	*Exporting*	*Commerce*	*Agriculture*	*Building*	*Industry*
1990	18	17–19	6–9	12–14	11–13
1991	18	17–19	6–9	12–16	11–13
1992	and above 18	17–19	9	12–16	13
1993	18	18–24	12–16	12–16	16–18
1994	18	18–24	13–16	15	16–18
1995	18	22–25	13–16	15–16	17–19
1996	18	22–25	13–16	15–16	17–19
1997	18	22–25	13–16	15–16	17–19
1998	18	22–25	13–16	15–16	17–19
1999	18	22–25	13–16	15–16	17–19
2000	18	22–25	13–16	15–16	17–19

Source: Central Bank, Statistic Centre (2002).

average rate of inflation for the period under consideration, 1989–2000, has been above 22 per cent, the expected rate of profit for most of the activities is less than 20 per cent. Table 6.2 indicates the rate of profit of investment deposits. Table 6.3 shows the ratio of the capital to assets and Table 6.4 indicates the capital trends. It is obvious that the Iranian banks faced capital inadequacy during 1986–98. Low capital–asset ratios are mainly due to the existence of huge risks in the Iranian economy. Table 6.5 indicates the summary of the Iranian banks' balance sheets.

Table 6.2 Profit rate of investment deposit in Iran by maturity (%)

Year	*Short run*	*One year*	*Two years*	*Five years*
1989	6	8.5	–	–
1990	6.25	9.8	10	13
1991	6.5	9	10.5	11.5
1992	7.5	10	11.5	13
1993	8	11.5	13.5	16
1994	8	11.5	13.5	16
1995	8	14	16	18.5
1996	8	14	16	18.5
1997	8	14	15	18.5
1998	8	14	15	18.5
1999	8	14	15	18.5
2000	8	14	15	18.5
2001	7.5	13.5	14.5	17

Source: Central Bank, Statistic Centre (2002).

Table 6.3 Ratio of capital to assets in Iranian banks, 1986–98 (%)

Year	*Commercial banks*	*Specialized banks*	*Total*
1986	0.9	9.6	2.5
1987	0.7	8.9	2
1988	0.5	6.4	1.3
1989	0.3	5.9	1.1
1990	0.0	4.7	0.7
1991	0.0	7.6	1.2
1992	1.4	6.6	2.2
1993	5.5	9.3	5.9
1994	4.3	16.2	5.7
1995	3.2	12.3	4.3
1996	2.4	9.7	3.4
1997	2.3	7.9	3.2
1998	2.1	6.0	2.7

Source: Central Bank of Iran (2000).

Table 6.4 Capital trends in Iranian commercial and specialized banks, 1986–99 (billion rials)

Year	*Commercial banks*	*Specialized banks*
1986	81.0	272.2
1987	98.7	216.5
1988	86.3	209.8
1989	81.1	200.1
1990	67.7	165.4
1991	85.1	179.9
1992	9.1	187.7
1993	22.4	409.7
1994	567.1	436.5
1995	3,680.9	765.5
1996	3,538.9	1,776.8
1997	3,466.3	1,797.4
1998	3,326.7	1,930.5
1999	4,346.2	2,130.0

Source: Central Bank of Iran (2000).

Table 6.5 Summary of balance sheet of Iranian banks

	1995	*1996*	*1997*	*1998*	*1999*
Net foreigner assets	199,533	2,969	–2,430	–3,101	–1,120
Foreigner assets	6,137	8,340	3,816	2,424	5,290
Foreigner debts	–6,104	–5,371	–4,059	–5,525	–6,410
Net domestic assets	74,366	100,368	112,378	144,729	171,690
Net debt of Central Bank to other banks	13,308	23,927	22,205	29,792	25,428
Debt of banks to the Central Bank	–10,420	–10,190	–14,930	–13,400	–24,329
Banks' deposits in Central Bank	22,369	33,104	35,721	41,794	47,963

Source: Central Bank of Iran (2000).

Analysis of the efficiency of Iran's interest-free banking

Now we examine the performance of the banking system, first from the point of view of mobilizing resources; second, according to the allocation of those resources; and finally, by some other relevant criterion. Table 6.6 shows resource mobilization by kind of deposits.

It can be seen from Table 6.6 that during the ten-year period studied (1989–99), there is considerable fluctuation in the case of demand deposits. That is, they go up in the first year, then decrease during the two following

Table 6.6 Changes in deposit mobilization of Iranian banks by kind of deposits, 1989–99 (billion rials)

Kind of deposits	*1989*	*1990*	*1991*	*1992*	*1993*	*1994*	*1995*	*1996*	*1997*	*1998*	*1999*
Demand	5,342	7,076	9,061	11,009	15,581	21,731	30,294	43,055	47,923	56,011	64,931
% change	23.5	32.5	28.0	21.5	41.5	39.5	39.4	42.1	11.3	16.9	15.9
Saving	1,281	1,392	869	2,441	2,983	3,495	4,616	6,039	8,693	12,420	16,269
% change	7.3	8.7	–37.6	180.9	22.2	17.2	32.1	30.8	43.9	42.9	31.0
Investment	8,007	9,695	11,740	14,647	19,053	22,517	28,417	35,847	47,103	62,429	79,532
% change	25.2	21.1	21.1	24.8	30.1	18.2	26.2	26.1	31.4	32.5	27.4
Short run	5,245	5,945	6,810	8,116	10,304	1,287	15,033	19,051	24,289	32,046	37,564
% change	23.1	13.3	14.5	19.2	27.0	17.3	24.4	26.7	27.5	31.9	17.2
Long run	2,762	3,750	4,930	6,531	8,749	10,433	13,384	16,796	22,814	30,383	39,968
% change	29.5	35.8	31.5	32.5	34.0	19.2	28.3	25.5	35.8	33.2	31.5

Source: Survey Office of Central Bank (2000).

Table 6.7 Balanced combination of granted facilities to non-governmental sectors, 1989–99 (%)

Contract	*1989*	*1990*	*1991*	*1992*	*1993*	*1994*	*1995*	*1996*	*1997*	*1998*	*1999*
Instalment selling	46.8	49.0	47.0	46.5	45.0	45.8	45.0	43.4	56.0	51.5	59.5
Civil partnership	12.8	14.5	17.8	17.6	17.4	18.1	19.6	19.6	11.6	9.7	10.3
Forward purchasing	6.7	5.3	5.0	6.7	6.9	6.2	5.5	5.0	5.2	6.2	6.7
Muḍārabah	10.7	10.2	9.7	8.5	7.5	7.3	6.8	6.7	6.4	6	6.3
Interest-free loans	7.5	5.7	4.2	3.6	4.6	4.4	4.7	4.5	4.6	5.9	4.6
Legal partnership	5.8	4.6	4.8	5.2	4.8	3.6	2.7	3.8	4.7	3.1	2.7
Ju'ālah	5.1	6.6	7.0	6.0	6.0	6.6	7.0	6.6	1.6	1.4	1.7
Direct investment	1.3	1.3	1.3	1.9	2.6	2.4	1.7	2.8	2.5	1.8	1.5
Ijārah	0.5	0.4	0.7	0.5	0.7	0.8	1.0	1.1	0.87	0.7	0.6
Debt purchasing	0.6	0.3	0.1	0.1	0.1	0.1	0	0	0	0	0
Other	2.2	2.1	2.4	3.5	4.3	4.7	6.2	6.5	6.4	7.4	0
Housing	–	–	–	–	–	–	–	–	–	6.3	6.1
Total	100	100	100	100	100	100	100	100	100	100	100

Source: Central Bank, Survey Office (2000).

years; in the middle three years the trend is relatively constant, and then it decreases sharply during the last three years. In the case of saving deposits, the pattern of change is more gentle. Except in 1990 and 1993, there is no severe fluctuation. Investment deposits also follow a relatively steady-state situation.

With regard to the financial facilities granted, Table 6.7 presents the relevant data. Before evaluating the results, we categorize the ways of utilizing banking resources in the interest-free system mainly into three groups. The first group concerns sharing contracts and direct investment. In sharing contracts (civil partnership, legal partnership and *muḍārabah*), 'in principle' (and legally),[12] definite profit is being determined (not really after the results of real economic activity are known). Direct investment, from this viewpoint, is like sharing contracts.

The second group includes instalment selling and *ijārah*, in which the profit is determined at the time of transaction. Debt purchasing and *juʿālah* (the third group) do have variable profits, the precise amount of which will be determined at the end of the period. We conclude (from considering Table 6.7) that the share of instalment selling and *ijārah* has increased considerably, from 47.3 per cent in 1989 to 60.1 per cent in 1999. The shares of *muḍārabah*, direct investment and interest-free loans has decreased from 19.5 per cent in 1989 to 12.4 per cent in 1999. In addition to the allocative performance of the banking system, its working also may be judged according to the profit paid to the depositors and profits received from granted facilities. Table 6.8 shows that the real profit received by depositors during the total period is almost negative. For simplicity, let us

Table 6.8 Profit paid on the deposits, 1989–2000 (%)

Year	*SRNP*	*LRNP*	*Inflation rate*	*SRRP*	*LRRP*
1989	6	8.5	17.4	–11.4	–8.9
1990	6.5	13	9	–2.5	4
1991	6.5	14	20.7	–14.2	–6.7
1992	7.5	15	24.4	–16.9	–9.4
1993	8	16	22.9	–14.9	–6.9
1994	8	18.5	35.2	–27.2	–19.8
1995	8	18.5	49.5	–41.4	–30.9
1996	8	18.5	23.1	–15	–4.5
1997	8	18.5	17.3	–9.3	1.2
1998	8	18.5	20.2	–12	–1.5
1999	8	18.5	20.4	–12.4	–1.9
2000	9	18.5	12.6	–4.6	5.9
2001	7.5	17	11.5	–4	5.5
Average	7.6	16.4	21.9	–14.3	–5.7

Source: Calculated from Central Bank, *Economic Reports*.

Table 6.9 Profit rate of bank granted facilities to the economic sectors, 2000–1 (%)

	Industry and mineral	*Housing and construction*	*Agriculture*	*Commerce*	*Exporting*
2000	17–19	15–16	13–16	22–25	18
2001	16–18	15–16	14–15	23 (floor)	18

Source: Central Bank, Economic Report (2002).

define some abbreviations; SRNP=short run nominal profit; LRNP=long run nominal profit; SRRP=short run real profit; LRRP=long run real profit. Also, Table 6.9 indicates the profit from facilities granted to the economic sectors. The profit rate of housing and the profit rate of the exporting sectors have remained unchanged.

However, we can see a 1 per cent decrease in the rate of profit for agriculture and the industry and mineral sectors. Other things being equal, this reduction in profit rate (which is equivalent to the interest rate charged on them) may increase the tendency to investment in those sectors.

Shortcomings of the Iranian banking system

We now outline the roots of the shortcomings and the challenges which are responsible for the existing inefficiencies in Iranian banking system. We demonstrate that most of the conclusive factors are outside the system. We believe that three factors are important in this respect, and the first is that the Iranian banking system is totally governmental. We feel that some deficiencies of the system are due to the absence of serious competitors from the private sector. In addition, since the banking system has been monopolized by government, banks are used as an instrument to resolve difficulties in the fiscal area. When government faces a budget deficit, it borrows from the banking system. This kind of policy will increase the rate of inflation.

Obviously, this governmental structure is not related to the interest-free banking system endogenously. Nevertheless, the nationalization of banking system has been stipulated in the constitution, but it is not incorrigible and it is not an eternal principle.[13] Of course, the monitoring and supervisory role of the Central Bank with regard to other banks is vital.[14] Table 6.10 shows some of the debts the government sector owes to the banking system. As can be seen, government companies in Iran borrow money independently from the government. Most of the government debts belong to the Central Bank, but government companies borrow money mainly from other banks. We can see from this table that the public sector debt in 1998 relative to 1997 has grown by more than 60 per cent. Table 6.11 indicates the annual budget ordinance to oblige the banking system. Here, we have shown the subject just in the framework of the 1998 budget, which is quite typical.

The situation in other years is similar to that of 1998. Another factor which is responsible for the inefficiencies of the banking system in Iran but,

Table 6.10 Public sector debts to banking system, 1995–8 (billion rials)

	1995	*1996*	*1997*	*1998*
Public sector debts:	11,528.4	8,089.7	13,174.1	18,457.1
To the Central Bank	2,583.7	3,836.7	5,664.2	9,038.7
To other banks	3,344.8	4,253.0	7,509.9	9,418.4
Government debts:	5,022.8	1,820.8	4,890.8	8,233.2
To the Central Bank	4,816.4	1,869.8	5,030.7	8,214.6
To other banks	216.4	–49.0	–140.0	18.6
Government company debts:	6,495.6	6,268.9	8,283.4	10,223.9
To the Central Bank	3,367.2	1,966.9	633.5	824.1
To other banks	3,128.4	4,302.0	7,649.9	9,399.8

Source: Calculated from Central Bank, *Economic Report* (1999).

Table 6.11 Change in ordinance facilities of banking system in annual budget, 1998 (billion rials)

The activity	*Change in facilities balances*		
	In the government sector	*In the non-government sector*	*Total*
Facilities with cultural goals	343	115	458
Employment-oriented facilities	46	2,285	2,331
Market regulating facilities	17	155	172
Production-oriented facilities	1,694	1,342	3,036
Total	2,100	3,897	5,997

Source: *Journal of Banking and Economics* (September 1999).

at the same time, is not related to the interest-free system, I think, is non-straightforward thinking and the behaviour of government agents involved in interest-free banking. Here, we do have both theoretical and practical bottlenecks. Of course, part of this question pertains to the law of interest-free banking (at least there are some ambiguities in that law) which will be mentioned in this section.

One example of this non-transparent behaviour is using profit instead of interest in some of the accounts, bills, and so on where both rates have the same nature. The Central Bank bills show that long-run profit payable to the deposits is 17 per cent (in June 2003). This profit is, in principle, at a constant rate and thus equivalent to interest. But the bankers pretend that it is not definite at constant rate but it is in part payment (subject to final accounting) so it is different from interest. But actually profit is not in part payment; it is a definite rate. In some other activities, the bankers use a 'piece-work rate' instead of profit and as a substitute for interest. Also, in the

Iranian banking system some bills are issued which do have a fixed nature really, but they are called '*mushārakah* bills'. This behaviour has led to some distrust in the minds of people which may reduce their incentive to open accounts in the banking system. This non-straightforward behaviour also leads to a kind of ambition and over-reaching behaviour with regard to policy makers and so adversely affects their planning for banking activities, and also their prediction of the trend of monetary variables and so forth.

It is argued that the straightforwardness of government agents in Iran (at least regarding banking) has increased relatively since 1997 (after the Reformist Movement of people on 23 May in that year). Although this argument should be analysed scientifically, some weak evidence confirms it. One bit of evidence is the gap between predicted and actual growth in liquidity, before and after 1997. Table 6.12 indicates this gap.

Finally, one reason which I think is responsible for the shortcomings of the Iranian banking system has to do with non-economic considerations, such as political, cultural and social elements, which also do not relate to interest-free banking per se. For example, some managers do not have enough incentive to go in the Islamic direction. Also, some of the bankers are not trained regarding the laws of Islamic banking and their implementation. Because of this fact, some studies show that the law of interest-free banking is not applied in some banks.

The absence of fiscal discipline and the existence of some non-banking, fiscal and monetary organizations over which Central Bank has no control are other factors. One of these is called the Boniad Fiscal and Credit Centre; it has 240 branches, and one million depositors are using it.[15] Not

Table 6.12 Gap between predicted and realized growth of liquidity in Iran, 1991–2002 (%)

Year	*Predicted liquidity growth*	*Actual liquidity growth*
1991	9.2	24.6
1992	5.9	25.3
1993	5.3	34.2
1994	–	28.5
1995	12.5	37.6
1996	12.5	37
1997	12.5	15.2
1998	12.5	27.1
1999	12.5	27.5
2000	19.9	25.1
2001	17.4	29.4
2002	15.3	30.2
2003	14	
2004	13	

Source: Calculated from *Journal of Iran Economics* (March 2000).

Table 6.13 Average inefficiency for Iranian banks, 1989–95

Name of the bank	*Average inefficiency*	*Rank*
Refah (welfare)	0.145	1
Sepah (corps)	0.16	2
Milli (National)	0.175	3
Sanat and Madan (Industry and Mineral)	0.20	4
Millat (nation)	0.21	5
Keshavarzi (agriculture)	0.286	6
Saderat (Exporting)	0.31	7
Maskan (Housing)	0.324	8
Tejarat (commerce)	0.32	9

surprisingly, it is understood among Iranian economists that at least 40 per cent of the Iranian economy as a whole and more than 45 per cent of its financial and monetary activities are beyond the control of the government. Such huge unregulated activities have choked the normal economy (especially its banking system). Inefficient bureaucracy in the government sector, the intervention of the Central Bank in the activities of other banks, the existence of corruption in public sector, dissatisfaction and distrust among people with regard to the monetary and fiscal system, have all aggravated the situation.[16] In spite of the above facts, when there is some improvement in the banking situation, we see considerable improvements in their efficiency. For example, three banks (the Welfare Bank, Sepah Bank and National Bank) among the commercial banks have had the least inefficiency, and the Industry and Mineral Bank (among the specialized banks) has performed relatively better. In comparing the banks, we find that these four banks are experiencing fewer/smaller problems than the other five (see Table 6.13).

There are nine banks with 15,000 branches in Iran. Table 6.13 has given inefficiency rankings for all the Iranian banks.[17] Generally speaking, this system has performed its activities with at least 76 per cent efficiency. From 1998 on, there has been a 27.5 per cent average growth in assets. The growth of facilities granted to non-governmental sector has been reported to be, on average, 30.2 per cent; non-governmental deposits have increased by 27.8 per cent; and growth in time deposits is reported to be 48.7 per cent. Also, Table 6.14 shows monetary targets for the year 2001. I conclude that in the case of Iran, if we used the Islamic teachings as our pattern and made an effort to resolve the difficulties around fiscal devices (the banking system, *zakāh* and *khums*), we would achieve a considerable level of SD; but, for the time being, we cannot show a significant relationship between the interest-free banking system and SD.

Concluding remarks and policy implications

SD is going to be one of the most important socio-economic problems, especially during the first decade of the twenty-first century. SD encourages economic development strategies that are environmentally and socially sustainable.[18] In this connection, economic systems and the environment are dynamically inter-related. One of these linkages is that between fiscal and monetary devices and SD. Bringing out this relationship from the Islamic point of view does have considerable significance.

Efficient financial devices, on the one hand, can be substituted for natural resource exploitation (and thus act as a supporter of SD) and, on the other, they can finance the expenditures needed to combat the negative externalities resulting from the depletion of the environment. Islamic teachings are in line with the protection of the environment, and thus helping SD. Emphasizing moderate consumption is another common element between Islamic teachings and SD. The reduction of material consumption is one of the preconditions of a sustainable society.

One of the obvious features of SD is that it is based on an efficient and equitable use of resources. This in turn depends critically on the ways in which property rights are defined and distributed.[19] In Islamic teachings, all resources originally belong to God and are given to the people as trustees. The Holy Qur'ān stipulates this fact as follows: 'Believe in Allah and His messenger and spend of that whereof He has made you trustees' (Qur'ān, 57:7). Doubtless if Muslims (in either the private or the public sector) were to obey the spirit of this verse, there would not actually be any serious problem regarding SD.

A moderate approach to the government's role in Islam is another link between it and SD. In the case of SD, the intervention of the government is necessary. Stiglitz points out that: 'Prices in general do provide signals concerning the scarcity of resources and in the absence of market failure lead to economic efficiency.'[20] When there is externality, or a resource is not priced, a private economy which governs it will not be efficient. I think the moderate role of government, together with Islamic teachings and its special fiscal devices, has organized a coherent system which is compatible with SD.

In this connection, Iran is a plausible case study (regardless of any conclusion we reach) because, first of all, about 80 per cent of its current and developmental expenditure is financed by using natural resources (especially gas/petrol). Second, it has a 100 per cent interest-free banking system. Third, the banking system in Iran is nationalized. When the government faces difficulty with regard to gas/petrol revenue, it forces the banking system to finance the deficit. So there is an ordered, regulated exogenous relationship (and not an economic, efficient and endogenous one) between fiscal and monetary policies.[21]

The monopoly of the banking system by the government, the lack of opportunities for private sector activities, the banking system being used as an instrument to resolve government difficulty, the banks' focus on short-run facilities, ultra-banking and (even) ultra-economic problems, property right difficulties, corruption in the government sector, the fact that over 40 per cent of the economic and monetary activities is unregulated, a high inflation rate, the absence of necessary discipline in fiscal management and so forth, are the current challenges facing Iran's banking system.

By resolving some theoretical problems in the interest-free system, training bankers and informing people about the new banking system, monitoring the monetary activities of non-bank institutions, encouraging competition among banks, combating all kinds of non-economic renters, maintaining the independence of the banking system, improving managerial techniques and using modern banking instruments could all generate some fiscal and monetary devices in the support of SD. At present, because of the absence of these conditions, there is no meaningful link between Iran's monetary financing devices and sustainable development. So we cannot achieve these goals in the short run, but we should plan mid-run strategies and organize all required instruments.

Comment

Kazem Sadr

This chapter is composed of three major parts: the first two are the meaning and implication of sustainable development, and the attributes of Islamic banking and its ability to provide a sustainable mechanism of finance for those economic activities which contribute to sustained development. The third part of the chapter examines the performance of the Iranian banking sector after the implementation of Interest-free Banking Law (IFBL) and highlights its achievements and drawbacks in the light of the expected relationship between an interest-free banking (IFB) system and the sustainable development of the Iranian economy.

A major point brought forth in this chapter is that Islamic banking is itself a component of a whole comprehensive system of Islamic economy in which all the economic functions carried out in product and factor markets are sustainable by their very nature; that is, they help the economy to follow a course of growth which would be sustainable. The tax and social security system, along with the financing of the government budget and of the private sector investment activities, are all carried out in such a way as to lead the economy to obtain the maximum level of income and preserve, at the same time, the quality of life and environmental capital for future generations.

Enjoying sustainable development requires that some principles concerning the utilization of renewable and exhaustible natural resources be followed. Among them are the rules that the latter resources should be used efficiently, such that their net present value will be maximized over the time they are utilized and, concurrently, a renewable resource will be developed as a substitute.

The author notices that the Iranian economy, at present, is mainly financed by export revenues of oil which is a non-renewable resource. He maintains that Islamic finance can substitute for oil income. I assume he means that if a renewable form of energy such as sunlight could be technologically developed so that it would be economically viable, then the interest-free financial system could finance the technological development of this investment as well as its utilization by firms and consumers.

There seems to be a general agreement about the meaning and implication of sustainable development, and therefore it needs no further clarification. Thus, the present comment is confined to a short review of the capabilities of Islamic finance and the performance of this system in Iran, and to point out the factors that have contributed to its success or otherwise.

Characteristics of the interest-free financing system

In the last three decades many economists have presented alternative models of Interest-free Finance (IFF) and have derived many behavioural hypotheses from it. Among them are the following propositions.

The real values of assets and liabilities (of financial institutions) would be equal at all points in time. The prospect of instantaneous equilibrium between the asset side of the banking system – driven mainly by the real sector of the economy – and the liability side means that there must necessarily be a close and direct relationship between investment and deposit yields. Also, since the return to liabilities of the banking system is a direct function of the return to the asset portfolio of the system, and since assets are created in response to investment opportunities in the real sector of the economy, it is the real sector that determines the rate of return to the financial sector rather than the reverse.

In an Islamic financial system, the adjustment to shocks leading to banking crises and disruptions in the country's payment mechanism is faster than in the conventional system. There will also be no disruption in the intermediation process of the banking system, and neither is there any reason to believe that the savings and investment process will be impaired.

Monetary policy can be effective in stabilizing the economy, and this has been shown in both the closed and open economy models. In an open economy context, to the extent that external resources mobilized through profit-sharing models are channelled to productive investments, such investments can be expected to generate a stream of returns which are at least sufficient to repay the associated external liabilities. Also, in an open economy context, there will be two-way capital flows; that is, there is no reason to expect only capital outflows, since net results will depend on the difference between domestic and external rates of return (Laleh, 1999).

The system provides a multitude of incentives for savings, and there is no indication that risk-averse consumers would not save as much as they do in a conventional system (Mirakhor, 1997).

The flow of information concerning the capital market conduct and performance is more inclusive and accessible by demanders and suppliers, because in a profit-loss sharing system suppliers of funds have a vested interest in the success of the investment activities and, therefore, provide all their market information to their partners (Sadr, 1999; Sadr and Iqbal, 2001).

Banks and other financial institutions would resolve adverse selection and moral hazard problems by monitoring the activity of their partners and also by asking for collateral, using restricted covenants, or other means suggested in the literature. The costs of monitoring will be paid using benefits accruing from supervision, which creates at least three advantages. The first is the close monitoring of the conduct of the agent to ensure that he is acting according to the terms of the contract. Second, stronger supervision provides greater knowledge of the market conditions under which the enterprise subject of the contract has to operate and this allows the supervisors greater ability to forecast further market developments. Finally, the stronger supervision provides broader knowledge of the comparative advantages of the region or locality in which the resources are invested. This will make it possible to obtain better estimates of the return to further investment in the region under consideration (Sadr, 1999; Sadr and Iqbal, 2001).

The overall risk of investment will be lower in the economy as a result of the increased flow of market information and supervision of investors by their financiers. The cost of capital will be lower to the entrepreneurs as a result of the lower risk of investment activities, and therefore the demand for it will be higher than in the conventional system (Haque and Mirakhor, 1987; Sadr, 1999; Sadr and Iqbal, 2001).

More investment will lead to a higher level of total output and employment of labour and productive inputs. Therefore, consumers in an economy in which IFF is practised (Sadr and Iqbal, 2001) will enjoy a higher level of social welfare.

Many of the above hypotheses have been verified by facts in many empirical studies. Mohsin Khan's proposition that Islamic banks absorb and rapidly adjust to external shocks was tested first by Darrat (2001) for the Tunisian economy. By assuming M1 (the money that bears no interest) and the total saving deposits (i.e., M2 minus M1) to which interest is paid, as representatives of the Islamic and traditional systems, respectively, he showed that demand for money is more stable in the former system than in the latter.

Having adopted an Islamic system, Iran's experience seems to present a good opportunity to test Khan's theory. Kavand (1999) completed a study in which all measures of money (that is, M1, M2 and M2–M1) carry no interest and therefore are correct representations of alternative definitions of money in an Islamic economy. The study uses various statistical techniques to test the stability of the demand for money and finds that demand is stable for all three definitions. Darrat (1988) repeats his study for the Iranian and Pakistani economies and verifies the former conclusion.

It is difficult to single out the share of interest-free intermediations in the development of the Iranian economy without undertaking substantial research studies. However, Haidari (1996) has shown that the agricultural finance in this system has contributed significantly to the growth of value added in that sector. His study encompasses periods both before and after the interest-free banking operation. It concludes that the new banking system has positively affected the growth of the agricultural sector in the Iranian economy and supports the proposition that Islamic interest-free finance can be growth-enhancing. After the Iran-Iraq war, the annual growth rates of fixed capital formation and that of GDP are, on the average, 0.5 and 5.7 per cent respectively in Iran.

In addition to growth promotion, the financing system has contributed to a reduction of the growth disparity among different regions in Iran. Toutounchian (1995) indicates in his study that financial resources have been distributed among the provinces such that their comparative degree of deprivation has been reduced.

The saving behaviour of the private sector during 1950–97 was found to be neither a function of interest rate which used to be paid by banks prior to the implementation of IFBL, nor a function of fixed rate of return which was payable after it. Instead, the ratio of private saving to GNP was found to be a positive function of per capita income and its rate of growth, and a negative function of the inflation rate and the ratio of net real value of private sector wealth to GNP (Toutounchian, 1995).

To substantiate the argument that supervision by financiers of the performance of their investor partners is itself an investment activity which creates new information that will be utilized in further allocation of financial resources among new demanders, regions and projects, and that the benefit of this endeavour will exceed the cost of monitoring incurred by the financier to overcome the asymmetric informational problems, a research project designed to explore the answer was carried out in the Agricultural Bank of Iran (Sadr, 2000). Being a development bank, it has continuously accompanied the supply of its major financial services with supervision. The findings of the study show that the Agricultural Bank of Iran has supplied financial capital to farmers over time as a positive function of the rate of return and a negative function of the risk of various modes of finance. The results further show that this bank selects among the alternative modes of finance a portfolio which seeks to maximize its expected profit. By investing in supervision, this bank seems to be able to learn about profitable investment opportunities in various agricultural regions and also about the entrepreneurial and moral characteristics of its partners. The bank uses this expertise to improve over time the allocation of its capital resources among the best alternative available projects and also to the best qualified farmers. The fact that this bank has continued monitoring its customers over time, while effectively expanding the domain of its activities, shows that it has enjoyed the benefits of close supervision and that this monitoring has been a profitable investment in gaining new and better information.

New developments in the Iranian financial system

Some new developments have taken place in the financial system of Iran recently. Banks no longer need to be public; some private banks and financial institutions have already been established and many more are obtaining licences. Although banks were considered to be public organizations in the Constitution, a lengthy communication and thoughtful discussion between the Guardian Council and the Central Bank experts ended up at the conclusion that the Constitution implies that central banking and monetary policy undertaking should be in the hands of public authorities, but commercial banking and finance could be carried out by both public and private bodies. Recently, the establishment of foreign banks in the free trade zones was also approved by Parliament. Thus, a multitude of financial institutions are today serving Iranian financial markets. They include public and private banks, private credit institutions, public and private insurance companies, private investment houses and *qurūd al-ḥasanah* cooperatives. On the other hand, the central bank is expanding its supervision of the performance of all financial institutions and has required them to report their net worth and balance sheet in a form that helps to implement monetary policy more effectively. As of 2002, the banks were required to pay the depositors a variable rate of return depending on the profit earned by each bank.

In 1995, an Act was passed by Parliament which granted permission to the government to issue partnership or *mushārakah* securities for financing specific infrastructure investments. Since then, many social overhead projects, including dams and irrigation canals, hospitals and housing construction, have been financed by partnership shares. This policy has helped in the process of mopping up excess liquidity as well as mobilizing new savings. In addition to the central government, municipalities and public institutions are also permitted to make use of this instrument for expansion of their activities. Last but not least, an important institution is the stock market. Although this market was in operation prior to the Revolution, it actually became activated by the Central Bank after the end of the war with Iraq in 1988. Since then, an increasing number of firms are being financed in this market by issuing shares.

Notes

1. See Dadgar and Najafee (2000).
2. Rees and Smith (1998), p. 178.
3. Solow (1992).
4. Turner (1987), p. 17.
5. Pearce (1992), pp. 2–3.
6. World Commission on Environment and Development (1987).
7. Dadgar (2002).
8. In some Muslim countries from 1960, some introductory efforts for an interest-free system have been initiated. At least one bank in Jordan and considerable numbers in Bahrain, Sudan, Pakistan and Saudi Arabia have been established on an interest-free basis since 1980.
9. Suhr (1988), p. 122.
10. Keynes (1960), pp. 351–3.
11. Creutz and Glotz (1997).
12. This statement is emphasized to show that in the Iranian system this lawful process has not been followed, and there is some unevenness related to that.
13. So, in order to apply some modifications to the Iranian banking system, it would be necessary to establish some reforms regarding the constitution law.
14. In Iran the monitoring role of government is very weak but its intervention is extensive and widespread.
15. The profits from the monetary activities of the Boniad Centre are reported to have been 2.8 billion Rials, in 1999. Also in that year it granted 970 billion Rials financing to its customers.

16. However, it should be noted that Iran is the first country to begin changing the whole banking system in such a way, so it is only to be expected that there will be some dificulties in the beginning.
17. This ranking has been estimated based on two indices of efficiency. One is technical efficiency, which deals with banking service production (most production by given factors), and the other concerns cost efficiency (combination of factors of production which contains least cost).
18. See Serageldine (1996), pp. 14–29.
19. World Bank (1992).
20. Stiglitz and Driffill (2000), pp. 351–60.
21. For example in 1998, government revenue from foreign exchange declined (because of an oil shock). This led to liquidity growth of 27.1 per cent, which in turn caused about a 20 per cent increase in inflation.

References

Central Bank of Iran (2000), *Banking Facilities*, Tehran: Economic Survey Office.

Creutz, H. and E. Glotz (1997), 'The How and Why of a New Monetary System', *Working Paper, University-Doz*, Vienna, Austria.

Dadgar, Y. (2002), 'Management of *Zakāh* in Iran', Paper presented to IRTI Training Seminar on Management of *Zakāh* in a Modern Economy, held in Islamabad.

Dadgar, Y. and M. Najafee (2000), *Summarization of 'Eqtesaduna'*, Kermanshah: Razi University Press.

Darrat, Ali (1988), 'The Islamic Interest-free Banking System: Some Empirical Evidence', *Applied Economics*, 20, 417–25.

Darrat, Ali (2001), 'On the Relative Efficiency of an Interest-Free Monetary System: Some Empirical Evidence', in Munawar Iqbal (ed.), *Islamic Banking and Finance*, Leicester: The Islamic Foundation.

Haidari, Bahram (1996), 'Estimating the Effect of Credit on the Agricultural Sector's Value Added in Iran', MS Thesis, School of Economic and Political Sciences, Shahid Beheshti University, Tehran.

Haque, Nadeem ul- and Abbas Mirakhor (1987), 'Saving Behaviour in an Economy without Fixed Interest', in Mohsin Khan and Abbas Mirakhor (eds), *Theoretical Studies in Islamic Banking and Finance*, Houston, TX: The Institute for Research and Islamic Studies.

Kavand, A. (1999), 'Stability of Demand for Money within an Islamic Banking Framework', MS Thesis, School of Economic and Political Sciences, Shahid Beheshti University, Tehran.

Keynes, J. M. (1960), *The General Theory of Employment, Interest and Money*, London: Macmillan.

Laleh, Muhammad (1999), 'Factors Affecting Saving Behaviour in Iran', MS Thesis, School of Economics and Political Sciences, Shahid Beheshti University, Tehran.

Mirakhor, Abbas (1997), 'Progress and Challenges of Islamic Banking', *Review of Islamic Economics*, 4 (2), 1–11.

Pearce, D. W. (1992), *World Without End*, Oxford: Oxford University Press.

Rees, Gareth and Charles Smith (1998), *Economic Development*, London: Macmillan.

Sadr, Kazem (1999), 'A Review of the Performance of Interest-free Banking in Iran', presented at the International Conference on Islamic Economics, Kuala Lumpur, Malaysia.

Sadr, Kazem (2000), *The Impact of Asymmetric Information and Monitoring upon the Choice of Modes of Finance*, Tehran: Centre for Economic Studies, Agricultural Bank of Iran.

Sadr, Kazem and Zamir Iqbal (2001), 'Choice Between Debt and Equity Contracts and Asymmetric Information', in M. Iqbal (ed.), *Islamic Banking and Finance*, Leicester: The Islamic Foundation.
Serageldine, I. (1996), 'Sustainable Development from Theory to Practice', *Finance and Development*, 33, 14–29.
Solow, Robert (1992), *An Almost Practical Step Toward Sustainability*, Washington DC: Resource for the Future.
Stiglitz, J. and J. Driffill (2000), *Economics*, London: Norton.
Suhr, Dietr (1988), 'Capitalism at its Best', in Margaret Kennedy (1988), *Interest and Inflation Free Money*, Stayerburg: Permaculture Institute.
Todaro, M. P. (2000), *Economic Development*, Boston, MA: Addison-Wesley.
Toutounchian, Iraj (1995), 'Resource Mobilization for Government Expenditure through Islamic Modes of Contract: The Case of Iran', *Islamic Economic Studies*, 2 (2), 35–58.
Turner, R. K. (1987), *Sustainable Environmental Management*, London: Methuen.
World Bank (1992), *Development and the Environment*, Washington, DC: World Bank.
World Commission on Environment and Development (1987), *Our Common Future*, Oxford: Oxford University Press.

7

Effects of Implementing a Non-interest Banking System on Monetary Policy Controllability and Policy–Goals Links in Iran

Karim Eslamloueyan and Morteza Heidari

Two important features of a monetary system are its policy controllability and reliability. Using an Autoregressive Distributed Lag (ARDL) approach, two models have been constructed to investigate the impact of implementing a non-interest-based banking system on monetary policy controllability and the monetary aggregate–economic goals link in Iran. The chapter studies both the short- and long-run effects. The models have been estimated for the narrow as well as the broad definitions of money. The results show that the Islamic banking system adopted in 1984 has not reduced the impact of money base growth on the growth rate of M1. More specifically, the estimation results of the M1 controllability model show that the non-interest-based banking adopted in Iran has not decreased the slope of the money base growth. Moreover, the results indicate that there was a significant positive shift in the intercept of the controllability model after the adoption of the interest-free banking system. In other words, M1 has become even more controllable in the new banking arrangement. When M2 is used as the policy variable, the results of the estimated model show that the degree of the controllability did not change after the implementation of the new monetary arrangement. The chapter also examines how the aggregate–economic goals link has been affected by the new system. The results show that non-interest-based banking has neither increased nor decreased the reliability of the monetary aggregates in Iran. These results hold both in the short run and the long run. Finally, the chapter concludes that M1 is more controllable than M2 , but M2 is more reliable than M1. Hence, the Iranian monetary authorities should take this fact into account before setting their monetary instruments.

Introduction

The Iranian financial system has gone through a structural change since 1984 when the Central Bank of the Islamic Republic of Iran officially adopted the interest-free banking system. This chapter intends to examine the performance of narrow and broad definitions of money,[1] as two alternative monetary aggregates, before and after the implementation of the new financial system in Iran.

In the literature of monetary economics, a monetary aggregate is subject to the problems of controllability and reliability, or policy–goal links. These are two important criteria for evaluating the performance of a monetary system. In other words, if the monetary aggregate is not controllable effectively by the monetary authority, it cannot be used to predict the policy moves. This might happen when it is affected by non-policy factors. Moreover, even if the aggregate is controllable, it might not be reliable because it may not be linked to the main goal of monetary authorities. That is, if the system misses its target, there might be no close link between a monetary aggregate and the goal set for the monetary system by the policy makers. Policy controllability and reliability are the two crucial requirements for usefulness of a financial aggregate. As Darrat (1988) mentions, an important criterion for relative superiority of a financial system is usefulness of a financial aggregate. In many countries, price stability is the ultimate objective of the monetary policy. If the relation between the goal of price stability and a particular monetary aggregate is weak, even if that aggregate is controllable, it is not useful for policy purposes.

The Islamic Republic of Iran implemented the non-interest-based banking system in 1984. This chapter examines how the new system has changed the effectiveness and usefulness of monetary policy instruments in Iran. The two important features of a monetary system – namely, policy controllability and usefulness – are examined under both the new and old monetary rules. Using an Autoregressive Distributed Lag (ARDL) approach, two models have been constructed to investigate the impact of the implementation of this new banking system on monetary policy controllability and the monetary aggregate–economic goals link in Iran. Thus, short- and long-run relationships are studied simultaneously. Moreover, it gives an efficient and unbiased estimator when the sample size is small. The model will be estimated for two definitions of money: the narrow and broad definitions of money M1 and M2 respectively.

The following section reviews the literature on the subject. The estimation method is discussed in the section after that, while the fourth section presents the basic econometric models for examining the degree of controllability of the monetary aggregates. It also contains the estimation results. The fifth section presents a basic econometric model to study the reliability of M1 and M2. In the same section, the empirical results are analysed. The final section contains conclusions.

Review of the literature

There are very few studies on the issues of controllability and usefulness of the monetary aggregates in Islamic countries. Using time series data on the banking system of Tunisia, Darrat (1988) studied the feasibility of an Islamic interest-free banking system. More specifically, using regression analysis he examined the relative stability and policy usefulness of Islamic banking in comparison with the conventional interest-based banking system. He showed empirically that a banking system with non-interest bearing assets (Islamic banking) is more stable than one with interest bearing assets (conventional banking system). Moreover, the monetary policy variable was found to be more controllable and reliable in the Tunisian monetary system. He therefore concluded that an Islamic financial system is superior to the conventional system.[2]

In Darrat's investigation, only M1 is considered to be the representative of an aggregate in an Islamic banking system. However, in some Muslim countries, such as Iran, with some history of interest-free banking, M2 is also used for policy purposes. Hence using M2 as a monetary aggregate is not unique to Western banking systems. Indeed, M2 is now an important monetary instrument in the Iranian monetary system.

Feldstein and Stock (1993) examine the possibility of using the broad monetary aggregate, M2, to target the growth rate of nominal GDP. Their results indicate that the monetary authority can guide M2 in a way that reduces not only the average rate of inflation, but also the variance of annual rate of growth of output. More specifically, using Vector Auto-Regression (VAR) and the single equation approach, they show that there is a stable relation between M2 and GDP in the USA, and that M2 can be used to reduce the variance of nominal GDP growth. Their findings also indicate that M2 is a useful predictor of nominal GDP.

Dotsey and Otrok (1994) study the controversy over using M2 as an intermediate target of monetary policy. It is argued that Feldstein and Stock's result, regarding the ability of M2 to reduce the variance of nominal GDP growth, depends highly on the assumption that M2 is completely controllable.

The above argument shows that it is important to study both the controllability and reliability of a monetary aggregate. Yousefi, Abizadeh and Mccormick (1997) replicate Darrat's work for examining the monetary stability of the interest-free banking system in Iran. Their results are mixed. Hence, they suggest that more work needs to be done to see whether an Islamic banking system is more stable than the conventional banking system. They also examine the policy usefulness of monetary aggregates in an Islamic banking system. Following Darrat, they assume that the monetary base is under the control of the central bank. Using regression analysis, they confirm Darrat's (1988) result that M1 is more controllable than M2. However, they do not explicitly examine how the controllability of M1 and M2 has been affected by the implementation of interest-free banking in Iran.

Yousefi, Abizadeh and McCormick (1997) also use a simple model to study the link between the monetary aggregates and price stability. After performing regression analysis for the period 1967–92, 1967–83 and 1984–92, their study fails to confirm Darrat's conclusion that M1 has a stronger and more reliable link with the goal of price stability than M2. However, the regression techniques used by Yousefi, Abizadeh and McCormick do not allow them to avoid the problem of spurious regression. The data might not be stationary, and they do not control for this problem. More important, their study does not examine how the controllability and ability of these two monetary aggregates have been affected since 1984 when the new banking arrangement was put in place.

Much of the debate has focused on the notion of stability. The argument in Yousefi, Abizadeh and McCormick (1997) is that if M1 is less controllable than M2, then the non-interest banking system is less useful in comparison with the conventional banking system. This argument basically misses the point. The method used in Yousefi, Abizadeh and McCormick (1997) is not an appropriate way to examine the usefulness of the monetary system after the implementation of the interest-free banking system in Iran. To evaluate the aggregate–economic goal link, a structural model with correct specifications must be used. Omission of any important variable from the model may cause a misspecification problem.

Darrat and Yousefi, Abizadeh and McCormick, in particular, examine the usefulness of an Islamic financial system by looking into the controllability and reliability of M1. For them, M1 is an interest-bearing variable and hence cannot be included in a non-interest banking system. In other words, the broad definition of money is specific to the conventional banking system. However, it is well known now that M2 is also an important monetary aggregate in the interest-free banking system of the Islamic Republic of Iran and so cannot be considered as a distinguishing feature of the conventional banking systems. Therefore, issues involving the controllability of M1 (or M2) and the structural relationship between these variables and economic goals have not been adequately addressed.

To fill these gaps, and also to find out to what extent the implementation of the non-interest banking system in Iran has changed the controllability and reliability of M1 and M2, we estimate four structural equations using the ARDL approach. Dummy variable techniques have been used to measure the exact impacts of the change.

The method of estimation

It is known that the Least Squares approach may lead to misleading results when there are non-stationary variables in the model. More specifically, t and F statistics are not valid in the presence of non-stationary variables. It is suggested that the problem might be overcome if first or second difference of non-stationary variables is used in the model. If a time series has to be differenced p times before it becomes stationary, it is integrated of order p, denoted by $I(p)$. However, it is possible to lose valuable long-run information when first or higher order differenced time series are used.

It is also known that different non-stationary variables might be used at levels in the model if they are co-integrated.[3] This means that the regression on the levels of these variables is not spurious. In this case, the usual econometric methods can be used to estimate the model. Hence, different methods have been developed to examine whether a vector of time series are co-integrated.

The concept of co-integration is now widely used in econometric analysis. It is a useful tool to model variables that are linked by economic forces. Two or more non-stationary time series might form a linear combination that is stationary. In this case, the variables are co-integrated. It means there is a long-run equilibrium relationship between them. Hence, the regression on the levels of these variables is not spurious.

Given that a long-run equilibrium relationship exists, there might be a deviation from this equilibrium path in the short run. This deviation must be stationary to have a sensible long-run relation. The method used by Engel and Granger to test whether different $I(1)$ series are co-integrated is based on checking the stationary condition of the estimated residual obtained from estimation of the long-run model. However, as it is shown the Ordinary Least Squares (OLS) estimator in small samples might be unbiased, but inconsistent.[4] To remove this inconsistency, it is suggested that one uses an over-parameterized model. In other words, using more lags is preferred to using fewer lags. Another reason that makes the use of lagged variables important is the fact that the adjustment process cannot be understood unless the short-run dynamics is known. This may allow us to see how a short-run disequilibrium error corrects itself through time. In order to have a complete picture, the long-run equilibrium and short-run relations have been estimated simultaneously. This can be done by using the ARDL modelling to co-integration analysis. Consider the following ARDL $(p, q_1, q_2, \ldots, q_k)$ model:

$$A(L)y_t = \sum_{i=1}^{k} B_i(L)X_{it} + \Phi W_t + u_t \tag{7.1}$$

where L is a polynomial lag operator $A(L) = 1 - \alpha_1 L - \alpha_2 L^2 - \ldots - \alpha_p L^p$, $B_i(L) = 1 - \beta_{i1}L - \beta_{i2}L^2 - \ldots - \beta_{iqi}L^{qi}$ $(i = 1, 2, \ldots, k)$, W_t is a vector of deterministic variables such as the constant term, dummy variables and exogenous variables with fixed lags, and Φ is a vector of parameters. The disturbance term, u_t, is assumed to be a white noise.

The above model will be estimated for all possible combinations of p and q $(p = q_i = 0, 1, 2, \ldots, m)$. After determining maximum lag (i.e., choosing m) in the model, $(m+1)^{k+1}$ different models are estimated. At this stage, using Akaike Information Criterion (AIC), Schwarz Bayesian Criterion (SBC) and Hannan–Quinn Criterion (HQC), the most appropriate estimated short-run model is chosen.[5] Hence it would be possible to find the estimated parameters of the long-run model. If a long-run equilibrium relation between variables exists (i.e., the null hypothesis of no co-integration in the long-run model is rejected), the error correction model (ECM) for two variables (i.e., y_t and x_t) can be reformulated as:

$$A(L)\Delta y_t = B(L)\,\Delta x_t + (1-\Pi)\,ECT_{t-1} + \Phi\,W_t + u_t \tag{7.2}$$

where *A(L)* and *B(L)* are the polynomial lag operators defined above, Δ denotes the first difference, ECT_{t-1} is the error correction term, and $\Pi = (\alpha_1 + \alpha_2 + \ldots + \alpha_p)$. In general, we have:

$$A(L)\Delta y_t = \sum_{i=1}^{k} B_i(L)\,\Delta X_{it} + \psi ECT_{t-1} + \Phi\,W_t + u_t \tag{7.3}$$

where ψ is a parameter. Consequently, this approach not only allows us to derive the long-run relation between variables, but also to see how quickly short-run disequilibrium is corrected.[6]

In the next two sections, we apply the above autoregressive distributed lag modelling approach to co-integration analysis to study policy controllability and the reliability of monetary system in Iran. Moreover, using the dummy variable approach, we compare the usefulness of the monetary aggregates in the Iranian financial system before and after the implementation of non-interest banking system in 1984.

The issue of policy controllability

Basic model

To see to what extent the controllability of monetary aggregates has been changed by the implementation of non-interest banking system, the following models have been used.

$$GM_{1t} = \alpha_0 + \alpha_1\,GMB_t + u_{1t} \tag{7.4}$$

$$GM_{2t} = \beta_0 + \beta_1\,GMB_t + u_{2t} \tag{7.5}$$

where GMB is the growth rate of monetary base, GM_1 is the growth rate of M1 and GM_2 is the growth rate of liquidity (M2), α_i and βj are parameters and u_{it} $(i = 1, 2)$ are disturbance terms. The more the monetary base can explain the increase in the growth of money balances, the better the control the monetary authority would have over the monetary policy. Since M1 and M2 might have different degrees of policy controllability, the ARDL approach is used to examine their behaviour before and after the implementation of the non-interest banking system in Iran. More specifically, the following model will be estimated for the Iranian economy:

$$(GM)_t = C + \sum_{j=1}^{p} \alpha_j (GM)_{t-j} + \sum_{h=1}^{q} \alpha_j (GMB)_{t-h} + \theta_1 D_1$$
$$+ \theta_2 D_2 GMB_t + \varepsilon_t \qquad (7.6)$$

in which GM can be the growth rate of either M1 or M2 , D_i (i=1, 2) is a vector of dummy variables and θ_i is a vector of its related coefficients. The vector of dummy variables contains the dummy representing the adoption of the non-interest financial system in Iran. In the following sections, the dummy to capture the implementation of the interest-free banking system in 1984 is denoted by DU84.

The estimation results of policy controllability

In this sub-section, we present the results of estimates of controllability of the monetary aggregates in Iran. This would allow us to compare the degree of monetary controllability of M1 and M2 before and after the implementation of the non-interest banking system in Iran. Before estimating the model, we used Augmented Dickey–Fuller test (ADF) and Phillips–Perron unit root tests. The results of these tests are presented in Appendix tables 7.17 and 7.18. As the results show, all variables are stationary.

The estimation results of policy controllability for M1

In this sub-section, equation (7.4) is estimated to see how the policy controllability of M1 has been affected by the adoption of a non-interest banking system in Iran.[7] DU84 and DU71 are added to the model to represent the dummy for the implementation of the new banking system in 1984 and the oil revenue shock of 1971, respectively. As Table 7.1 shows, based on the Schwarz Bayesian Criterion, the selected order of our ARDL is (1, 0).

The above results indicate that the coefficient of lagged value of GM_1 is positive but insignificant at the 5 per cent significance level. The coefficient of GMB is positive and significant. Hence, GMB has a positive impact on GM_1. The coefficient of DU84GMB is negative but insignificant at the 5 per cent level.[8] However, DU84 has positively affected the GM_1.

As the results of diagnostic tests of the above model (presented in Table 7.2) show, the model passes the regular serial correlation, functional form, normality and heteroscedasticity tests.

Table 7.3 presents the results of the long-run model. As the table shows, a 1 per cent increase in the growth rate of money base will increase the growth rate of M1 by about 0.99. As the table shows, the coefficient of DU84GMB is negative (–0.45922), but not significant at the 5 per cent level.

Table 7.1 Controllability of M1 model

Autoregressive distributed lag estimates ARDL(1,0) selected based on Schwarz Bayesian Criterion dependent variable is GM_1 36 observations used for estimation from 1963 to 1998

Regressor	*Coefficient*	*Standard error*	*T-ratio[prob]*
$GM_1(-1)$	0.19487	0.10703	1.8206[0.079]
GMB	0.79387	0.12667	6.2672[0.000]
C	−0.00845	0.03016	−0.28009[0.781]
DU84GMB	−0.36973	0.20548	−1.7993[0.082]
DU84	0.09585	0.04431	2.1631[0.039]
DU71	0.01475	0.04854	0.30391[0.763]

R-Squared 0.75055 R-Bar-Squared 0.70897
S.E. of Regression 0.056252 F-stat. F (5, 30) 18.0528[0.000]
Mean of Dependent Variable 0.20963 S.D. of Dependent Variable 0.10427
Residual Sum of Squares 0.094930 Equation Log-likelihood 55.8047
Akaike Information Criterion 49.8047 Schwarz Bayesian Criterion 45.0542
DW-statistic 1.8648 Durbin's h-statistic 0.52897[0.597]

Table 7.2 Diagnostic tests of controllability of M1 model

Test statistics	*Lm version*	*F version*
A: Serial Correlation	$\chi^2(1) = 0.031899[0.858]$	$F(1, 29) = 0.02572[0.874]$
B: Functional Form	$\chi^2(1) = 2.4757[0.116]$	$F(1, 29) = 2.1416[0.154]$
C: Normality	$\chi^2(2) = 0.59471[0.743]$	Not applicable
D: Heteroscedasticity	$\chi^2(1) = 2.3479[0.125]$	$F(1, 34) = 2.3722[0.133]$

A: Lagrange multiplier test of residual serial correlation
B: Ramsey's RESET test using the square of the fitted values
C: Based on a test of skewness and kurtosis of residuals
D: Based on the regression of squared residuals on squared fitted values

Table 7.3 Estimated long-run coefficients of controllability of M1 model

Estimated long-run coefficients using the ARDL approach ARDL (1,0) selected based on Schwarz Bayesian Criterion dependent variable is GM_1 36 observations used for estimation from 1963 to 1998

Regressor	*Coefficient*	*Standard error*	*T-ratio[prob]*
GMB	0.98602	0.16556	5.9558[0.000]
C	0.01049	0.038029	0.27589[0.785]
DU84GMB	0.45922	0.26316	1.7451[0.091]
DU84	0.11905	0.057266	2.0789[0.046]
DU71	0.01832	0.059889	0.30595[0.762]

Since this coefficient is only significant at the 10 per cent level, we cannot strongly conclude that the form of non-interest banking adopted in Iran has decreased the slope of GMB. Thus, we might say that there is not a major structural change in the model. In other words, the presence of the new system has not decreased the controllability of M1. Moreover, the coefficient of DU84 is positive and significant at the 5 per cent level. Hence, the intercept of the model has increased after the implementation of the new system in Iran. From the change of the intercept, it may be concluded that the controllability of M1 has increased after the adoption of the non-interest banking in Iran. However, the coefficient of DU71 is insignificant, and so the oil shock of 1971 in which oil price tripled had no impact on the growth rate of M1 in Iran.

Table 7.4 presents the result of the ECM. As the results indicate, the coefficient of ECM (–0.8) is significant. Hence, about 80 per cent of disequilibrium is corrected each period.

Since the variables used in the above model are stationary at levels, we know that there is no problem of spurious regression and hence we do not have to test for cointegration.[9]

The estimation results of policy controllability for M2

To see how the adoption of the new financial system in Iran has affected the controllability of M2, equation (7.6) has been estimated. As before, the dummy variables are introduced into the model to examine the impact of the new monetary system (DU84); the oil revenue shock of 1971 (DU71); and the closure of banks before the victory of Islamic Revolution in 1979 (DU79).

Table 7.4 Error correction representation for controllability of M1 model

Error correction representation for the selected ARDL model ARDL (1,0) selected based on Schwarz Bayesian Criterion dependent variable is DGM_1 36 observations used for estimation from 1963 to 1998

Regressor	*Coefficient*	*Standard error*	*T-ratio[prob]*
DGMB	0.793873	0.12667	6.2672[0.000]
DC	0.008447	0.030159	0.28009[0.781]
DDU84GMB	0.369731	0.20548	1.7993[0.082]
DDU84	0.095853	0.044313	2.1631[0.039]
DDU71	0.014753	0.048543	0.30391[0.763]
ECM(–1)	–0.80513	0.10703	–7.5221[0.000]

R-Squared 0.70800 R-Bar-Squared 0.65933
S.E. of Regression 0.056252 F-stat. F(5, 30) 14.5477[.000]
Mean of Dependent Variable 0.0049256 S.D. of Dependent Variable 0.096377
Residual Sum of Squares 0.094930 Equation Log-likelihood 55.8047
Akaike Information Criterion 49.8047 Schwarz Bayesian Criterion 45.0542
DW-statistic 1.8648

The results are presented in Tables 7.5 and 7.6. Based on the Schwarz Bayesian Criterion, the selected order of our ARDL is (1, 0).

As Table 7.5 shows, the coefficient of lagged value of GMB is not significant at the 5 per cent level. The growth rate of the money base (MB) has a positive and significant impact on the growth rate of M2 . The coefficients of dummy variables for implementing the non-interest banking system in 1984 are insignificant. The coefficient of DU79 shows that the closure of banks during the Islamic revolution (1978–9) had a negative impact on GM2.

As the result of diagnostic tests in Table 7.6 show, the model does not have serial correlation, functional form, normality and heteroscedasticity problems.

Table 7.5 Controllability of M2 model

Autoregressive distributed lag estimates ARDL (1,0) selected based on Schwarz Bayesian Criterion dependent variable is GM_2 34 observations used for estimation from 1965 to 1998

Regressor	*Coefficient*	*Standard error*	*T-ratio[prob]*
GM2(–1)	0.23918	0.12885	1.8563[0.074]
GMB	0.52559	0.17117	3.0707[0.005]
C	0.052603	0.040103	1.3117[0.201]
DU84GMB	–0.062612	0.22364	–0.27997[0.782]
DU84	0.020617	0.047918	0.43026[0.670]
DU71	0.051191	0.050338	1.0169[0.318]
DU79	–0.17089	0.070564	–2.4218[0.022]

R-Squared 0.67431 R-Bar-Squared 0.60193
S.E. of Regression 0.050806 F-stat. F(6, 27) 9.3167[0.000]
Mean of Dependent Variable 0.22126 S.D. of Dependent Variable 0.080526
Residual Sum of Squares 0.069693 Equation Log-likelihood 56.9862
Akaike Information Criterion 49.9862 Schwarz Bayesian Criterion 44.6440
DW-statistic 1.7915 Durbin's h-statistic 0.92111[0.357]

Table 7.6 Diagnostic tests of controllability of M2 model

Test statistics	*Lm version*	*F version*
A: Serial Correlation	$\chi^2(1) = 0.31696[0.573]$	F(1, 26) = 24466[0.625]
B: Functional Form	$\chi^2(1) = 1.2044[0.272]$	F(1, 26) = 95486[0.337]
C: Normality	$\chi^2(2) = 1.1092[0.574]$	Not applicable
D: Heteroscedasticity	$\chi^2(1) = 0.47237[0.492]$	F(1, 32) = 45085[0.507]

A: Lagrange multiplier test of residual serial correlation
B: Ramsey's RESET test using the square of the fitted values
C: Based on a test of skewness and kurtosis of residuals
D: Based on the regression of squared residuals on squared fitted values

Table 7.7 presents the results of the long-run model. As the table shows, a 1 per cent increase in the growth rate of the money base will increase the growth rate of M2 by 0.7 per cent. But, from Table 7.3, we know that a 1 per cent increase in GMB will increase the growth rate of M1 by more than 0.98 per cent. This indicates that M1 is more controllable than M2 .

The coefficients of dummy variables for implementing the non-interest banking system in 1984 (i.e., DU82 and DU84GM) are not significant. It means that controllability of M2 has not been affected by the new financial system in the long run. However, the coefficient of DU79 shows that the closure of banks during Islamic revolution (1978–9) had a negative impact on the growth rate of M2 .

Table 7.7 also shows that the oil shock of 1971 which tripled oil prices, so that the government revenue from oil had no impact on the M2 growth rate.

As the results of the dynamic model in Table 7.8 show, the impact of the growth rate of the monetary base on the growth rate of M2 is lower in the short run than in the long run. The dummies capturing the effect of the non-interest banking system on policy controllability of M2 are not significant in the short run as well. The coefficient of the ECM is significant and negative. It shows that about 76 per cent of error is corrected each period.

Table 7.7 Estimated long-run coefficients of controllability of M2 model

Estimated long run coefficients using the ARDL approach ARDL (1,0) selected based on Schwarz Bayesian Criterion dependent variable is GM_2 34 observations used for estimation from 1965 to 1998

Regressor	*Coefficient*	*Standard error*	*T-ratio[prob]*
GMB	0.69083	0.22177	3.1150[0.004]
C	0.069140	0.048885	1.4143[0.169]
DU84GM	–0.082296	0.29349	0.28041[0.781]
DU84	0.027099	0.062937	0.43056[0.670]
DU71	0.067284	0.065148	1.0328[0.311]
DU79	–0.22462	0.097228	–0.3102[0.029]

The monetary aggregate–economic goals link

It is not sufficient to evaluate the usefulness of a monetary system by simply examining the degree of controllability of the monetary aggregates in that system. For that to be the case, M2 must be controllable and must have an effect on economic variables that the monetary authority wishes to influence.

Basic model

To study the link between the monetary aggregate and the goal of price stability (inflation rate in this model), the following model is used:

Table 7.8 Error correction representation for controllability of M2 model

Representation for the selected ARDL model ARDL (1,0) selected based on Schwarz Bayesian Criterion dependent variable is DGM_2 34 observations used for estimation from 1965 to 1998

Regressor	*Coefficient*	*Standard error*	*T-ratio[prob]*
DGMB	0.52559	0.17117	3.0707[.005]
DC	0.052603	0.040103	1.3117[.201]
DDU84GMB	–0.062612	0.22364	–0.27997[.782]
DDU84	0.020617	0.047918	0.43026[.670]
DDU71	0.051191	0.050338	1.0169[.318]
DDU79	–0.17089	0.070564	–2.4218[.022]
ECM(–1)	–0.76082	0.12885	–5.9046[.000]

R-Squared 0.61431 R-Bar-Squared 0.52860
S.E. of Regression 0.050806 F-stat. F(6, 27) 7.1674[0.000]
Mean of Dependent Variable 0.0033979 S.D. of Dependent Variable 0.073998
Residual Sum of Squares 0.069693 Equation Log-likelihood 56.9862
Akaike Information Criterion 49.9862 Schwarz Bayesian Criterion 44.6440
DW-statistic 1.7915

$$\Pi_t = \omega_0 + \omega_1 (GM_1)_t + \omega_2 (GM_1)_{t-1} + \cdots + \omega_i (GM_1)_{t-i} + \lambda W_t + v_{1t} \tag{7.7}$$

$$\Pi_t = \eta_0 + \eta_1 (GM_2)_t + \eta_2 (GM_2)_{t-1} + \cdots + \eta_i (GM_2)_{t-i} + \delta W_t + v_{2t} \tag{7.8}$$

in which Π_t is the inflation rate, GM_1 and GM_2 are defined as before, W_t is a vector of all other variables that affect inflation rate, λ, $\delta\omega_i$, η_j are parameters, and v_{it} are disturbance terms. To avoid the problem of misspecification, we introduce the growth rate of official exchange rate (GOR), and the real output growth (GY) as other explanatory variables.

More specifically, the following ARDL model will be estimated for the Iranian economy:

$$\Pi_t = C + \sum_{j=1}^{p} \alpha_j \Pi_{t-j} + \sum_{j=0}^{q^1} \beta_{1j} GM_{t-j} + \sum_{j=0}^{q^2} \beta_{2j} GOR_{t-j} + \sum_{j=0}^{q^3} \beta_{3j} GY_{t-j}$$
$$+ \theta_1 D_{84} + \theta_2 D_{84} GM_t + \eta_1 Du_1 + \eta_2 Du_{93} + \varepsilon_t \tag{7.9}$$

where GOR_t is the growth of official exchange rate, GY_t is the real output growth, DU_{71}, DU_{84} and DU_{93} are dummies to capture the oil revenue shock of 1971, the implementation of the non-interest banking system in 1984, and the exchange rate reform of 1993, respectively. The disturbance term ε_t is assumed to be a white noise.

Results of aggregate-economic goals link model

In order to examine the degree of reliability of money balances and to study the aggregate-goal link, using the ARDL approach, we estimate equation (7.9). The results of ADF and Phillips–Perron unit root tests of the variables are presented in Appendix Tables 7.17 and 7.18. As these tables show, all variables except GY are stationary at the 5 per cent level. GY is also stationary at the 10 per cent level.

Estimation of M1 reliability

Using the SBC which economizes in the use of lags, the optimal lags of variables in our ARDL model for inflation is ARDL(2, 2, 2, 2). The results are presented in Table 7.9.

The above results have been used to derive the long-run coefficients given in Table 7.11. But before the validity of model needs to be tested, the result of diagnostic tests is presented in Table 7.10. As the result shows, the model passes the regular serial correlation, functional form, normality and heteroscedasticity tests.

Table 7.9 Reliability of M1 model

Autoregressive distributed lag estimates ARDL (2, 2, 2, 2) selected based on Schwarz Bayesian Criterion dependent variable is π 37 observations used for estimation from 1962 to 1998

Regressor	*Coefficient*	*Standard error*	*T-ratio[prob]*
Π (−1)	0.28950	0.15933	1.8170[0.083]
Π (−2)	−0.43390	0.18551	−2.3389[0.029]
GY	−0.019364	0.13819	−0.14013[0.890]
GY(−1)	0.054957	0.14820	0.37084[0.714]
GY(−2)	−0.36841	0.14133	−2.6068[0.016]
GM_1	0.10580	0.12678	0.83452[0.413]
GM1(−1)	0.13561	0.11765	1.1527[0.261]
GM1(−2)	0.27269	0.10757	2.5351[0.019]
GOR	−0.0053651	0.054650	−0.098172[0.923]
GOR(−1)	0.12712	0.057471	2.2118[0.038]
GOR(−2)	0.11980	0.077674	1.5424[0.137]
C	0.015355	0.028219	0.54413[0.592]
DU84GM1	0.092373	0.21130	0.43716[0.666]
DU71	−0.0012150	0.044585	−0.027251[0.979]
DU84	0.047996	0.051425	0.93332[0.361]

R-Squared 0.86494 R-Bar-Squared 0.77899
S.E. of Regression 0.045287 F-stat. F(14, 22) 10.0634[0.000]
Mean of Dependent Variable 0.12910 S.D. of Dependent Variable 0.096332
Residual Sum of Squares 0.045121 Equation Log-likelihood 71.6219
Akaike Information Criterion 56.6219 Schwarz Bayesian Criterion 44.5400
DW-statistic 2.2776

Table 7.10 Diagnostic tests of reliability of M1 model

Test statistics	*Lm version*	*F version*
A: Serial Correlation	χ^2 (1) = 2.5920[0.107]	F(1, 21) = 1.5820[0.222]
B: Functional Form	χ^2 (1) = 2.5717[0.109]	F(1, 21) = 1.5687[0.224]
C: Normality	χ^2 (2) = 0.78579[0.675]	Not applicable
D: Heteroscedasticity	χ^2 (1) = 1.8579[0.173]	F(1, 35) = 1.8504[0.182]

A: Lagrange multiplier test of residual serial correlation
B: Ramsey's RESET test using the square of the fitted values
C: Based on a test of skewness and kurtosis of residuals
D: Based on the regression of squared residuals on squared fitted values

After selecting the best ARDL model, the estimated coefficients of the long-run and the short-run ECMs have been derived. Table 7.11 shows the results of the estimated coefficients of the long-run model. There exists a stationary long-run relation between inflation rate, growth of M1, real output growth, and growth of real exchange rate. The coefficients of variables influencing the inflation rate have the expected signs.

According to this result, real output growth has a significant negative impact on inflation. The growth of the official exchange rate and M1 have positive impacts on the inflation rate. However, since the coefficients of $DU84GM_1$ and DU84 are not statistically significant, the implementation of the new banking system in Iran has neither increased nor decreased the impact of M1 growth on the inflation rate. As Table 7.11 shows, the oil shock of 1971 has not affected the inflation rate in Iran either.

The results of estimating the error correction model are shown in Table 7.12. As the table shows, the behaviour of the short-run and long-run models is similar. Hence the adoption of the new monetary system has not changed the impact of the M1 growth rate on the inflation rate either in the short run or in the long run.

Table 7.11 Estimated long-run coefficients of reliability of M1 model

Estimated long run coefficients using the ARDL approach ARDL (2, 2, 2, 2) selected based on Schwarz Bayesian Criterion dependent variable is π 37 observations used for estimation from 1962 to 1998

Regressor	*Coefficient*	*Standard error*	*T-ratio[prob]*
GY	−0.29082	0.13193	−2.2045[0.038]
GM1	0.44924	0.098197	4.5749[0.000]
GOR	0.21108	0.11947	1.7668[0.091]
C	0.013418	0.024714	0.54291[0.593]
DU84GM1	0.080718	0.18319	0.44063[0.664]
DU71	−0.0010617	0.038932	−0.027270[0.978]
DU84	0.041940	0.042699	0.98223[0.337]

Table 7.12 Error correction representation for reliability of M1 model

Error correction representation for the selected ARDL model ARDL (2, 2, 2, 2) selected based on Schwarz Bayesian Criterion dependent variable is dπ 37 observations used for estimation from 1962 to 1998

Regressor	*Coefficient*	*Standard error*	*T-ratio[prob]*
DΠ1	0.43390	0.18551	2.3389[0.028]
DGY	0.019364	0.13819	0.14013[0.890]
DGY1	0.36841	0.14133	2.6068[0.015]
DGM1	0.10580	0.12678	0.83452[0.412]
DGM11	−0.27269	0.10757	−2.5351[0.018]
DGOR	−0.005365	0.054650	−0.098172[0.923]
DGOR1	−0.11980	0.077674	−1.5424[0.136]
DC	0.015355	0.028219	0.54413[0.591]
DD83GM1	0.092373	0.21130	0.43716[0.666]
DDU71	−0.0012150	0.044585	−0.027251[0.978]
DDU84	0.047996	0.051425	0.93332[0.360]
ECM (−1)	−1.1444	0.18252	−6.2701[0.000]

R-Squared 0.77122 R-Bar-Squared 0.62563
S.E. of Regression 0.045287 F-stat. F(11, 25) 6.7420[.000]
Mean of Dependent Variable 0.0040124 S.D. of Dependent Variable 0.074016
Residual Sum of Squares 0.045121 Equation Log-likelihood 71.6219
Akaike Information Criterion 56.6219 Schwarz Bayesian Criterion 44.5400
DW-statistic 2.2776

The estimation results for M2 reliability

To examine how the policy maker can rely on M2 to affect the inflation rate, M2 has been used on equation (7.9) instead of M1 and run with the aggregate-economic goals model. Based on the SBC the optimal lags of inflation rate, real output growth, M2 growth rate, and exchange rate growth are determined. As Table 7.13 shows, the order of ARDL is (2, 0, 2, 2).

As the regular diagnostic tests in Table 7.14 show, the model has no problem of serial correlation, functional form, normality and heteroscedasticity.

The estimated long-run coefficients of the reliability of the M2 model depicted in Table 7.15 indicate that the growth of real output, the growth of M2 and the official exchange rate growth have the expected impacts on the inflation rate. However, the coefficients of the dummy variables used for the adoption of non-interest banking (i.e., DU84GM2 and DU84) are statistically insignificant. This means the implementation of the new style of banking in 1984 has not changed the impact of M2 growth on the inflation rate.

As Table 7.15 shows, the coefficient of GM_2 is about 0.6, and from Table 7.11 it can be seen that the coefficient of GM_1 is about 0.45. The comparison between these results shows that M2 is more reliable than M1 in the long

Table 7.13 Reliability of M2 model

Autoregressive distributed lag estimates ARDL (2, 0, 2, 2) selected based on Schwarz Bayesian Criterion dependent variable is π 37 observations used for estimation from 1962 to 1998			
Regressor	*Coefficient*	*Standard error*	*T-ratio[prob]*
Π(−1)	0.50760	0.15730	3.2269[0.004]
Π(−2)	−0.24147	0.14638	−1.6496[0.113]
GY	−0.37636	0.11103	−3.3898[0.003]
GM2	0.21591	0.13078	1.6509[0.112]
GM2(−1)	−0.16290	0.13622	−1.1959[0.244]
GM2(−2)	0.38899	0.11922	3.2627[0.003]
GOR	0.023835	−0.057161	−.41698[0.681]
GOR(−1)	0.19468	0.053086	3.6672[0.001]
GOR(−2)	0.11630	0.063601	1.8286[0.080]
C	0.0012393	0.030121	0.041144[0.968]
DU84GM2	0.088248	0.22957	0.38440[0.704]
DU79	−0.15990	0.050291	−3.1795[0.004]
DU84	−0.017223	0.052361	−0.32894[0.745]
DU93	−0.0097249	0.043855	−0.22175[0.826]

R-Squared 0.87842 R-Bar-Squared 0.80970
S.E. of Regression 0.042024 F-stat. F(13, 23) 12.7824[0.000]
Mean of Dependent Variable 0.12910 S.D. of Dependent Variable 0.096332
Residual Sum of Squares 0.040618 Equation Log-likelihood 73.5670
Akaike Information Criterion 59.5670 Schwarz Bayesian Criterion 48.2906
DW-statistic 2.0287

Table 7.14 Diagnostic tests of reliability of M2 model

Test Statistics	*Lm Version*	*F Version*
A: Serial Correlation	χ^2 (1) = 0.1160[0.733]	F(1, 22) = 0.0692[0.795]
B: Functional Form	χ^2 (1) = 0.5855[0.444]	F(1, 22) = 0.3537[0.558]
C: Normality	χ^2 (2) = 0.3346[0.846]	Not applicable
D: Heteroscedasticity	χ^2 (1) = 0.3968[0.529]	F(1, 35) = 0.37945[0.542]

A: Lagrange multiplier test of residual serial correlation
B: Ramsey's RESET test using the square of the fitted values
C: Based on a test of skewness and kurtosis of residuals
D: Based on the regression of squared residuals on squared fitted values

run. Hence, if price stability is the main goal of the monetary authorities in Iran, they should choose M2 as the policy instrument.

As Table 7.16 indicates, the dynamic model also mimics the long-run behaviour. According to this table, about 73 per cent of error is corrected each period.

Table 7.15 Estimated long-run coefficients of reliability of M2 model

Estimated long run coefficients using the ARDL approach ARDL (2, 0, 2, 2) selected based on Schwarz Bayesian Criterion dependent variable is π 37 observations used for estimation from 1962 to 1998

Regressor	*Coefficient*	*Standard Error*	*T-ratio[prob]*
GY	−0.51284	0.16540	−3.1006[0.005]
GM2	0.60229	0.16853	3.5738[0.002]
GOR	0.39127	0.17222	2.2719[0.033]
C	0.001688	0.041049	0.041139[0.968]
D83GM2	0.12025	0.30838	0.38994[0.700]
DU79	−0.21788	0.083428	−2.6116[0.016]
DU84	−0.023469	0.071893	0.32644[0.747]
DU93	−0.013251	0.059718	−0.22190[0.826]

Table 7.16 Error correction representation for reliability of M2 model

Error correction representation for the selected ARDL model ARDL (2, 0, 2, 2) selected based on Schwarz Bayesian Criterion dependent variable is $d\pi$ 37 observations used for estimation from 1962 to 1998

Regressor	*Coefficient*	*Standard Error*	*T-ratio[prob]*
DΠ 1	0.24147	0.14638	1.6496[0.112]
DGY	−0.37636	0.11103	−3.3898[0.002]
DGM2	0.21591	0.13078	1.6509[0.111]
DGM21	−0.38899	0.11922	−3.2627[0.003]
DGOR	−0.023835	0.057161	−0.41698[0.680]
DGOR1	−0.11630	0.063601	−1.8286[0.079]
DC	0.0012393	0.030121	0.041144[0.968]
DD83GM2	0.088248	0.22957	0.38440[0.704]
DDU79	−0.15990	0.050291	−3.1795[0.004]
DDU84	−0.017223	0.052361	−0.32894[0.745]
DDU93	−0.0097249	0.043855	−0.22175[0.826]
ECM(−1)	−0.73387	0.13437	−5.4617[0.000]

R-Squared 0.79405 R-Bar-Squared 0.67765
S.E. of Regression 0.042024 F-stat. F(11, 25) 8.0617[.000]
Mean of Dependent Variable 0.0040124 S.D. of Dependent Variable 0.074016
Residual Sum of Squares 0.040618 Equation Log-likelihood 73.5670
Akaike Information Criterion 59.5670 Schwarz Bayesian Criterion 48.2906
DW-statistic 2.0287

Concluding remarks

Two important features of a monetary system are its policy controllability and reliability. Using an ARDL approach, two models were constructed in this chapter to investigate the impacts of implementing a non-interest-based banking system on monetary policy controllability and the monetary aggregate–economic goals link in Iran. This approach allowed the study of both the short-run and the long-run effects. Dummy variable technique has been used to examine for the existence of structural break in the models. The models are estimated for the narrow and broad definitions of money.

The results of controllability of M1 show that the non-interest style of banking adopted in Iran has not decreased the slope of money base growth (GMB). It means that the implementation of the new banking system in 1984 has not reduced the impact of money base growth on the growth of M1 and, hence, has not decreased the controllability of the narrow definition of money. Moreover, the estimation results indicate that the intercept in the M1 controllability model has increased since the implementation of the new system in Iran. From this positive shift in the intercept, it may be concluded that M1 has become even more controllable in the new banking arrangement.

When M2 is used for policy purposes, the results of our estimated model show that the degree of M2 controllability has not changed since the new financial arrangements were implemented in 1984. Hence, the financial innovation in the 1980s which resulted from the adoption of the new banking system in Iran has not affected the usefulness of monetary aggregates negatively.

The chapter also examines how the aggregate–economic goals link (or the policy reliability) has been affected by the adoption of the new monetary system. The results show that the new financial arrangement has neither increased nor decreased the reliability of the monetary aggregates in Iran. These results hold both in the short and the long run.

Moreover, it is found that M1 is more controllable than M2, but M2 is more reliable than M1. The Iranian monetary authorities should take this fact into consideration when deciding about which policy instrument to use for achieving the goal of price stability.

In general, it may be concluded that the adoption of the new banking system in Iran has not caused any major change in the usefulness of the Iranian monetary system. This might be attributed to the fact that the new system after 1984 still mimics the pre-non-interest banking arrangement in which the authorities used to influence the interest rate and allocate the financial resources among economic sectors. After the implementation of the new banking system, Bank Markazi Iran (BMI), the central bank of Iran, determines the expected rate of returns on deposits and loans and allocates the financial resources in the economy more or less in the same fashion as it was doing before. While there is no official interest rate in the system, the expected profit rate is set administratively by the monetary authorities.

Indeed, BMI sets administratively the banks' rates of return on investment (time) deposits according to the maturity of deposits. The lending rates are also set differently by BMI based on the expected rate of return of the sector to which credit is extended. In practice, the administratively determined lending rates denote the profit rate that borrowers have to obtain and which the banks will collect from them. This causes some problems. First, it seems that this type of lending and borrowing operation is, in practice, against the Islamic principle of profit-loss sharing advocated by most Muslim economists. Second, the administratively managed profit rate cannot freely respond to changes in the economy and accommodate the economic shocks. Third, it might mislead the economy by sending wrong signals to the market, since it does not necessarily reflect the true profit rates. *Ex-post* profit rates may be higher or lower than the administratively quoted rates. Hence the implementation of a pre-determined profit rate system might be an important source of inefficiency in the Iranian monetary sector. Fourth, in an economy with relatively limited financial assets operating under the government supervision, and in the presence of an administratively controlled profit rate, we should witness the rise of parallel underground financial markets. Therefore, the Iranian financial system should move faster towards the implementation of a real profit-loss sharing system.

In the end, it may be pointed out that the Iranian financial system has recently witnessed important structural changes. Hence, it may be noted that the results of this study regarding the usefulness of monetary aggregates in Iran are confined to the period under investigation and cannot be extended to the years after 1998. One may also note that the words 'Islamic banking system' have not been used in this chapter. It may be argued that the true Islamic banking system has not yet been fully practised in Iran. However, the adoption of *non-interest banking* is considered as an important positive move towards establishing an Islamic banking system; but this move is not complete yet and requires more efforts.

Appendix: unit root tests

Table 7.17 Augmented Dickey–Fuller test

Variable	*ADF stat.*	
	Without trend	*With trend*
GM_1	–3.10	–3.19
GM_2	–3.33	–3.27
GMB	–3.30	–3.22
Π	–2.45	–5.00
GOR	–3.15	–3.77
GY	–2.63	–2.90

Critical Value at 5 per cent (a) without trend –2.94; (b) with trend –3.53

Table 7.18 Phillips–Perron test

Variable	*Phillips-Perron test for first difference*	
	Without trend	*Withtrend*
GM_1	–2.93	–3.14
GM_2	–3.31	–3.27
GMB	–3.22	–3.14
Π	–2.21	–3.89

Critical Value at 5 per cent (a) without trend –2.94; (b) with trend –3.53

Comment

Iraj Toutounchian

The findings of the study are solid and firm. It may be observed that, until now, not enough attention has been directed to the philosophy of Islamic banking which encourages cooperation and mutual support in relationships to emerge as activities pertinent to Islamic economics. The philosophy of Islamic banking is implicit in the PLS. It is within the spirit of the principle of sharing: two alternative monetary aggregates, M1 and M2, will be both controllable and reliable. The authors, using the new method of co-integration, have come up with the following conclusions, which will be reviewed in this comment:

1 The degree of controllability of M2 has not changed after the implementation of the new monetary arrangement.
2 The results show that non-interest banking has neither increased nor decreased the reliability of the monetary aggregates (i.e., M1 and M2) in Iran.
3 The new banking system in Iran has not caused a major change in the usefulness of the Iranian monetary system. This might be attributed to the fact that the new system after 1984 still mimics the pre-non-interest banking arrangements.
4 While there is no official interest rate in the system, the profit rate is set administratively by the monetary authorities.
5 In practice, the administratively determined lending rates denote the profit rate that the borrower has to obtain and the bank will collect from them.
6 The implementation of a pre-determined profit rate system might be an important source of inefficiency in the Iranian monetary sector.

Most important of all is the fact that the writers, being aware of the Islamic banking and of the interest free banking law of 1983, have written: 'it seems that this type of lending and borrowing operation is, in practice, against the Islamic principle of profit-loss sharing advocated by most Muslim economists'. Thus, they have recommended that the Iranian financial system should move faster toward the implementation of a real PLS system.

The Interest Free Banking Operations of Iran (1983) may be considered as one of the best pieces of law concerning usury-free banking, and it may also be the best law passed in post-revolutionary Iran. Although 'the law' has its own critics, who find it flawed in minor items, their critique does not appear to be very convincing for the work was an unprecedented effort intended to prevent ambiguities. The criticisms can be partially justified and/or accounted for on the grounds that the authorities had no previous examples to follow.

There is much evidence indicating that the banks in Iran have been operating on a conventional basis under an Islamic guise. This is due to unnecessary misinterpretations of 'the law'. These flaws have been pointed out by some religious scholars as well as by some economists. Even the ordinary citizens of Iran have a view that banks operate on a conventional rather than on an Islamic basis. These opinions reveal that people are outraged by interest rates of over 30 per cent; that firms are suffering from high interest costs which have brought them to the brink of bankruptcy; and that inflation has caused inequitable distribution of income and wealth so that the country's official statistics show an unemployment rate of over 14.2 per cent.

The *muḍārabah* contracts are conducted operating with interest rates of 30 per cent and above. The *mushārakah* contracts are either not administered or they constitute a small percentage of total loans (one may note that *mushārakah* contracts are long term and that there is no conceivable termination year). So, the accounts are not cleared and figures are carried forward from the previous to the next years. This is contrary to other Islamic contracts that enjoy high rates of turnover and are cleared within short time periods. That is why some observers wrongly reached the conclusion that the number of *mushārakah* was considerable.

The new law, if properly practised, looks at any demand for finance as a project (however small it may be, such as a domestic plumbing repair or the purchase of a photocopying machine). That is to say, a value-added will be created in society. Thus, every unit of money that is to exit the Iranian banks will be linked to a project. In other words, it is the unutilized output potentialities which determine the money supply, not vice versa. That is, utilizing the change in relative profit share compared with capital share and without interfering in market mechanism, we can either upgrade or limit demand for project finance. This task is fulfilled along with placing an absolute sanction against interest (usury). This would eliminate speculation and hence, Say's Law (which is the necessary condition for full employment) will be realized in the system. In this situation (and in an ideal theoretical setting), the general level of prices will be stabilized, full employment will be realized and income distribution will be directed towards equity. This is so because depositors will be benefiting from real profits, the sum of which is several times larger than that of the interest rate. Finally, the manufacturing costs of commodities will be reduced, thanks to the elimination of interest, and the purchasing power of the public will increase.

In short, in such a system, first of all, investment is a function of profit rate. This rate would emerge as a result of competition among producers in each area of the private sector. Its mathematical expectation as well as its standard deviation, and also its risk situation, will be the basis upon which decisions are made. Second, as a result of state banks' participation and because of their close supervision, financial discipline will prevail and fiscal reports will be prepared properly and correctly. Third, as a result of the existence of various contracts applicable in all areas, whether the request for finance is put forward by a real or legal entity, the money market will be diminished and ultimately this will eliminate the context in which excess demand appears, excess demand being the main cause of inflation.

Now, if the experience of banking in Iran after 1984 is far from the above-mentioned results, we must be doubtful whether law and practice correspond with each other. If Islamic banking as envisaged in the new Law were practised in Iran, it would have passed both the controllability and reliability tests. Under those circumstances, money supply would have attained the above capability, not because of a change in interest rate (which is forbidden) but due to the inseparable links it has with economic projects. The authors certainly expect that after the implementation of the new law, M1 and M2 would both become controllable and reliable. In fact no perceptible change was observed. We can therefore conclude that problem lay in implementation of the law. The concluding remarks by the authors attest that this seems to have been the case.

Notes

1. That is, M1 and M2 , respectively.
2. Treichel (1997) uses a vector co-integration approach to study the relation between money base and M2 and M4 in Tunisia. It shows that money supply is controllable by the monetary authority.
3. If two or more non-stationary time series are integrated of the same order, they are on the same wavelength.
4. See, for example, Pesaran and Shin (1997) and Harris (1995).
5. Pesaran and Shin (1997) suggest using SBC because it economizes in using the lags.
6. The coefficient of error correction term shows the speed of adjustment towards long-run equilibrium.
7. Throughout this paper, a Microsoft software package was used which is designed for the econometric modelling of time series data.
8. It may be noted that it is significant only at 10 per cent level.
9. However, even if we carry out a unit root test of the null hypothesis of no co-integration. The sum of $\hat{a}_i$ $(i=1,\ldots p)$ in (1) must be less than one for the dynamic model to converge to a long-run solution. Thus, dividing $(1-\Sigma\hat{a})$ by the sum of their associated standard errors provides a t-type test statistic, which can be compared against the critical values given by Banerjee, Dolado and Mestre, in order to test the null hypothesis. This test was conducted for the M1 controllability model and the null hypothesis of no co-integration was rejected.

References

Banerjee, A., Dolado, J. J., and Mestre, R. (1998), 'Error-Correction Mechanism Tests for Cointegration in a Single-Equation Framework', *Journal of Time Series Analysis*, 19(3), 267–83.

Darrat, Ali F. (1988), 'The Islamic Interest-free Banking System: Some Empirical Evidence', *Applied Economics*, 20, 417–25.

Dotsey, M. and C. Otrok (1994), 'M_2 and Monetary Policy: A Critical Review of the Recent Debate', Federal Reserve Bank of Richmond, *Economic Quarterly*, 80 (1) (Winter), 41–60.

Feldstein, Martin and James H. Stock (1993), 'The Use of Monetary Aggregate to Target Nominal GDP', *Working Paper 4304*, Cambridge, MA: National Bureau of Economic Research, March.

Harris, R. I. D. (1995), *Using Cointegration Analysis in Econometric Modelling*, New York: Harvester Wheatsheaf: Padstow Press.

Pesaran, M. Hashem and Yongcheol Shin (1997), *An Autoregressive Distributed Lag Modelling Approach to Cointegration Analysis*, Department of Applied Economics, Cambridge: University of Cambridge.

Treichel, Volker (1997), 'Broad Money Demand and Monetary Policy in Tunisia', *IMF Working Paper /97/22*, Washington, DC: IMF.

Yousefi, M., S. Abizadeh and K. McCormick (1997), 'Monetary Stability and Interest-free Banking: The Case of Iran', *Applied Economics*, 29, 869–76.

8

The Role of Islamic Finance in Industrial Projects in the State of Kuwait

Javed Hussain and Sherifa Marafi

This chapter seeks to evaluate the cost-effectiveness of Islamic finance when combined with conventional finance for industrial projects in the State of Kuwait. The chapter analyses a deal which was structured for Equate Petrochemical Company and co-financed by Islamic and conventional financial institutions. It compares aspects of Islamic project finance with conventional banking practices, and examines the appropriateness of Islamic financing for industrial projects to see whether Islamic finance combined with conventional finance reduces the weighted average cost of capital (WACC). The empirical results using conventional with Islamic finance failed to corroborate the perceived benefit of combining Islamic with conventional finance, which raises a number of questions. Finally, the chapter reports some recent trends, together with the deterrents and stimulants for the growth and development of the Islamic financial system.

Introduction

Financing policies of firms are universal in raising finance for new projects. However, a standard firm's capital structure is composed of retained earnings, debt or equity; this capital structure defines ownership in both developing and developed countries (La-Porta, Lopez de Silanes and Shleifer, 1999). Firms operating in Islamic countries mirror a similar capital structure due to historical reasons. The capital structure of firms is important and it affects corporate behaviour. Applying Hutton and Kenc's (1998) analysis, we may deduce that firms financed through the Islamic mode of finance also exhibit similar characteristics which may influence the cost of capital. Thus, financing policy, capital structure and ownership behaviours are linked through costs and returns, which are also affected by the taxation and depreciation provision policies of governments. Hence, combining conventional and Islamic modes of finance for companies and projects will influence the cost of capital, return and ownership, irrespective of how the cost/return is built into the deal.

Modigliani and Miller (1958, 1963), King (1974, 1977) and practitioners in industrialized countries have developed complex models to study the impact of combining debt and equity on the cost of capital. Prasad, Green and Murinde (2001), Brada and Singh (1999) studied capital structure-related issues of developing countries, but there is a conspicuous gap in the empirical research on the impact of co-financing (combining conventional with Islamic finance) on projects and businesses and on a company's cost of capital.

Over the last decade, Islamic banking has become more internationalized as it began to compete with conventional banks, particularly in Western countries where a considerable Muslim population is present (for example, the UK has over 1.5 million Muslims). A large number of Western financial institutions, following the lead of Citibank, now have their own subsidiaries or Islamic Divisions serving their Muslim clientele. The assets of financial institutions have grown more than forty-fold, and are now estimated to be worth over $230 billion (Warde, 2001). Islamic banking literature is now easily accessible to Western economists and practitioners, and the research brief has shifted from description to product innovation, regulatory compliance and the application of Islamic principles to package existing conventional products in order to mobilize vast pools of financial assets held by Muslim populations the world over. Citibank, Dresdner Kleinwort Benson, the ANZ Group and others have long recognized the importance of the pool of financial assets held by the Muslim world, but more recently, HSBC, Lloyds/TSB and Barclays in the UK have begun to tap into this niche or to sensitize the existing products to comply with Islamic principles.

To mobilize funds, Islamic banks use profit-sharing as a substitute for the payment of interest, where return is neither fixed nor guaranteed. The banks' prudence is not affected through profit-sharing (Siddiqi, 1983; Murinde, Naser and Wallace, 1995; Bokhari, 2000). Conventional banks raise funds through deposits and debt, where fixed interest is paid, whereas Islamic banks' capital structure comprises a high proportion of profit-sharing funds collected via investment accounts (Deehani al-, Karim and Murinde, 1999). Such different capital structures of conventional and Islamic banks will have inherently different charging structures for lending money to firms, and this has implications for the firm's cost of capital. Earlier work by Modigiliani and Miller (1958, 1963), Modigiliani (1988), Myers (1986, 2001) and Miller (1977) considers capital structure in the context of debt and equity. Though Al-Deehani, Karim and Murinde (1996) consider the capital structure for Islamic banks, there is a dearth of empirical studies which examine how co-financing deals impact upon the firm's cost of capital.

This chapter investigates co-financing issues for industrial companies in the State of Kuwait using equity, conventional and Islamic finance. This introduction is followed by a section on methodology used. After that, we present a case study of a co-financed deal structured for a company in

Kuwait, Equate Petrochemical Company (Equate). The final section draws conclusions and suggests lines of exploration for further case studies to examine the issue of Islamic finance and the problems encountered in structuring co-financed deals.

The background: reconciling Islamic finance

The prohibition of *ribā* in Islam means that Islamic banks cannot incur or earn interest in their financial transactions, in order to prevent exploitation, maximize social benefits and encourage enterprise. The Islamic model encourages equity financing and seeks to reward the entrepreneurial spirit that shares distribution of risk and reward (Duncan, 1996).

Islamic banks have developed various financing techniques for trade and project financing, such as *muḍārabah, mushārakah, murābaḥah, istiṣnā*ʿ and *ijārah* (Iqbal, 1997a, 1997b). However, a capitalist economy consists of a complex monetary system. Monetary agents seek to maximize profit by raising the interest rate 'spread', the difference between earnings on loans and costs of servicing deposits. Such a system would continue to operate as long as monetary agents provide facilities for savers, 'rewards' for their deposits and monetary resources for borrowers, who in turn pay interest for these resources. Shirazi (1990), Keynes (1931), Fisher (1930) and Veblen (1904, cited in Dar and Presley, 1999) saw interest as a destabilizing force in the economy, reducing liquidity. Dar and Presley (1999) argue that a monetary equilibrium would result in the stagnation of an economy since entrepreneurs would no longer seek to expand or contract their activities.

Conversely, Laliwala (1994) argues that an Islamic approach contributes to the saving prosperity of an economy because; it encourages economic activity through labour, enterprise, saving, innovation and justice without exploitation; this view is consistent with the Keynesian liquidity preference of interest theory, which suggests that if savings are not invested or utilized for production, then interest paid on these savings cannot be justified since refraining from consumption leads to economic recession (Keynes, 1936, cited in Laliwala, 1994). Statistics indicate that usury leads to wealth inequality and debt crisis, so that developing countries have become heavily indebted to Western lenders. For example, the external debts of Mexico, Indonesia and Brazil reached US$165.7 billion, US$107.8 billion and US$159.1 billion in 1998, respectively, and Pakistan, Egypt, Turkey, Morocco and Algeria similarly highly indebted countries, which leaves them with limited funds for essentials, such as food, healthcare and education (UNDP Human Development Report, 1998). Such inequalities are a recipe for social, political and economic exclusion, which in turn has other adverse impacts on the fabric of a society.

Effective economic growth can be achieved in Muslim countries if innovative methods in interpreting principles of Islamic jurisprudence are used to maximize the potential resources of investors (Ebrahim, 1999). However, one of the major criticisms of Islamic banking is the lack of standard interpretation of the *Sharīʿah*, especially on issues related to debt and equity financing (Parker, 1995; Martin, 1997). While conventional systems compensate for high risk with high return, incorporating high interest, Islamic funds lack such a direct relationship. High returns will carry high risk but there is no additional compensation, as is the case in conventional finance. Therefore the synthesis of new methods of Islamic finance is insufficient without the skill to select an appropriate method in order to maximize return and minimize risk for the financier (Fernandez, 1997). Ebrahim (1999) demonstrates the importance of innovation in Islamic financing techniques by developing mathematical models. *Muḍārabah* can be financially engineered in accordance with clientele risk preferences by adjusting the profit sharing in proportion, and in accordance with the financial objectives of the investor, such that the investor can share profits as with an income bond, share project appreciation as with a participating bond, or sell the *muḍārabah* contract in the secondary market rather than terminating it at an inopportune moment. Such liquidity encourages participation and enhances the development of financial markets.

Siddiqi (1991) describes *muḍārabah*, where the bank provides finance and the other party is responsible for management, as creating an agency relationship, capable of exploiting business potentials and maximizing net worth. In this case, financiers may be reluctant to employ *muḍārabah* in project finance, as the financier provides only capital, with no management input, thereby leading to high agency cost and risk exposure. The financier is fully responsible for capital losses as well as for claims from third parties when the project is unsuccessful, provided the borrower is not guilty of wilful negligence (Fernandez, 1997).

In contrast, *mushārakah* (joint venture), characterized with more certainty than *muḍārabah*, is a more widely used technique of project finance whereby losses are borne by both parties to the deal according to the proportions of their capital contribution to the project. The sharing of financial risks and rewards in an Islamic financial system implies that the relationship between Islamic banks and their clients involves more banker–client interaction such that information asymmetry is minimal, unlike the relationship of conventional banks. In an Islamic financing deal such as *mushārakah*, it could be inferred that the agency problem, where conflicts arise between the stakeholders of a business due to differences in their interests (Watson and Head, 2001), becomes less of an issue between the bank and the client, as both parties share the same information.

On the contrary, Khalil and Rickwood (1999) demonstrate through an empirical study that a *muḍārabah* contract creates a typical principal-agent problem, where the bank is the principal delegating authority of managing an investment to the client who represents the agent, which implies that the agent has inside information related to the outcomes of the project, thereby creating a situation of asymmetric information between the bank and the client, making it vital for the bank to monitor the client's entrepreneurial effort efficiently and effectively to avoid opportunistic behaviour. As for the client, Islamic banks usually select their agents in a *muḍārabah* contract based on several critical factors including reputation, experience and frequency of transactions with the bank, and having a good borrower's credit record (Khalil and Rickwood, 1999). However, the efficiency and effectiveness of the contractual governance structure of *muḍārabah* remains questionable since the agent selection process may be arbitrary, lack a full information set to arrive at a decision, be biased, inadequate or may limit the number of transactions it can undertake, thereby constraining the scope of an operation.

It is suggested that Islamic banks lack expertise in appraising projects, in particular in the case of *mushārakah*, where the partnership requires that (amongst other aspects) the bank should share in the management of the project with the client, a prospect rarely expected to materialize in the real business environment. In allocating funds, the banks' primary concern is to maximize their return. Therefore wider economic, political and social factors are useful in as much as these can help the banks protect their interests. It remains untested whether an Islamic financier would be more willing to enter into a co-financed deal under *mushārakah* if the conventional financier's portion was greater than that of the Islamic financier, such that the majority of the risk is borne by the latter.

Ijārah (leasing), a similar structure to that of conventional leasing which conforms to the laws of many countries, is consistent with Islamic principles (Fernandez, 1997). Fernandez has classified *ijārah* and *bay' bi thaman al-'ājil* under debt finance, which can be recognized as leasing contracts and forward purchase contracts of interest-based conventional financial systems, respectively (Ghalayini, 1995). An *ijarah* facility is a flexible facility since the lease payments can be short term or long term, while financing and prices can be on a fixed or floating basis, unlike fixed-term or fixed-date trading contracts (e.g., *murābaḥah* and *istiṣnā'*). The flexibility of *ijārah* has allowed this facility to experience an accelerated growth in the Arabian Gulf region, although there is an absence of corporate tax, such that an *ijārah* transaction would not bring any tax benefits to either party to the deal (this is a major taxation benefit in Western countries which makes leasing an attractive alternative for firms). Another possible reason for the growth of *ijārah* in the Gulf region is its similarity to a conventional leasing facility, which means that the conventional lease contract is enforceable in the Gulf region, whereas it could be difficult to enforce other interest-based financial contracts in the courts of some Gulf countries. A third advantage of *ijārah* is that, unlike other financing techniques, there is no exposure to credit risk from the lessee, since a lease transaction is by definition asset-backed.

Moreover, from the bank's perspective, *ijārah* can generate returns that are in excess of the cost of the asset, and over a longer term than those offered by other financing instruments.

There is some ambiguity in the cases of *murābaḥah* and *istiṣnāʿ*, where transactions can be interpreted as a form of *ribā* since the profit is predetermined and bears no risk (Siddiqi, 1983). However, it can be argued that the compliance of *murābaḥah* and *istiṣnāʿ* with the *Sharīʿah* depends on the nature of the transaction. In order for these financing vehicles to comply with *Sharīʿah*, it is necessary to physically perform the trading transactions such that the financier bears the risk of default or damage during the transit time of transporting and owning the asset up to the time of sale to the client. Such a transaction has a time lag before the ownership of the asset is passed over and can be a useful 'bridging', cost-free facility, but the provider will build into the contract a time value of money for the transit period. It is perceived that most Islamic banks fail to realize the physical aspect of a transaction, such that the whole trading transaction is performed through the signing of documents of purchase, sale and transfer of goods, hence avoiding the risks involved in handling.

Fernandez (1997) has distinguished between equity and debt finance, finding a close resemblance between Islamic equity project finance and conventional financial systems, such that the concepts of *mushārakah* and the joint-stock company both involve equity participation. *Muḍārabah* can be associated with the conventional portfolio management business in the sense that in both cases one party is a mere provider of equity while the other party is responsible for management. However, in the case of conventional portfolio management, investments are diversified across a range of projects for the purpose of minimizing risk. Losses from one project can be compensated by profits from another (Arnold, 1998), while in the former case the purpose is to encourage the selection of projects that will contribute to economic growth and maximize wealth whilst complying with Islamic moral rules (i.e., projects that do not involve activities which have an adverse impact on human beings or society or which may create social, economic or political disorders).

Ethical considerations

Islamic finance is concerned with the profitability of the project and, more importantly, its viability, while the size of the collateral is a major concern for conventional banks (Ariff, 1988). This implies that some feasible and economically viable projects may be rejected by conventional banks due to lack of collateral negatively impacting on entrepreneurial activities. Lack of collateral and the high cost of borrowing creates barriers for start-ups and for expanding businesses (Deakins and Hussain, 1993). Therefore, conventional funding structures are an impediment to economic progress, which is considered to be unethical in Islamic banking. In contrast, Islamic banks are capable of financing such projects on a PLS basis without the need for collateral. This improves access to finance for businesses and combines a fair return with an ethical orientation in investments. Moore (1997) states that there is evidence of ethical equity funds (e.g., for projects concerned with environmental protection) outperforming conventional funds; hence, theoretically, Islamic funds should also outperform conventional ones. He ascribes the outperformance of ethical funds to the more stringent scrutiny of the fund managers, in comparison with conventional fund managers, and the increase in global awareness about ethical issues, which in turn increases the popularity of ethically oriented projects.

El-Gamal (1997) demonstrates through a theoretical model that, in order for Islamic banking to survive in the long run, it is necessary to maintain a heterogeneous banking environment for devout Muslims who never engage in usurious transactions, and traditional economic agents who deal in interest-based transactions which depend greatly on uncommitted Muslims, who deal symmetrically with interest-based and non-interest-based transactions. The Malaysian hybrid banking system is a model of such a heterogeneous environment, which appears to follow a more liberal school of jurisprudence and is not necessarily more widely accepted than the conservative approach. Several Islamic bankers support the view of co-existence and interaction between Islamic and conventional finance and suggest that ethically oriented investors, such as Church Commissions or Charities in Western Europe, should entrust some of their resources to Islamic investment managers (Moore, 1997).

However, a heterogeneous banking environment implies that Islamic financiers may invest in shares of companies that have interest-based income, thereby becoming religiously unethical or unacceptable. Iqbal (1997a) explains that it has been considered acceptable by various religious authorities to invest in companies with negligible interest income and low debt ratio, provided that profits are 'purified'. The 'profit-purification' process involves the distribution of profit earned through interest to charities, thereby abiding by the *Sharī'ah*. El-Gamal (1997) considers it unethical for Islamic financiers to invest in companies that deal with interest-based products and argues that Islamic banks are not really abolishing interest; they are merely mimicking an interest-free system (Ahmad, 1992, cited in El-Gamal, 1997).

Given the heterogeneous environment, there is no evidence of large-scale projects being fully financed by Islamic funds (Esty, 2000). The co-existence of Islamic and conventional banks in an economy could generate competition that might be beneficial to investors, such that a highly competitive environment will force Islamic and conventional banks to be more innovative in creating more competitive financing tools in order to gain competitive advantage.

Academics and practitioners argue that these criticisms do not take into consideration the fact that Islamic jurisprudence consists of various schools of thought based on diversified opinions and there is a lack of clarification of the concept of usury: what may be considered acceptable by one school might be regarded unacceptable by the other. Irrespective of the different schools of thought, from the investor's perspective, it is clear that indulging in interest-bearing co-financing deals is unlawful.

Some schools of thought argue that the use of conventional funds in a project introduces the element of *ribā*, in which case both the Islamic financier and the investor would be contravening the *Sharīʿah*. This creates an ethical dilemma for both the Islamic financier and the investor, as an ethical decision will have to be made on whether to involve conventional, interest-based funds in the financing of the project or not. Consider the dilemma from a deontological perspective, in which conduct is ethical if it is an act of goodwill out of respect for a moral law (Hoffman and Frederick, 1995). The *Sharīʿah* acts as the moral law, which prohibits interest. Therefore, some argue that disrespecting this moral law by introducing conventional, interest-based funds to a project is deontologically unethical and un-Islamic. Asserting that an organization's responsibility is to maximize profits, Friedman (1970, cited in Green, 1993) overlooks the ethical, religious, social and economic considerations that positively impact on a company's profile and profitability.

It has been suggested that to investigate the effect of a co-finance deal on its stakeholders, it might be more reasonable to analyse the ethical dilemma using Neutral Omni-partial Rule-Making (NORM), whereby all stakeholders' views are taken into consideration, such that:

> an action is right if each person might reasonably think of that action as being accepted by anyone who looked at the matter in an informed and omni-partial way as a moral rule, that is, as an abiding form of conduct known by everyone and open to everyone in similar circumstances.
>
> (Green, 1993)

Evaluation of co-financed projects using NORM is acceptable provided it does not contravene Islamic principles, is beneficial to the investor and enhances the prospect of success of the project. Moreover, abiding by Islamic laws and avoiding interest ensures the social responsibility of the investor, thereby gaining political, social and economical advantage (Pearson, 1995).

Ethical issues are clearly pertinent for project appraisal and financing, as ethics encourages the implementation of more transparent and productive projects, enhancing economic growth and encouraging socially beneficial activities. This approach is consistent with Islamic principles, as it explicitly facilitates a fair and equitable system that empowers and rewards all rather than a few.

Evolution of Islamic finance

The origin of Islamic finance is enshrined in the *Holy Qur'ān* (2:275–6), so Islamic banking and finance prohibits *ribā* (Esty, 2000) and encourages the earning of profits. To ensure social justice, equality and property rights in Islam, borrowers and lenders become equity holders and share both profits and losses, leading to fair distribution of wealth accumulation and distribution in the economy (Iqbal, 1997a).

Islam, Judaism and Christianity share the principle of the prohibition of interest. The Old Testament (Exodus, XXII: 24) encourages interest-free loans to the poor. The fact that the prohibition of interest can be traced back to religions before Islam indicates that it is a matter of morality and is important to prevent exploitation and maximizing social benefits. The traditional world of finance, dominated by interest-based principles, limits entrepreneurship through the rationing of funds and gives rise to theological issues (Moore, 1997). Financial practices in pre-Islamic Arabia were largely interest-based, and the socially constructive nature of basic Islamic banking practices can be traced back to the early seventh century. Islam enshrined commitment to private property, free enterprise and the sanctity of the contract which accelerated trade and economic prosperity.

The main impetus behind the acceptance of Islamic finance lies in its strict ethical framework. The Middle Ages experienced a well-established, highly sophisticated financial system that fostered trade and business activities (Iqbal, 1997b; Ebrahim, 1999). Muslims at the time of the Ottoman Empire financed their maritime projects with a profit-sharing financial instrument, *muḍārabah*. However, during the nineteenth century, when Muslim territories became colonized by the West, the Islamic economic system was replaced by the capitalist system (Meenai, 1989, as cited in Moore, 1997, p. 6), though European financiers and businessmen later adopted many concepts, techniques and instruments from Islamic finance.

The resurgence of Islamic finance may be traced back to the discovery of oil in the Gulf Region in the 1920s, which led to economic independence and major concessions from Western oil companies in the 1960s (Razavi, 1996). This was followed by the formation of the Organization of the Islamic Conference group (OIC) in 1970, which recognized positive correlation between the role of financial institutions and economic growth, and hence initiated the development of Islamic institutional infrastructure, financial markets and the framework to facilitate the growth of Islamic finance through improving liquidity and standardizing tradable instruments that abide by the *Sharīʿah*, while accommodating modern financial techniques (Presley, 1988).

This led to the creation of the Islamic Development Bank (IDB), which was followed by the establishment of the Dubai Islamic Bank in 1975, initiating the Islamization of all banks in Pakistan in 1979. Sudan and Iran followed suit in 1983. Prior to the 1970s, several sporadic and unrelated efforts were made to establish Islamic banks in Malaysia, Pakistan and Egypt, which failed due to structural, management, regulatory and possibly political reasons. Nevertheless, the experiment was an inspiration that promoted movements towards new Islamic financial systems (Presley, 1988) and led to the creation of the Nasser Social Bank in 1972 (Omar al- and Abdel-Haq, 1996). Islamic banking in the 1970s was very much based on private individual initiatives and hence mostly small-scale, which made its survival in the banking industry alongside the well-established conventional banks difficult (Presley, 1988).

The diminishing of political inhibitions in the 1970s enhanced the growth of Islamic financial institutions; it encouraged governments to establish Islamic financial institutions and create new structures at state level. This led to the establishment of the International Association of Islamic Banks in 1977 (Presley, 1988) to coordinate and develop a close relationship between Islamic and other financial institutions, and also to promote banking free of usury internationally, which led to the establishment of other Islamic banks over the 1970s and 1980s in Dubai, Egypt, Sudan, Jordan, Bahrain and Kuwait (Abdul-Gafoor, 1995).

Currently, over 200 interest-free institutions operate worldwide. In addition, many major UK banks also have their own divisions which offer Islamic finance, reflecting the robustness of the principle when working alongside the conventional banking structure, creating a competitive environment in the banking industry. Martin (1997) reports that several hundred Islamic institutions are operating in more than 40 countries in Africa, Asia and Europe (e.g., Denmark, Luxembourg, Switzerland and in the UK), and the figure increased to 75 countries by 2001 (Warde, 2001). This suggests that Islamic banking has come a long way since the 1970s. Areas such as micro finance, Islamic mutual funds, venture capital and stock markets, provided they are compliant with Islamic principles, have grown rapidly (Warde, 2001).

Moore (1997) ascribes the emergence of the Islamic banking industry as being partly due to the domestically proactive organizations which had their operations limited to within a country; partly due to the domestically retroactive institutions (banks formed in response to legal, political or constitutional changes, as in Sudan and Iran, where economies have been officially 'Islamized' and are required by law to operate under an interest-free system); partly due to the international catalyst that resulted from the proliferation of Islamic banks reaching a certain critical mass in both Muslim and Western countries; and also due to the internationally retroactive: global banks which have supported international Islamic banking movements and identified the potential that the industry offers (e.g., Citibank, Dresdner Kleinwort Benson and others that realized the need to satisfy the demands of the numerous Muslim individuals, institutions and companies controlling large amounts of assets). These conventional banks have established either fully Islamic subsidiaries or Islamic banking departments or windows within their Headquarters where the Islamic banking system continues to co-exist with interest-based banks in Western and Muslim countries, (e.g., Jordan, Egypt, Indonesia, Bangladesh and Kuwait).

The liberalization of financial systems in the West and technological change during the 1990s produced a major adjustment in international finance (Warde, 2000) and equally, had a positive impact on the economic environment in the world. This was accompanied by rising stock market prices, adding to financial assets of oil-rich nations in the Middle Eastern countries, which attracted conventional financiers to explore Islamic finance. Deregulation, technological advances, the process of 'slicing and splicing' of interest and the principal components of a bond enabled conventional financiers to develop tailor-made Islamic products. These are being used as tools for fund mobilization, portfolio diversification and investment management of an investor's funds, which had a positive influence on the Western banks (Bokhari, 2000). However, the extent to which such a growth is compliant with Islamic principles remains under scrutiny.

Islamic finance is a global industry, its assets exceeding $230 billion, compared with $1 billion in 1975 with an annual growth rate of 15 per cent (Martin, 1997). The renewed impetus behind this boom lies in the excesses of global finance (Sadowski, 1996), and the erosion of Judaeo-Christian finance principles through market domination. The new paradigm reflects the diversity of the Islamic world (Warde, 2001); it takes a global perspective and welcomes forward-thinking solutions to philosophical concerns. The phenomenal growth in Islamic finance has influenced Western institutions to offer Islamic products which are compliant with ethical values. The customer base of Islamic banks is continuously increasing, and ranges from individuals to corporate giants. For example, General Motors, IBM and Xerox have raised funds through a US-based Islamic leasing fund set up by the United Bank of Kuwait, and the multinational mega-corporations such as Enron and Shell have used Islamic banks to finance their activities in the Arabian Gulf and Malaysia (Martin, 1997). This suggests that Islamic finance can be used for start-ups and existing small and large businesses, in both developing and developed countries. Therefore, there is a case for enhancing technical expertise, instilling rigour in the system and developing products which are compliant with the *Sharīʿah*.

Background to co-financed projects

The purpose of establishing Equate Petrochemical Company was to diversify the Kuwaiti economy, encourage foreign investment, create jobs and training opportunities for the Kuwaiti population and reduce dependence on oil revenues. Equate Petrochemical Company, based in Kuwait, is a joint venture established in 1995; it is owned by Union Carbide (a worldwide company, recently merged into The Dow Chemical Company, USA) with a 45 per cent share, Petrochemical Industries Corporation (PIC, a state-owned petrochemical corporation in Kuwait) with a 45 per cent share and Boubiyan Petrochemical Corporation (publicly listed) with a 10 per cent share. Equate obtains technology, world-class marketing and operational expertise from Union Carbide and low-cost feedstock and infrastructure from PIC.

Equate project consists of an olefins plant which is used to produce end products; polyethylene at a rate of 600,000 tons/annum and ethylene glycol at a rate of 400,000 tons/annum. The plant is located in Shu'aiba Industrial Area in Kuwait, which has a world-scale plant infrastructure, and a reliable dedicated industrial port with the capacity to meet present and future shipping demands.

Equate's share capital is over $1 billion and the total cost of the project was $2 billion: $800 million of equity and subordinated debt, $600 million of term debt from international and regional banks, $400 million of term debt from local banks and $200 million of Islamic finance (representing 10 per cent of total financing) in the form of *ijārah* (leasing facility) from the Kuwait Finance House (KFH) and funds raised from regional Islamic institutions. The maturity of loans ranged between eight and ten years.

Equate says that the main reason for introducing Islamic funds to the project was to reduce the cost of capital; implicitly, there is a presumption, first, that the cost of Islamic finance is lower than conventional finance, and second, as Kuwait is an Islamic country, that the Kuwaiti government wished to support the development of the Islamic capital market, especially since it owned a relatively large portion of Equate shares. Furthermore, Equate considers the use of an *ijārah* facility to be a cost-efficient method of financing, since the leased equipment can last for 20 years without significant maintenance; hence, depreciation and disposal costs are avoided for up to 20 years.

Methodology

This study assesses the cost effectiveness of combining conventional and Islamic finance by Equate Petrochemical Company and evaluates the effect of replacing conventional debt with an Islamic mode of finance on the WACC in particular; it also examines views of providers and practitioners in Kuwait.

This study draws upon Islamic philosophy and the principles of Islamic financing, using a combination of a phenomenological and positivistic approach and employing various methodologies, both qualitative and quantitative. Both positivistic and phenomenological approaches inform the study (Hussey and Hussey, 1997), which uses 'an array of interpretative techniques which seek to describe, translate and otherwise come to terms with the meaning, not the frequency of certain more or less naturally occurring phenomena in the social world' (Van Maanen, 1983).

The choice of the project was made following a round of exploratory interviews with a number of practitioners, and having examined a number of projects and access to information available from such projects. Information about Equate has been obtained from both secondary and primary sources, mainly meetings/informal interviews with executive officers of Equate Petrochemical Company and KFH, conducted in April 2001 in Kuwait.

The primary data is obtained through questionnaires and follow-up of information through meetings and telephone enquiries. The main institutions were visited by one of the authors. This method proved extremely useful in gaining an insight into what formed their decisions and face-to-face interviews lasted up to two hours, during which their motives for combining Islamic with conventional finance, the nature of the deal, size of the loan and the views of the Islamic regulatory authorities were discussed.

Three variants of questionnaires were developed, the first directed primarily to Equate Petrochemical Company, seeking information about the outcomes of the co-financed deal and its implications for the company's future investment strategies; the second questionnaire was for other Kuwaiti industrial companies, a sample of 15 (excluding Equate), to obtain an indication of their attitudes towards Islamic finance, and their awareness of the trends in demand for Islamic finance; and a third questionnaire was sent to a sample of 100 Kuwaiti individuals to estimate the potential market for Islamic finance in Kuwait and its growth potentials.

The co-existence of Islamic with conventional financial institutions

The co-existence of conventional and Islamic institutions over the short term is a necessity as the Islamic financial market grows. Such a situation exists in Malaysia where conventional banks operate alongside Islamic banks (Parker, 1995), under regulation from the Central Bank; this is unlike Islamic institutions in other countries, such as KFH, which operates under a special law customized to comply with the *Sharīʿah*. The experience of Malaysia and Bahrain suggests conventional banks have responded to competition by changing the range of products offered, whereas Islamic banks have not yet acquired the sophistication to be proactive in response to changing business conditions.

Viewing Islamic finance as cost free is a rather naive over-simplification, suggesting they have no costs of operation. For example, the PLS method involves time-consuming complicated assessment procedures and negotiations, requiring expertise and experience, and it can be cumbersome (Martin, 1997). However, it can be argued that PLS and other products offer a dynamic risk and return relationship that reduces agency cost. Yasseri (1998) suggests that Islamic finance is a viable alternative source of capital that can be crucial to the success of a project, leading to an increase in demand; hence, 'Islamic bankers are no longer so eager to offer financing at any price' (Martin, 1997). In Kuwait, Islamic institutions have become proactive, offering product innovation, training and a customer-focused approach that has generated greater demand for Islamic banking services.

However, competition and legislation have been cited as constraints for Islamic institutions. To overcome competition, Moore (1997) and Parker (1995) suggested that in over-banked countries, such as Malaysia and Kuwait, Islamic banks may form strategic alliances with foreign Islamic institutions or acquisitions of existing financial institutions. Legislation raises major issues, especially in non-Muslim parts of the world; for example, in the USA, federal banking laws bar banks from holding stakes in their clients' business (Martin, 1997). However, in the case of the UK, there is a move to enable conventional banks to operate and offer products which comply with *Sharīʿah* law and also comply with UK legislation.

Findings

The results indicated that Equate used Islamic finance to reduce the cost of finance, and Islamic principles were not an influential factor. The main reason cited for using an *ijārah* facility amongst others was its similarity to conventional leasing; Equate showed willingness to combine the two. However, when Equate's responses were compared with other industrialists, 33.3 per cent (including Equate) of the sample did not consider Islamic principles important. They were motivated solely by profit maximization or cost reduction, while a larger portion of industrialists (66.7 per cent) were motivated by their religious beliefs as well as profit maximization.

Industrialists are aware of the existence of Islamic financial institutions in Kuwait and in the Gulf Region. It was found that 50 per cent of the industrialists have used Islamic finance, 66.7 per cent of which were recent transactions (within the last six years). However, those who have used Islamic funds for their projects appear to be relatively small-scale, with loans ranging between KD50,000 and KD500,000; Equate seems to be the only large-scale project that was partially financed using the Islamic mode of finance. Furthermore, Islamic funds represent the smaller portion of a project, not exceeding 20 per cent, compared with conventional loans or equity funding. All the industrialists in the sample showed a willingness to use Islamic finance in the future, as a 100 per cent positive response indicated a high level of satisfaction. Moreover, of those 50 per cent who have never used Islamic finance, all of them do not believe in it, yet 33.3 per cent of them would consider using it for their projects; however, 66.7 per cent are not sure whether they would use Islamic funds. This suggests there may be a lack of awareness amongst industrialists about Islamic finance that prevents them from getting involved with unfamiliar financing techniques. There also appears to be a lack of awareness about the different modes of financing available. For example, out of the sample of 15, one of them mentioned the use of a *murābaḥah* facility and commented on its suitability for the purpose of the project. There seems to be a general understanding amongst industrialists that Islamic banking involves the sharing of both profits and losses, with the exception of one who understood Islamic banking as being interest-free. 'Islamic financing works the same way as conventional banking, only the name is different. There is no such thing as interest-free, banks will not lend when the risk is greater than return'; this view is rejected by Islamic jurisprudence.

It may be noted that 50 per cent of industrialists consider Islamic banks to be for Muslims only, and that only Muslims can run such banks. This negative perception could have an adverse impact on the market segment that is managed by non-Muslims, especially in the case of Western capital markets. Such ignorance can be considered prejudice and may exclude non-Muslims who possess substantial knowledge and innovative skills that can contribute greatly to the development and growth of Islamic financial markets. In addition, the role and social responsibility of Islamic banks are not fully appreciated as 83 per cent of the industrialists believed that an interest-free banking environment is inefficient for the enhancement of the community, thereby agreeing with Shirazi (1990) and Dar and Presley (1999), but they were unable to provide an explanation as to why that was the case.

The Industrial Bank of Kuwait (IBK) manages a portfolio of Islamic funds from KFH for industrial clients but the *muḍārabah* is the only Islamic product provided by the bank. Other conventional banks manage their clients' money in Islamically approved activities, but there seems to be no evidence of Islamic financing provided by conventional banks, as confirmed by the respondents in the sample of the industrialists, yet many of them showed a willingness to use Islamic products if they were offered by the conventional banks. From the questionnaire, it is apparent that the behaviour of the customers in Kuwait is influenced by the cultural environment in which there is a 'core' belief in Islam, since 50 per cent of industrialists would prefer to use an Islamic bank, even if non-Islamic banks offered loans based on the principles of Islamic banks, and this is where an element of competition can arise between Islamic and non-Islamic banks in Kuwait. Conventional banks may want to prepare for such competition, as banks in the UK have begun to respond to such potential expectations by offering Islamic products.

Respondents in our sample believed that Islamic banks do not necessarily provide better services than non-Islamic banks and it is not necessarily easier to obtain finance for a project from an Islamic bank. There is a lengthy routine procedure to be followed. However, 66.7 per cent believed that Islamic banks are capable of serving projects of all sizes, while 33.3 per cent felt that for all project sizes Islamic banks are not competitive; and 83.3 per cent suggested that Islamic institutions lacked variety and flexibility: 'Islamic banks do not have enough products to compete with conventional banks.' This suggests there is scope for innovation and improving upon existing Islamic products. One-third of the industrialists suggested that Islamic banks lack motivation to collect payment on time, while a larger portion, 66.7 per cent, claim that they do not exert any less pressure in collecting their funds. Clearly, there is diversity of opinion on many issues regarding Islamic finance. This is probably because opinions are based on personal experiences. The survey suggests there is a lack of understanding of Islamic finance and there is ample scope for education.

The opinions of conventional financiers

To gain an insight into how conventional financiers view co-finance, the IBK was selected, as it is a conventional bank and is the only one in Kuwait which specializes in the financing of industrial projects. Hence, the questionnaire was modified accordingly. The bank ran an Islamic portfolio, and they considered Islamic principles to be important for financing purposes. The bank's management agreed that if conventional banks operating in Kuwait offered services that complied with Islamic principles, more people would utilize such banks and their services. However, IBK felt that the religious and community motivations have to complement profit too. Furthermore, the bank has to offer cost-effective products, which comply with Islamic principles and compare favourably with conventional products.

The respondents from IBK accepted the principle of partnership-based financing but did not favour pre-determined interest charges on loans for investment projects. They would prefer to share in the profits of their clients according to pre-determined proportions, rather than receive a fixed interest. At the same time, they consider interest-free loans to be an inefficient method for economic development. It cannot be inferred that this behaviour is typical of profit-oriented conventional banks or unique to IBK.

Converting the whole banking system in Kuwait to an Islamic banking system (as in Iran and Sudan) was considered to be impractical at the current 'budding' stage, but respondents favoured the idea of all conventional banks offering Islamic products in Kuwait. However, lack of legislation in Kuwait was seen as a barrier since the Islamic facilities in conventional banks would have to operate separately under *Sharī'ah* customized regulations. The IBK manages Islamic funds and receives fees for portfolio management, which is similar to several conventional banks worldwide that run units and departments for their Islamic funds. Where the conventional bank owns

Islamic funds, regulation problems will arise, such as accounting regulations, as international accounting standards do not cater for Islamic finance (Drummond, 2000). For this reason, it would probably be more appropriate to adapt the Malaysian dual banking model in Kuwait.

To establish the level of awareness, potential demand and trends, a survey on views of individuals living in Kuwait was conducted. The survey included Muslims, non-Muslims, Kuwaitis, non-Kuwaitis, males and females living in Kuwait. A total of 100 questionnaires were distributed, out of which 69 responded and 66 were usable, bringing the response rate to 66 per cent.

Although the questionnaire was comprehensive, only selective responses are analysed here, focusing on the questions relevant to Islamic project finance. Moreover, refinements have been made for analysis purposes:[1] five-point Likert scales, which were used for measurement (Strongly Agree, Agree, Neutral, Disagree, Strongly Disagree), have been regrouped into two categories (agreement and disagreement), disregarding any 'Neutral' responses.

Table 8.1 gives the demographic characteristics of the sample. The sample is predominantly male (80.3 per cent). Furthermore, the age group lies within the range of 20–59 years; because the questionnaires were distributed to employed individuals, this is typical for the working population in Kuwait. However, the male dominance and the age group should not obstruct the analysis since these characteristics are representative of the portion of the population in Kuwait that is most likely to be exposed to issues of Islamic financing.

Table 8.1 Sample demographic of individual respondents in Kuwait ($N = 66$)

	Factor	*Frequency*	*Percentage*
Sex	Male	53	80.3
	Female	13	19.7
Total		66	100.0
Religion	Muslim	52	78.8
	Non-Muslim	14	21.2
Total		66	100.0
Nationality	Kuwaiti	41	61.5
	Non-Kuwaiti	25	38.5
Total		66	100.0
Age	Under 20	0	0.0
	20–39	34	51.5
	40–59	29	43.9
	60+	3	4.5
	Total	66	100.0

The sample consists of 21.2 per cent non-Muslims (mainly Christians, Hindus and Atheists), 78.8 per cent Muslims, 38.5 per cent non-Kuwaitis (mainly British, Australians, Indians, Pakistanis, Syrians, Lebanese, Jordanians and Palestinians) and 61.5 per cent Kuwaitis. It is worth noting that all the Kuwaitis are Muslims and they represent 78.8 per cent of the total Muslims. The rest of the 21.2 per cent Muslims are non-Kuwaiti but they use the banks for personal and business purposes (see Table 8.1).

It was found that 14.8 per cent of individuals own businesses; of the 85.2 per cent who do not own businesses, 63.9 per cent are Muslims and 21.3 per cent are non-Muslims. Some 30.8 per cent have borrowed money recently for personal purposes or purchasing real estate, and 24.2 per cent of individuals have borrowed from Islamic banks previously, of whom 21.2 per cent were Kuwaitis and 1.5 per cent were non-Kuwaiti Muslims; 75.8 per cent have never borrowed from an Islamic bank, suggesting a large proportion of untapped potential for Islamic banks. In the sample, 53 per cent have previously borrowed from non-Islamic banks, of which 45.4 per cent were Muslims and 7.6 per cent non-Muslims. Since Muslims are dominant in the sample, representing 78.8 per cent, it would therefore be unreliable to compare in relative terms. However, of the 14 non-Muslims, only 7.1 per cent have borrowed from Islamic banks whereas 35.7 per cent have borrowed from non-Islamic banks. Moreover, of the 52 Muslims, 28.8 per cent have borrowed from Islamic banks and 57.7 per cent have borrowed from non-Islamic banks. Therefore the borrowing rate from Islamic banks is lower for both groups. However, lower participation of non-Muslims can be explained by the nature of their employment and the legal constraints involved in setting up a business.

Figure 8.1 suggests that Muslims form the core customer base for Islamic banks and there is a significant potential market for Islamic banks in Kuwait. The survey yielded the result that 22 per cent would prefer Islamic banks as a source of finance as opposed to other sources of borrowing (e.g., from family, friends or conventional banks), and 14.7 per cent indicated they would prefer borrowing from conventional banks to Islamic banks. This indicates that there is fairly high competition between Islamic and conventional banks in the Kuwaiti market. In total, 20.6 per cent of individuals never borrow money, and 13.2 per cent think that the source of money is irrelevant. The latter category of individuals represent the segment of disloyal customers who have a tendency for 'switching' between different sources of finance.

There is a contradiction in the views of respondents as 46.2 per cent would prefer to use an Islamic bank and 53.8 per cent showed a preference for a pre-determined interest rate. Furthermore, if a non-Islamic bank were to offer loans based on Islamic principles, 41.4 per cent of individuals would use it, suggesting the provider is not important but the principle is. At the same time, 60 per cent agree that if the number of Islamic banks were to

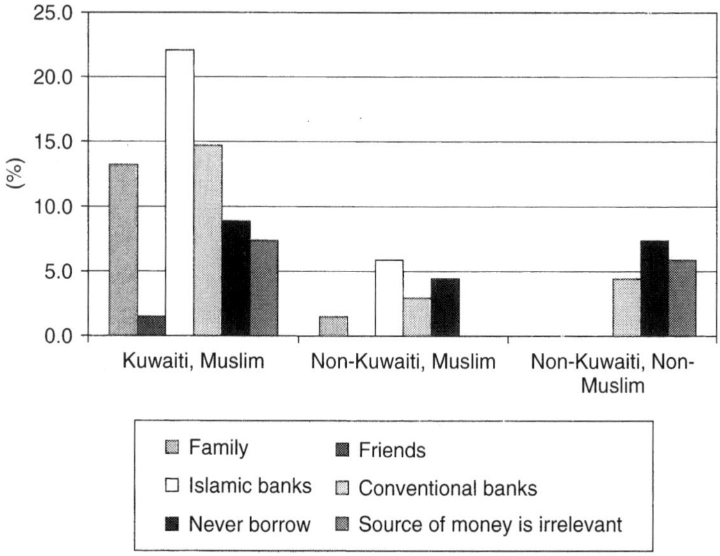

Figure 8.1 Sources from which individuals would borrow to buy substantial assets

increase in Kuwait, more people would utilize the service of Islamic banks. This would have implications for conventional banks offering interest-bearing products.

Results show that Islamic banking does not necessarily offer a better service than non-Islamic banks, and it is not necessarily easier to obtain a loan from an Islamic bank relative to a conventional bank. At least in this case the opinion of consumers coincides with those of industrialists. Furthermore, there are diverse opinions on whether or not Islamic banks put less pressure on loan repayments. Judging from the opinions of the industrialists and individuals, it can be deduced that the issue of banks pressurizing their clients on loan repayments, whether Islamic or non-Islamic, will differ from case to case, depending on the degree of conservatism that the bank management has and the creditworthiness of the client. Although Islamic banks may not charge interest for delayed payments, as do conventional banks, they may prosecute their clients for non-payment in other ways.

Figure 8.2 shows individuals in Kuwait are aware of Islamic banking facilities available in Kuwait and in the Gulf region, but this awareness amongst non-Muslims is limited. This suggests that neither conventional nor Islamic financiers are reaching a large segment of this untapped market. Results also show that individuals have diverse understandings about the concept of Islamic banking. Although a majority, 60.7 per cent, thought they understood Islamic banking, some were 'confused' and felt that 'Islamic

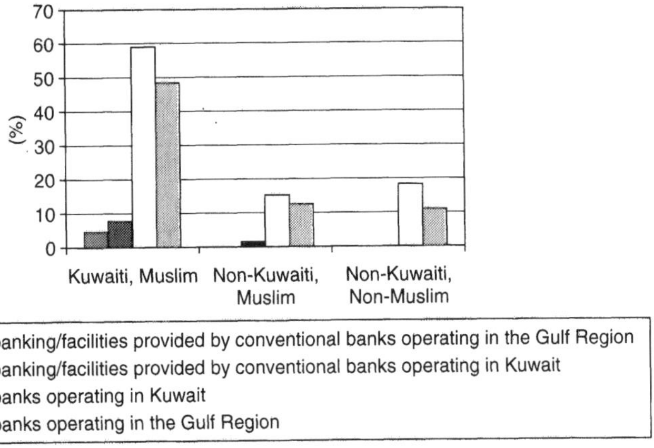

Figure 8.2 Awareness of individuals in Kuwait about Islamic banking

banking includes practical and spiritual aspects', and some described it as 'the exploitation of religious beliefs' for earning profits. A minority, 9.2 per cent, of both Muslims and non-Muslims regard Islamic banks as 'banks run by Muslims for Muslims only', which suggests there is scope for further education and informed opinion.

Although most non-Muslims do not believe in Islamic banking, they might be motivated to use Islamic finance if they were offered a facility in the form of Islamic banking that is competitive and beneficial when compared with conventional banks. However, 31 per cent of Kuwaitis do not believe in Islamic banking and, in total, 28.8 per cent of Muslims do not believe in Islamic banking either. The main motive for Muslims to use Islamic banks is religion (30 per cent), and 20 per cent cited profit as well as religion. However, 71.4 per cent of individuals (69 per cent Muslims and 2.4 per cent non-Muslims) believe that Islamic principles are important for borrowing purposes. This confirms that there is a 'core' belief in Islam amongst Kuwaitis, and the significant numbers of Muslims who do not believe in Islamic banking may be explained by a lack of confidence in the existing system that seeks 'loopholes' to overcome restrictions of *ribā*, and not a lack of belief in the Islamic banking concept itself.

Theoretical analysis of Islamic finance: cost-effectiveness

Co-financing has proved to be popular in the West and its use is rapidly growing. However, there is no empirical research that examines cost-effectiveness when Islamic finance is combined with conventional finance. The key principle of Islamic finance is to mobilize resources for productive purposes and link money with the real economy. Projects such as Equate comply with this principle. The relationship between conventional debt and equity and Islamic finance is analogous to studies of capital structure by Jean (1970), Schwartz (1959) and Modigliani and Miller (1958). In an economy where there are positive incentives for the cost of debt, it has been proved that the cost of capital falls up to a point, and then rises. A debt usually entitles a lender to a pre-specified rate of return and schedule of repayments, irrespective of the financial outcome of the investment project. Due to uncertainty regarding the financial outcome of the investment, Islamic fund providers may not receive any profit or even their initial investment.

Whilst recognizing that combining different Islamic products, (*ijārah*, *Sharī'ah* and the *muḍārabah*, etc.), and blending with conventional Islamic finance will impact differently on the WACC, it is assumed in the case of Equate that solely debt and equity will be used. Based on these assumptions, and referring to Watson and Head (2001), the WACC is calculated for different weightings of Islamic, conventional and equity finance by using the following formula:

$$WACC = \left[\left(\frac{K_e V_e}{D + V_e}\right) + \left(\frac{K_d(1 - C_t)D}{D + V_e}\right)\right] \tag{8.1}$$

where K_e and K_d are the cost of equity and debt respectively; D and V_e represent the value of equity and debt respectively, and C_t is the tax rate.

Since it has been assumed that all debts are bank borrowings, K_d can be approximated as the interest rate paid on the loan (Watson and Head, 2001). The cost of equity can be determined using the Gordon's growth model, which is usually used to value ordinary equity shares, as follows:

$$K_e = (D_0(1 + g) + g)/P_0 \tag{8.2}$$

where D_0 is dividend to be paid shortly, P_0 is the ex-dividend share price/market value and g is expected annual growth rate in dividends. The expected annual growth rate is estimated as:

$$g = [(d_n/d_0)^{1/n} - 1] \tag{8.3}$$

where n is number of years the share is held, d_n is dividends at year n and d_0 is initial dividends.

The Equate project's capital structure consists of \$1 billion debt, \$800 million in equity and \$200 million in Islamic funds (*ijārah*). Corporation tax is not enforced in Kuwait but, for closed shareholding companies, around 4 per cent of the profit is taxable; this is then given to the Kuwait Foundation

Table 8.2 Summary accounts for Equate Petrochemical Company, 1996–2001

($ millions)	*1996*	*1997*	*1998*	*1999*	*2000*	*2001*
Profit before interest and tax	(2.4)	150.6	251.3	334.2	342.1	361.3
Cash available for dividends	–	98.1	99.2	143.2	35.6	141.2

for the Advancement of Science (KFAS). Equate is a closed shareholding company with very limited information. Therefore, a number of assumptions are made for analytical purposes, acknowledging the fact that hypothetical figures may not necessarily hold when compared with the actual data.

Table 8.2 gives summary accounts for Equate. The estimates are based on the Boubiyan Petrochemical Company Offering Memorandum (24 April 1995 to 7 May 1995) and Equistar Chemicals (North America's largest producer of ethylene and polyethylene), LP (Equistar Funding Corporation) Form S-4, filed 16/4/99.

Equate uses the $200 million *ijārah* facility in addition to debt and equity. Whether it complies with the *Sharīʿah* law is queried as the financial leasing is not considered as a permissible mode of financing (Usmani, 2000). This study has not attempted to investigate whether Equate complied with the *Sharīʿah* law.

The deal is structured over 18 years, a period sufficient to return a profit to the lessor, after meeting the capital and interest costs (Puxty and Dodds, 1991). Typically, the *ijārah* structure is a variable-rate instrument requiring semi-annual payments (Millet, 1999). Equate's *ijārah* facility was split into two $100 million tranches, one for 8 years and the second for a further 10 years' maturity. For simplicity, the lease payments will be considered as fixed-rate annual payments. The standard *ijārah* contract sets the lease profit, based on a benchmark interest rate (e.g., six-month LIBOR) plus a fixed spread (Millet, 1999). Moreover, Millet (1999) states that bankers expected that the Equate deal would be priced at 160 to 200 Basis Points (BP) over 6-month LIBOR for conventional loans. Given that 6-month LIBOR = 6.375 per cent in December 1995, then a rate of 8.25 per cent (LIBOR + 175BP), as estimated by Millet (1999), will be assumed for both the lease profit and conventional debt rate. Hence, the Islamic financier's profit for providing a $200 million lease is $200 million × 8.25 per cent = $16.5 million, and Equate's total liability for the *ijārah* facility would be $200 million + $16.5 million = $216.5 million. The liability per tranche is $216.5 million/2 = $108.25 million.

Having assumed fixed-rate annual payments, the payments for each tranche ($108.25 million) are as follows:

Annual payment for an 8-year maturity: $108.25 million/8 years = $13.53
Annual payment for a 10-year maturity: $108.25 million/10 years = $10.825

Thus, re-writing equation (8.1), after introducing the Islamic lease financing, the equation becomes:

$$WACC = \left[\frac{(K_e E) + K_d(1 - C_t)D + K_{l1}(1 - C_t)L_1 + K_{L2}(1 - C_t)L_2}{(D + E + L_1 + L_2)}\right] \quad (8.4)$$

where L_1 is the value of lease facility for 8 year maturity, L_2 is the value of lease facility for 10 year maturity, K_{L1} the total lease payment for 8 year maturity and K_{L2} total lease payment for 10 year maturity.

The cost of equity (K_e) is estimated using equations (8.2) and (8.3), then from Table 8.2, D_0 (which equals d_n) is \$141.2 million at year 2001, assuming that all the available cash is distributed, and d_0 is \$98.1 million in 1997, as no dividends were paid in the first year of operation (1996); hence, from 1997 to 2001, $n=4$. There are insufficient data to determine P_0, since the company is not public and the share price and number of shares are unknown. However, we use the sectoral average multiple to estimate the market value of the company, roughly estimated by assuming a multiple of 7 for its income before interest and tax. Hence, from Table 8.2, profit before interest and tax is \$361.3 million for the year 2001 and, using the multiplying factor 7, the market value of the company is estimated as \$2.529 billion.

According to Esty (2000), the conventional funds required for the Equate project had maturities of approximately 8 years for international bank and 10 years for regional bank debt. Therefore, an average of 9 years' maturity will be assumed for total conventional debt. To calculate the annual interest payment, K_d, for an 8.25 per cent interest rate, and assuming that the rate is fixed with a 9-year maturity, K_d=(\$1billion × 8.25 per cent)/9years = \$9.167 million. Having established all the required information for the calculation of the WACC, then substituting it into equation (8.3):

$$g = (141.2/98.1)^{1/4} - 1 = 0.0953 = 9.53 \text{ per cent}$$

and substituting g into equation (8.2):

$$K_e = 141.2\,\frac{(1 + 0.0953)}{2529} + 0.0953 = 0.156 = 15.6 \text{ per cent}$$

The weightings for each source of financing are equity 40 per cent, debt 50 per cent and Islamic financing 10 per cent (5 per cent for each tranche). We deduct 4.5 per cent KFAS tax in accordance with Millet's projections, which gives a WACC of 11.78 per cent.

Now, consider the scenario where the Islamic finance portion increases from 10 per cent to 50 per cent of total financing. Equate would have \$1 billion in the form of *ijārah* which gives least cost, 8.25 per cent of a billion dollars, or $82.5 million, thereby creating a total liability of *ijārah* facility to be $1,082.5 million. Assuming fixed-rate annual payments once again, and assuming that the two tranches are equal, payments for each tranche are $67.65 per annum for 8 years and $54.125 million for 10 years. Now we assume that the weighting of equity is constant and the conventional debt weighting is 10 per cent, such that the effect of replacing Islamic funds with conventional funds can be tested.[2] The interest payment on conventional loans becomes K_d=($200 million × 8.25 per cent)/9years = $1.83 million. Now by holding everything else constant, WACC becomes 29.25 per cent, indicating that, by using *ijārah*, the cost of capital rises which would have an adverse impact on the company's rating and evaluation of future projects.

Simulating for various weightings of Islamic funds and conventional debt, using similar calculations, it may be observed that the change in WACC as the Islamic portion of funds increases until it fully replaces conventional debt. The WACC increases considerably from 11.78 per cent to 29.25 per cent, as shown in Figure 8.3. A constant cost of the *ijārah* facility over the two periods, 8 to 10 years, was used. The situation appears to be quite realistic as expected; hence, the costs of the *ijārah* facility will vary too. This has implications for long-term projects financed using the *ijārah* facility, and the assertion that cost of the *ijārah* facility is lower than conventional finance does raise a number of questions, particularly for Islamic countries which do not have taxation regimes that are parallel to Western countries. However, the *ijārah* facility offered by the companies, which can offset *ijārah* facility costs against taxation, will benefit (and has importance for) joint ventures.

We now examine other options that Equate might have used as Islamic funds: for instance, a *murābaḥah* facility, which is a fixed-rate financing tool

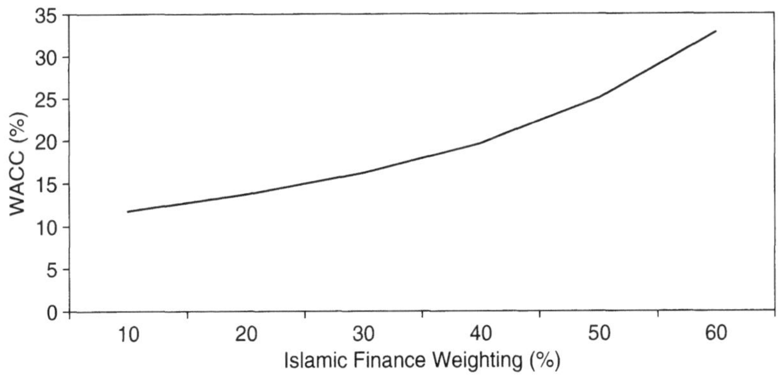

Figure 8.3 Relationship between WACC and proportion of Islamic funds (*ijārah*) in company capital

for which the cost of debt is tax-deductible, similar to *ijārah* as it has been assumed that the *ijārah* facility is also fixed-rate, and the lease profit was based on the benchmark interest rate used for conventional financing. Hence, if the mark-up price of the *murābaḥah* contract is calculated on the same basis as the lease profit of the *ijārah*, then it is logical that both financing tools will behave in a similar manner. However, it is recognized that replacing conventional debt with *murābaḥah* or *ijārah* without this assumption will impact differently on WACC. The situation changes further when the two-tier *istiṣnāʿ* is used to finance projects (Usmani, 2000); it is a temporary form of financing which involves advanced payments, an issue not considered here. Considering *muḍārabah* or *mushārakah*, however, both of which were excluded when structuring the co-financed deal, the Islamic funds become part of the equity as they are forms of partnerships. Hence increasing the portion of equity which will incorporate the Islamic fund, and simulating for various weighting, we can estimate the WACC using equation (8.1).

Using the original capital structure for Equate ($1 billion in term debt, $800 million in equity and $200 million in Islamic funds), for a *mushārakah* or *muḍārabah* facility the total equity becomes $1 billion ($800 million+$200 million). The interest payment on conventional loans, as calculated previously, is K_d=$9.167 million. If all else remains constant, the WACC is 12.2 per cent, where 50 per cent of equity consists of 40 per cent shareholders and 10 per cent Islamic funds.

Simulation results plotted in Figure 8.4 shows that, whilst holding the company's equity constant at 40 per cent, and increasing the Islamic finance portion from 10 per cent to 60 per cent (replacing conventional debt

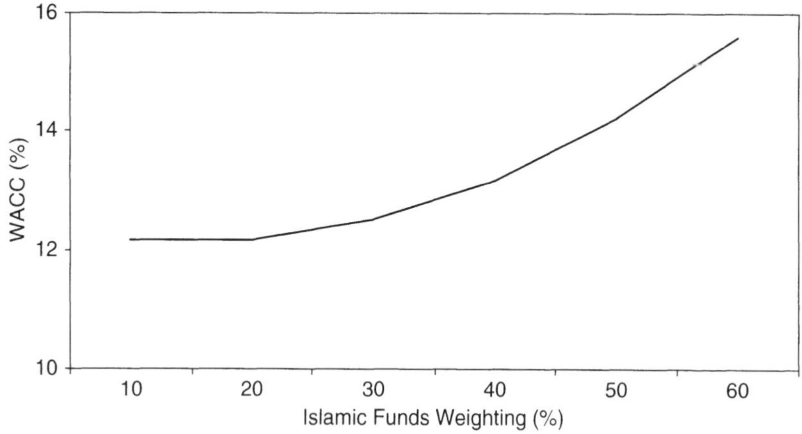

Figure 8.4 Relationship between WACC and proportion of Islamic funds (*mushārakah*/*muḍārabah*) in company capital

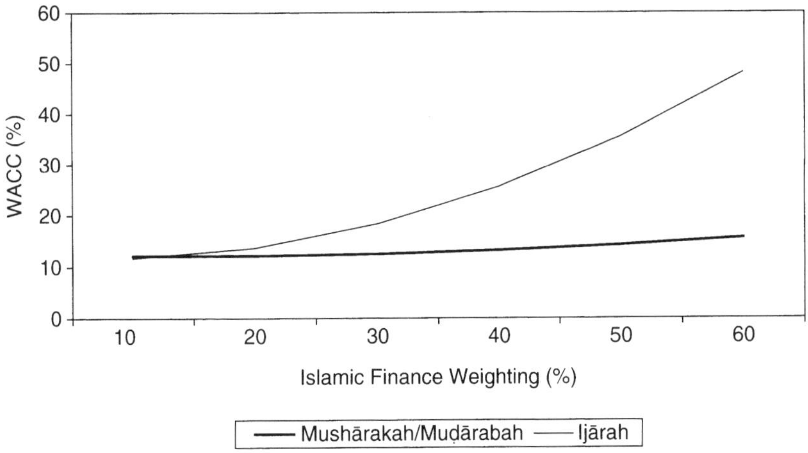

Figure 8.5 Comparison of WACC for varying proportions of *ijārah* and *mushārakah/muḍārabah* in company capital

finance fully), the WACC increases gradually as the portion of Islamic funds increases, reaching 15.6 per cent at full replacement of conventional debt (60 per cent), and the same is observed when debt is replaced with conventional lease. In comparison with the *ijārah* facility, in Figure 8.5, it is clear that the *ijārah* facility has a greater effect on the WACC of a company than *mushārakah/muḍārabah* facilities, which may be due to not using Islamic products with *ijārah*, an issue that needs further evaluation. However, in cases where larger proportions of external funds are required for project financing, *mushārakah* or *muḍārabah* would be preferable over *ijārah*, as its cost is lower and the risk of financial loss or gain is equally shared.

Since Islamic financing requires profits and losses to be shared equally between the company and financiers, the shareholders thus bear the cost of forgoing a portion of their dividends that are paid to the Islamic financiers. At the same time the shareholders' risk is reduced, as a company is not obligated to make any interest payments to the Islamic financier in the case of losses being incurred. In this case, for the Islamic financier, the uncertainty of the company generating profits creates an opportunity cost and where there exists a principal agent relation, it also incurs an agency cost (an area not fully explored in contextualizing the relationship between the provider and the users of funds).

Literature on credit rationing, asymmetric information and collateral suggests that, to account for these, interest can be charged. While Islamic financing avoids usurious interest, it might have been expected that using Islamic funds instead of conventional interest-based funds could reduce the agency cost. However, in the previous analysis, WACC rises when *ijārah* replaces conventional bank borrowings, reflecting the inability of this model to take account of qualitative factors. These preliminary findings suggest that there is a need for further investigation to explain this major deviation from the expected effects on WACC. Given the widespread dominance of conventional finance, it is important to construct an empirical study, with full access to co-financing projects' data, to examine the efficiency of such deals.

With Islamic finance, it is not possible to estimate the cost to the finance provider in advance, as profit made is shared proportionately; if profit is higher, the cost to the borrower can be much higher. Hence, with an interest-free facility, costs are not ascertained until the end of the period, which makes a comparison and evaluation of a project using a certain cost of capital much more difficult. Therefore, it is difficult to infer whether Islamic financing is more cost effective than conventional finance. However, traditional theories suggest that it would be sensible to incorporate a certain level of debt in the capital structure such that the cost of capital is optimal (Arnold, 1998), and the same is applicable to co-financing deals, irrespective of front- or back-loading of the cost of using funds. What makes Islamic finance more acceptable is its equitable share of worse outcome; and the fact that it is less onerous in seeking collateral to provide finance minimizes the chances of financial exclusion and the need for less government intervention.

In estimating WACC, a number of assumptions have been made. For example, the actual market value of the company could not be determined without sufficient information, and an *ijārah* with a variable rate rather than a fixed rate would have a varying level of impact on the value of the WACC. Furthermore, the projections used in Table 8.3 are hypothetical as Equate did not make profits in 1999, but suffered losses of $210 million due to a drop in crude oil prices, and a subsequent recession in the petrochemical market (Esty, 2000). This is likely to have affected K_e since no dividends were paid in that year.

Concluding remarks

This chapter examined the cost-effectiveness of Islamic finance and other issues related to co-financing deals with the help of the Equate case. Second, the chapter also considered the views of industrialists and finance providers, and evaluated the preferences and knowledge of the Kuwaiti population.

This research has shown that although Islamic principles are important for project financing, they are not necessarily the primary considerations for investors; profit maximization is still the dominant consideration for most investors. Though generalization might be inappropriate at this stage, this study opens the possibility of further investigation. Interest-free loans implicitly have a cost in the form of profit sharing, an end-loaded project cost (though not necessarily borne by entrepreneurs should they make losses).

With the exception of *ijārah*, both *mushārakah* and *muḍārabah* modes of finance indicate that their cost varies with the level of the project's profit. By attributing shared profit as cost, it is observed that projects with higher profits have higher costs than those which make a limited profit or loss. Hence the validity of the traditional analysis poses interesting questions, such as what cost should be used to evaluate projects? These questions have policy implications for both the providers and recipients of funds that warrant investigation to estimate cost for evaluation purposes, to negotiate financing deals, and finally to arrive at the overall cost of a finance deal in the end.

The appropriateness of co-financing for industrial project financing is a debatable issue. This study provides some insight into how co-financing, a growing area of applied finance in Islamic and Western economies, impacts on a company's cost of capital and examines the rationale for companies for using co-financing. There are other issues concerning whether co-financing deals comply with *Sharīʿah*, and to what extent the existing deals mimic conventional practices disguised in manipulated terminologies. However, evidence suggests that the rapid growth in number and size of co-financing deals worldwide creates a competitive environment in the banking industry to which both conventional and Islamic financial institutions are responding by offering Islamic financing facilities for projects.

The analysis has shown that to develop Islamic financial institutions which can deal with large deals and mass lending, there is a need to acquire expertise and experience in the structuring of co-financed deals that may involve complications, such as legal ones, and the compatibility of conventional and Islamic laws. The continuous growth of Islamic economies can be achieved by consistent efforts in innovation to create and develop efficient financing facilities or products. Evidence suggests Islamic institutions are striving to shift their focus from small-scale, less risky projects to financing long-term projects such as the Hub River Power Project in Pakistan, the Thuraya Space Telecommunications Company in the Middle East and the Equate Petrochemical plant. The pursuance of this trend will ensure maximum exploitation of the economic possibilities of Islamic finance and will satisfy the needs of less developed economies, such as Kuwait. 'International corporations that dismiss Islamic finance as a grab bag of weird practices to fund terrorists ought to think again. They are missing out on one of the world's fastest growing capital pools – and one that is beginning to be drawn into the mainstream of the global financial system' (Shepherd, 1996, p. 44).

Comment

Ridha Muhammad Saadallah

The main objective of the chapter is to evaluate the cost-effectiveness of Islamic finance when combined with conventional finance. The analysis is primarily based on a case study of a $2 billion petrochemical project in the state of Kuwait, which was co-financed by Islamic and conventional financial institutions. The project was financed using equity, interest-bearing long-term loans and *ijārah*, the Islamic counterpart of leasing.[3] The method of analysis consists in appraising the effect of introducing Islamic finance, specifically *ijārah* and *mushārakah*, on the WACC of the financed project. The main conclusion of the chapter is negative in nature: an 'interest-free banking system does not necessarily reduce the weighted average cost of capital of a project'. Put in other words, it means that empirical results failed to corroborate the perceived benefit of combining Islamic finance with conventional finance.

The present comments will focus on the discussion of the validity of such a conclusion.

Co-financing: rationale and lawfulness

Is there a need for co-financing? The chapter addresses this issue both theoretically and empirically, using a questionnaire directed to the Equate Petrochemical Company, to a random sample of 15 other industrial companies in Kuwait, to another sample of 100 individuals living in Kuwait and to a conventional financial institution, the Industrial Bank of Kuwait.

On the question of theory, it is first suggested that a heterogeneous banking environment, where Islamic finance co-exists with conventional finance, will probably lead to the co-financing of projects. It is then argued that co-existence is useful and could generate more competition and thus bring about more efficient allocation of resources. It is even suggested that a heterogeneous banking environment is a necessary condition for the survival of Islamic banking in the long run. A further argument in favour of co-financing is added in the particular case of *mushārakah* financing. It may be summarized as follows: as *mushārakah* is rather risky proposition, a substantial contribution from a conventional financier, in the form of a long-term loan, would act as a sign of the creditworthiness of the project and would, therefore, constitute an incentive to the Islamic financier to enter into a co-financed deal through *mushārakah*.

What are we to think of these arguments? Admittedly, the co-existence of the two financial systems in the same country or region may facilitate the structuring of co-financed deals. However, it is neither a sufficient condition for co-financing nor a necessary condition for the survival of the Islamic financial system. A priori, the two systems may co-exist and yet function independently of each other. The supposedly positive effect on competitiveness and efficiency is related to the distribution of market power in the banking industry rather than to its heterogeneous nature: a fully and exclusively Islamic banking industry may theoretically reach a high level of competitiveness if it is formed of a large number of Islamic financial institutions, each having a moderate market share. The argument conditioning the survival of the Islamic financial system on the heterogeneity of the industry is rather unsubstantiated and, more importantly, seems to contradict the Islamic faith: being prohibited, *ribā* could not be a necessary and long-lasting component of an Islamic financial system. Co-existence may be accommodated as a transitory arrangement but, ultimately, an Islamic system completely purified from *ribā* should be able to survive on its own.

On an empirical basis, the chapter provides useful first-hand information on the attitudes of industrialists, bankers and individuals regarding the use of either Islamic or conventional financial tools, as well as on the motives for combining the two, when applicable. The information collected shows the following.

There is a demand for both types of finance. Half of the industrial firms have used Islamic finance and another one-sixth of them would consider doing so. However, one-third of them have relied only on conventional finance and declared that they would continue to do so. The same heterogeneous attitudes are also observed in case of individuals, even among Muslims: 22 per cent of the Kuwaiti respondents show a preference for Islamic banks as a source of finance, while less than 15 per cent indicate that they prefer conventional borrowing. The source of financing is said to be irrelevant for around 13 per cent of the respondents.

There is some evidence in favour of co-financing industrial projects. Islamic finance, whenever used by industrialists, was supplemented by conventional finance. Moreover, the former did not exceed 20 per cent of the total funds.

Religious belief may be an important factor in decision making regarding the sources of funds, but it is not the only one. Cost-effectiveness is also an important and, in some cases (as in the case of the Equate project), the most influential factor.

The reported attitudes show that there is a de facto case for co-financing industrial projects between Islamic and conventional banks. However, it remains to be checked whether a combination of the two sources of finance is acceptable from the *Sharī'ah* point of view or not.

Is co-financing lawful? In the case of PLS, an objection to co-financing may be raised: the Islamic financier would share in an impure income, on the one hand, and he may be considered, on the other hand, to be indulging in *ribā* transactions as a partner. This question is much debated among Islamic jurists and no definite conclusion has been reached yet. The OIC *Fiqh* Academy has discussed the issue in a number of seminars and in its seventh and eighth annual sessions. It agreed to postpone the decision until further in-depth studies have been conducted.

If an Islamic bank enters into a co-financed transaction, using sale-based modes, such as *murābaḥah*, instalment sales or *ijārah*,[4] it will receive payments which have nothing to do with the interest paid by the investor to the conventional co-financier. Moreover, it will not share in the ownership of the project and so will not bear any responsibility in the management's decisions to indulge in interest-bearing transactions. Therefore, co-financing appears to be lawful in this case.

Some methodological considerations

The method used in the chapter to assess the cost-effectiveness of Islamic finance consists of evaluating the effect of replacing conventional debt with an Islamic mode of financing on the WACC. This is defined as the sum of the costs of the various sources of financing used in the project, weighted by their respective shares in the total cost of the project.

The chapter starts with calculating the WACC of the Equate project, using the actual shares of the different sources of financing: 40 per cent equity, 50 per cent interest-bearing long-term debt and 10 per cent *ijārah*. Then, it examines the behaviour of the WACC following a gradual replacement of conventional debt with *ijārah* or by PLS modes (*mushārakah* or *muḍārabah*). From there, a general conclusion is drawn. Introducing Islamic finance, whatever mode is used, would result in an increase of the weighted average cost of capital of the project (any project). This method calls for a number of observations.

The conclusion is a generalization from the empirical results obtained in a special case, the Equate case. A priori, nothing guarantees that the results are not specific to the selected case, and that a similar exercise undertaken for another project would not lead to a different conclusion. An alternative method may be more appropriate to establish analytically the effect on the WACC of introducing Islamic finance and of using the Equate case as an illustration.

The conclusion concerns Islamic finance in general, while the calculations which led to it were based only on the use of *ijārah* or *mushārakah/muḍārabah*. Two other modes, *murābaḥah* and *istiṣnāʿ*, were also considered, but ultimately discarded. In the case of *murābaḥah*, it is argued that 'if the mark-up price of the *murābaḥah* contract is calculated on the same basis as the lease profit of the *ijārah*, then it is logical that both financing tools will behave in a similar manner'. However, it is not clear why this is logical. Indeed, if it is accepted that *ijārah* and *murābaḥah* are the Islamic counterparts of leasing and loan respectively, and recalling that the WACC varies when leasing replaces loans or vice versa, one should expect the WACC to behave differently, according to whether conventional debt is replaced with *ijārah* or with *murābaḥah*. As for *istiṣnāʿ*, it was not considered a suitable tool for project finance, as 'it is a temporary form of financing which involves advanced payments'. However, *istiṣnāʿ*, or more precisely two-tier *istiṣnāʿ*, may well be used to finance projects on the lines explained below. The investor orders the bank 'to manufacture' the required equipment, with the payment being deferred to any agreed-upon date or dates. The bank, in its turn, orders a manufacturer to manufacture the same, with payment possibly made in advance or at the time of delivery.[5]

The effect on the WACC of introducing an Islamic finance tool such as *ijārah* is calculated on the basis of substituting it for a conventional loan. But one would rightly think that if the loan is replaced with a conventional lease, the WACC would also change. So it is not justifiable to attribute the calculated change in the WACC only to the Islamic financial tool. A more accurate method of evaluation of the effect of Islamic finance would be to introduce an Islamic financial tool in lieu of a conventional one of the same category: *ijārah* in lieu of leasing, PLS modes in lieu of equity or deferred payment sales (e.g., *murābaḥah* or two-tier *istiṣnāʿ*) in lieu of loans.

In addition to the above-mentioned methodological remarks, the empirical conclusions reached in the particular case of Equate are unlikely: interchanging the weights of *ijārah* and conventional debt (10 per cent and 50 per cent) results in almost a three-fold increase in the WACC. This result is a priori surprising, if it is also recalled that the tax rate on profits is very low (4.5 per cent) and that the *ijārah* profit is based on a benchmark rate which is equal to the interest rate on the loan. Therefore, we will try to scrutinize in what follows the calculations on which was based the central conclusion of the chapter.

The capital structure of the Equate project is as follows: 50 per cent nine-year maturity debt, 40 per cent equity and 10 per cent *ijārah*, divided into two tranches of equal amounts and at eight and ten-year maturity, respectively. Denoting k_d, k_e and k_l, the after-tax cost of the three components of capital respectively, the weighted average cost of capital of the Equate project may be written as:

$$\text{WACC} = 0.5\ k_d + 0.4\ k_e + 0.1\ k_l$$

Cost of equity. The cost of equity is determined using the Gordon model, which assumes a constant growth rate of dividends over a very long period of time (theoretically infinite):

$$k_e = D_1/P_0 + g \qquad (8.5)$$

where P_0 is the intrinsic value of the firm at time 0, D_1 is the cash dividend expected to be paid in period 1, starting at time 0, and g is the constant future growth rate of dividends.

The applicability of the Gordon model requires first that k_e is greater than g and, more fundamentally, that the firm is not in its pioneering phase, so that dividends may be expected to be reasonably stable. It is clear that the last condition is not satisfied in the Equate case. Furthermore, the estimation of the growth rate on the basis of expected dividends for only four years is quite inaccurate, as it is very sensitive to any change in the figures. In fact, the study reports that the expected profits of $334 million turned out to be an actual loss of $210 million. The unavailability of the relevant data to estimate the cost of equity more accurately may, however, justify the method used, in spite of its shortcomings. Taking 1997 as the starting period, the application of the method gives a cost of equity equal to 19.72 per cent.

Cost of ijārah. When using *ijārah*, all lease payments are tax-deductible,[6] while only interest payments are deducted when a loan is used. But the use of *ijārah* implies that the asset is not owned by the investor (the lessee) who is, therefore, not allowed to benefit from the tax deductions on depreciation. The after-tax cost of *ijārah* should reflect both the gains and losses of tax deductions.

The determinant factor of the cost of *ijārah* is the benchmark rate used by the lessor to determine his required return. One could assume that the interest rate on loans of the same maturity is naturally used as a benchmark rate. This is, in fact, the assumption made in the study. However, it could be otherwise for at least two reasons: first, being asset-backed, *ijārah* may be considered less risky than a term loan of the same maturity, and as such a lower benchmark rate would be required. Second, the lessor, as owner of the asset, may benefit from investment tax credit and depreciation tax deductions. He may be willing, under some circumstances, to pass on part of these benefits to the lessee in the form of lower lease payments.

Having no information on the benchmark rate actually used by the lessor, Kuwait Finance House, the assumption used in the chapter may be retained and assumed a fixed benchmark rate of 8.25 per cent per year may be presumed. It may fully assume straight-line depreciation and constant annual lease payments.

The annual lease payments, A, are given by the following equation:

$$(1+r)^T * L - a \sum_{t=0}^{t=T-1} (1+r)^t = 0 \Leftrightarrow A = \frac{L}{\frac{1-1+r^{-T}}{r}} = \frac{L}{PVa(T,r)} \qquad (8.6)$$

where L is the amount of the lease (here $100 million for each tranche); T is the maturity of the lease (8 years for the first tranche and 10 years for the second); r is the benchmark rate (8.25 per cent); and $PVa(T, r)$ is the present value of $1.00 received per year for the next T years, discounted at r per cent. Using the above equation, we found that the annual lease payments amounted to \$17.567 million for the first tranche and to \$15.071 million for the second tranche.

With τ denoting the tax rate, equal in the present case to 4.5 per cent, the cost of each tranche is given by the following equation:

$$\sum_{t=1}^{t=T} \frac{(1-\tau)A+\tau * \frac{L}{T}}{(1+k_1)^t} = L \quad \Leftrightarrow$$

$$\left[(1-\tau).A+\tau.\frac{L}{T}\right] * \left(\sum_{t=1}^{t=T} \frac{1}{(1+k_l)^t}\right) = L \quad \Leftrightarrow$$

$$\frac{1-(1+k_l)^{-T}}{k_l} = \frac{L}{(1-\tau)\left(.A+\tau.\frac{L}{T}\right)} \quad \Leftrightarrow$$

$$PVa(T,k_1) = \frac{L}{(1-\tau).A+\tau.\frac{L}{T}} \tag{8.7}$$

Using data corresponding to the first tranche of *ijārah*, equation (8.7) may be rewritten as follows:

$$PVa(8,k_1) = \frac{100}{(1-0.045)*17.567+0.045.\frac{100}{8}} = 5.767 \tag{8.8}$$

The resolution of equation (8.8), using the trial-and-error method, provides the cost of capital for the first tranche *ijārah*, which is equal to 7.90 per cent.

Similarly, applying data corresponding to the second tranche of *ijārah* to equation (8.7) gives the following specification:

$$PVa(10,k_1) = \frac{100}{(1-0.045)*15.071+0.045.\frac{100}{10}} = 6.737 \tag{8.9}$$

Equation (8.9) is also resolved using the trial-and-error method. The corresponding cost of capital is found to be equal to 7.91 per cent. The weighted average cost of capital is shown by:

$$\text{WACC} = 19072\% * 0.4 + 7.88\% * 0.5 + 7.90\% * 0.05 + 7.91\% * 0.05 = 12.62\%$$

The effect on Equate's WACC of substituting ijārah *for conventional debt.* It is clear from the previous calculations that there is a very slight difference between the cost of capital through *ijārah* and through conventional debt. This result is not surprising; for, on the one hand, the benchmark used to determine the lease profit was assumed to be the same as the interest rate applied to conventional debt; and, on the other hand, the tax rate is very low.

Under these conditions, a substitution of *ijārah* for debt is not expected to modify significantly the weighted average cost of capital. Indeed, it is found that, when the WACC is expressed with two digits after the decimal point, it remains unchanged following an increase of the share of *ijārah* up to 30 per cent (and a decrease of conventional debt down to 30 per cent). The WACC increases by only 0.01 per cent (to 12.63 per cent) when the share of *ijārah* ranges between 40 per cent and 60 per cent (the latter corresponds to a full replacement of conventional debt by *ijārah*).

The effect of replacing ijārah *and/or debt by* mushārakah. If we admit the assumption of the chapter (i.e., the cost of *mushārakah* is the same as the cost of equity), then the introduction of *mushārakah* would obviously result in a significant increase of the weighted average cost of capital of the project. This is understandable, recalling that *mushārakah* is much more risky than either *ijārah* or loans.

Concluding remarks

The discussion above shows that the Equate case does not provide empirical support for the main conclusion of the chapter regarding the negative impact of Islamic finance on the firm's cost of capital. Furthermore, the calculated effect of substituting *ijārah* for conventional debt will equally be observed if the latter is replaced by conventional lease.

In order to avoid mixing up the effects of introducing financial tools of different types (e.g., debt versus equity or leasing) with the effects of using financial tools of different nature (i.e., Islamic versus conventional), one should start by selecting a certain category of financial tool. Next, one should compare the cost of capital corresponding to the use of the Islamic and the conventional versions of that financial tool. The above discussion shows that, in this case, the WACC will not be affected, unless the benchmark rate used to determine the required rate of return on the Islamic version of the tool differs from the rate applied to the conventional version. Research aimed at assessing the effect of introducing Islamic finance on the firm's cost of capital should, therefore, focus on the factors which would explain why the benchmark rate used to find out the required rate of capital on an Islamic financial tool may differ from the rate applied to its conventional counterpart.

Notes

1. Note that the frequency of response is not necessarily equal to the sample size ($N=66$) since some individuals may not have answered a particular question or may have given more than one answer.
2. It is accepted that Islamic financial products, used instead of conventional loans would provide different results.
3. *Ijārah* is not equivalent to the well known financial leasing. Among its distinctive features, we may note the following: (i) all the liabilities emerging from the ownership of the lease asset are to be borne by the lessor; (ii) The lease period commences only on the delivery of the asset to the lessee; and (iii) rentals are no longer due if and when the asset loses the function for which it is leased. For more details, see Usmani (2000).
4. *Ijārah* is a sale of the usufruct of an asset.
5. See Usmani (2000), pp. 198–200.
6. Tax-deductibility depends, in fact, on the fiscal system of each country: for instance, in the USA lease payments are fully deductible only for true leases.

References

Abdul-Gafoor, A. (1995), 'Interest-free Commercial Banking', http://users.bart.nl/~abdul/chap4.html

Ahmad, K. (1992), *Towards Interest-free Banking*, New Delhi: International Islamic.

Ariff, M. (1988), 'Islamic Banking', *Asian Pacific Economic Literature*, 2 (2), 46–62.

Arnold, G. (1998), *Corporate Financial Management*, London: Financial Times Professional.

Bokhari, F. (2000), 'Islamic Banking and Finance', *Financial Times Survey*, 26 October, p. 4.

Brada, J. C. and I. Singh (1999), *Corporate Governance in Central Eastern Europe: Case Studies of Firms in Transition*, London: Sharpe.

Dar, H. and Presley, J. (1999), 'Islamic Finance: A Western Perspective', *International Journal of Islamic Financial Services*, 1 (1), 1–5.

Deakins, D. and Hussain, J. G. (1993), 'Risk Assessment with Asymmetric Information: Case Study of Lending Decisions by Bank Officers', United Kingdom Enterprise Management and Research Association 16th (*UKEMRA*), National Small Firms Policy and Research Conference, 24–25 November.

Deehani T. al-, Rifaat A. A. Karim and V. Murinde (1999), 'The Capital Structure of Islamic Banks under the Contractual Obligation of Profit Sharing', *International Journal of Theoretical and Applied Finance*, 2 (3), 1–39.

Drummond, J. (2000), 'Islamic Banking and Finance', *Financial Times Survey*, 26 October, p. 4.

Duncan, R. S. (2003), 'Securitisation and the Development of an Islamic Secondary Market', *The 2nd Annual Islamic Finance Summit*, 2003, Kuala Lumpur, Malaysia.

Ebrahim, M. (1999), 'Integrating Islamic and Conventional Project Finance', *Thunderbird International Business Review*, 41 (4/5), 583–609.

Esty, B. (2000), 'The Equate Project: An Introduction to Islamic Project Finance', *Journal of Project Finance* (Winter), 5 (4), 7–20.

Fernandez, P. (1997), 'Project Finance under International Islamic Capital Market', *The Journal of Contemporary Issues in Business and Government*, 3 (1), 54–62.

Fisher, I. (1930), *Theory of Interest*, New York: Macmillan.

Friedman, M. (1970), 'The Social Responsibility of Business is to Increase its Profits', *New York Magazine*, 30 September.

Gamal, M. El- (1997), *Can Islamic Banking Survive? A Micro-evolutionary Perspective*, Madison, Wisconsin: University of Wisconsin.

Ghalayini, B. (1995), 'The Growth of Leasing in Islamic Finance', *Arab Banker*, 11 (2), 22.
Green, R. (1993), *The Ethical Manager – A New Method For Business Ethics*, London: Macmillan.
Hoffman, W. and R. Frederick (1995), *Business Ethics – Readings and Cases in Corporate Morality*, London: McGraw-Hill.
Hussey, J. and R. Hussey (1997), *Business Research – A Practical Guide for Undergraduate and Postgraduate Students*, New York: Palgrave.
Hutton, J. and T. Kenc (1998), 'Tax Policy and Financial Structure', *Working Papers*, I. 28, Institute of Financial Research (IFS), Birkbeck College, London.
Iqbal, Z. (1997a), 'Equity and Ethics', *The Banker*, February, pp. 64–6.
Iqbal, Z. (1997b), 'Islamic Financial Systems', *Finance and Development*, 34 (2), 42–5.
Jean, W. H. (1970), *The Analytical Theory of Finance*, New York: Holt, Reinehart & Winston.
Keynes, J. M. (1931), *The Treatise of Money*, vol. 2, London: Macmillan.
Keynes, J. M. (1936), *The General Theory of Employment and Money*, London: Macmillan.
Khalil, A. and C. Rickwood (1999), 'Identifying Agency Problems in *Muḍārabah* Contracts: An Empirical Study', *Middle East Business Review*, 3 (2), 85–105.
Khatib, M. M. (1986), *The Bounteous* Qur'ān (Translation of Holy Qur'ān), London: Macmillan.
King, M. A. (1974), 'Taxation and the Cost of Capital', *Review of Economic Studies*, 41, 21–35.
King, M. A. (1977), *Public Policy and the Corporation*, London: Chapman & Hall.
Laliwala, J. (1994), *Theories of Interest, Money and Banking – Secular and Islamic*, Gujarat, India: Ismail Rajab Institute of Research in Economics and Policy-Making.
La Porta, R., F. Lopez-de-Silanes and A. Schleifer (1999), 'Corporate Ownership Around the World', *Journal of Finance*, 54 (2), 417–517.
Martin, Josh (1997), 'Islamic Banking Raises Interest', *Management Review: The American Management Association Magazine* (November), 86 (10), 25–30.
Meenai, S. A. (1989), *The Islamic Development Bank: A Case Study of Islamic Co-operation*, London and New York: Kegan Paul International, distributed by Routledge, Chapman & Hall, New York.
Miller, M. H. (1977), 'Debt and Taxes', *Journal of Finance*, 32, 261–75.
Millet, M. (1999), *The International Investor: Islamic Finance and the Equate Project*, Boston, MA: Harvard Business School.
Modigliani, F. (1988), 'MM – Past, Present, Future', *Journal of Economic Perspectives* 2, 149–58.
Modigliani, F. and M. H. Miller (1958), 'The Cost of Capital, Corporation Finance and the Theory of Investment', *American Economic Review*, 48, 261–96.
Modigliani. F. and M. H. Miller (1963), 'Taxes and the Cost of Capital: A Correction', *American Economic Review*, 53, 433–43.
Moore, P. (1997), *Islamic Finance – A Partnership for Growth*, London: Euromoney.
Murinde, V., K. Naser and R. S. O. Wallace (1995), 'Is it Prudent for Islamic Banks to Make Investment Decisions without the Interest Rate Instrument?', *Research in Accounting in Emerging Economies*, 3, 123–48.
Myers, C. (1986), 'Corporation Tax: Finance and the Cost of Capital', *Review of Economic Studies*, 53, 93–112.
Myers, S. C. (2001), 'Capital Structure', *Journal of Economic Perspectives*, 15 (2), 81–102.
Omar, Fuad al- and M. Abdel-Haq (1996), *Islamic Banking: Theory, Practice and Challenges*, Karachi: Oxford University Press.
Parker, M. (1995), 'Islamic Finance', *Arab Banker*, 11 (2), 23–4.
Pearson, G. (1995), *Integrity in Organizations – An Alternative Business Ethic*, London: McGraw-Hill.

Prasad, S., J. C. Green and V. Murinde (2001), 'Company Financing Structure, and Ownership: A Survey and Implications for Developing Economies', *Economic Research paper No. 01/3*, Loughborough: Loughborough University.

Presley, J. (1988), *Directory of Islamic Financial Institutions*, London: Croom Helm.

Puxty, A. and J. Dodds (1991), *Financial Management – Method and Meaning*, London: Chapman & Hall.

Razavi, H. (1996), 'Financing Oil and Gas Projects in Developing Countries', *Finance and Development*, 2–5 June.

Sadowski, Y. (1996), 'Just a Religion: For the Tablighi Jamā'at, Islam is not totalitarian', *The Brookings Review*, 14 (3), 34–5.

Schwartz, E. (1959), 'The Theory of Capital Structure of the Firm', *The Journal of Finance*, 14 (1), 18–39.

Shepherd, J. R. W. (1996), 'Integrating Islamic and Western Finance', *Global Finance*, May, 44–50.

Shirazi, H. (1990), *Islamic Banking*, London: Butterworths.

Siddiqi, M. N. (1983), *Banking without Interest*. Leicester: The Islamic Foundation.

Siddiqi, M. N. (1991), 'Some Economic Aspects of *Muḍārabah*', *Review of Islamic Economics*, 1 (2), 21–33.

UNDP (1998), *UNDP Human Development Report*, Washington, DC: UNDP.

Usmani, M. T. (2000), *An Introduction to Islamic Finance*, Karachi: Idaratul Maarif.

Van Maanen, J. (1983), *Qualitative Methodology*, London: Sage.

Warde, I. (2000), *Islamic Finance in the Global Economy*, Edinburgh: Edinburgh University Press.

Warde, I (2001), 'The Prophet and the Profits: Islamic Finance', *Le Monde diplomatique*, <http://mondediplo.com/2001/09/09> accessed 14 January 2003.

Watson, D. and A. Head (2001), *Corporate Finance – Principles and Practice*, London: Pearson Education.

Yasseri, A. (1998), 'Recent Global Trends in Islamic Banking', *Iran Today Economic Magazine*, 20, 50–3.

9

The Role of Islamic Banks in Economic Growth: The Case of Jordan

Said Al-Hallaq

This chapter investigates the practice of the Jordan Islamic Bank (JIB) as a case study during the period 1980–2000. The Two Stage Ordinary Least Square method has been used to capture the direct and indirect effects of the JIB on the real per capita income as a proxy for the rate of economic growth. The indirect effect of total financing and investment by the JIB as a percentage of total credit was relatively small (0.048) compared to that by conventional banks (0.50). However, this contribution made by a single Islamic bank should be looked at as a good start given the fact that the Islamic banking experience is only 20 years old compared to conventional banks.

Introduction

The history of Islamic financial institutions in Jordan is not very long. The Jordan Islamic Bank for Finance and Investment was established in 1979 with a capital of JD4 million divided into 4 million shares. The Bank's capital increased over the years to reach JD38.5 million by 2000. The Bank aims to accommodate the diversified economic and social needs of citizens in the fields of banking, financing and investment on a non-usurious basis. This is realized through the Bank's 51 branches and 11 offices, spread all over Jordan. The Bank has been growing rapidly. The number of clients as well as the volume of mobilized and invested funds reflect this rapid growth. The Bank's success led the Arab Bank Corporation (the largest financial institution in Jordan) to establish the International Arab Islamic Bank in 1996 to conduct *murābaḥah* transactions, leasing and other investment instruments according to Islamic principles.

The entrance of the International Arab Islamic Bank into Islamic banking industry is expected to increase competition between the two Islamic banks in Jordan and reduce the monopolistic position of the Jordan Islamic Bank, which had previously been the only Islamic bank in the country. It is expected that the performance of the Jordan Islamic Bank will tend to improve due to the presence of a new competitor. However, we must keep in mind that the Jordan Islamic Bank is facing some obstacles, as outlined below (Omar al- and AbdelhHaq, 1996):

1 JIB has the disadvantage of not being able to use the Jordan Central Bank as a lender of last resort, which confines most of its financing to the short or medium term, and forces it to hold high levels of liquidity in the form of cash to deal with unforeseen emergencies.
2 It lacks a variety of financial instruments, such as bonds. If the JIB could hold listed securities issued by high-quality corporations, the need to hold cash could be minimized.
3 The JIB has found itself forced to take a tougher line on guarantees when it agrees to finance any project. The reason for this is that, in the past, some clients have tried to take advantage of the fact that the JIB is not able to charge interest on late payments of bills as conventional banks do. It is generally held in Islamic banking circles that there is no penalty for late payment under Islamic law.

Thus, when comparing the impact of the JIB on the economic growth of Jordan relative to the conventional banks, one should not be surprised if the impact of the JIB is found to be minimal.

The importance of this study lies in the fact that there is a serious lack of empirical studies on the evaluation of the performance of Islamic banks compared with that of the conventional banks. In this regard a study carried out by Iqbal (2001) stands alone. The study by Iqbal was based on a sample of 12 Islamic banks and 12 conventional commercial banks. It showed that, in general, Islamic banks have done fairly well during the period 1990–98. The present study is an attempt to extend the empirical research work on Islamic banking.

Data and methodology

The present study makes an attempt to examine the role of the Jordan Islamic Bank in economic growth during the period 1980–2000. The required statistical data have been collected from the annual reports of the Jordan Islamic Bank, and the annual reports and quarterly statistical bulletins of the Central Bank of Jordan. The suggested model is a simultaneous macroeconometric one consisting of two behavioural equations, which will be estimated using the Two Stage Ordinary Least Squares method (2SLS).

Development of the Jordan Islamic Bank

Before examining how the JIB could contribute to the economic growth of the Jordanian economy through its financing and investment, it is worth having an overview of the development of the JIB itself during the period under consideration (see Table 9.1).

Table 9.1 Development of the Jordan Islamic Bank, 1980–2000

Financial year	*Total assets (millions JD)*	*Total deposits (millions JD)*	*Total financing and investment by JIB (millions JD)*	*Total financing by conventional banks (millions JD)*	*Growth rates of total assets (%)*	*Growth rates of total deposits (%)*	*Growth rates of total financing and investment by JIB (%)*
1980	15.5	11.6	6.8	563.9	–	–	–
1981	31.6	25.3	14.2	721 .3	103.8	118.1	108.8
1982	45.2	35.8	26.5	887.2	43.0	41.5	86.6
1983	71.5	58.6	37.6	1,030.9	58.2	63.7	41.9
1984	102.0	82.8	63.0	1,184.8	42.7	41.3	67.6
1985	126.8	102.8	71.0	1,274.4	24.3	24.2	12.7
1986	161.7	127.6	95.5	1,395.4	27.5	24.1	34.5
1987	197.4	158.5	109.0	1,513.0	22.1	24.2	14.1
1988	222.6	177.8	124.1	1,634.0	12.8	12.2	13.9
1989	242.3	187.2	144.1	1,729.2	9.0	5.3	16.1
1990	244.8	190.3	148.9	1,863.5	1.0	1.7	3.3
1991	356.7	296.9	193.1	1,965.8	45.7	56.0	29.7
1992	435.3	369.5	243.1	2,218.3	22.0	24.4	25.9
1993	528.3	420.6	306.7	2,616.9	21.4	13.8	26.2
1994	570.0	462.1	356.1	3,248.4	7.9	9.9	16.1
1995	621.9	508.5	418.2	3,705.7	9.1	10.0	17.4
1996	618.7	502.3	422.1	3,920.3	–0.5	–1.2	0.9
1997	650.6	513.4	461.8	3,979.7	5.2	2.2	9.4
1998	706.7	527.8	481.4	4,285.3	8.6	2.8	4.2
1999	756.7	543.6	490.2	4,466.6	7.1	3.0	1.8
2000	853.3	564.6	531.8	4,546.5	12.8	3.9	8.5

Sources: Central Bank of Jordan, Monthly Statistical Bulletin, different issues; Jordan Islamic Bank for Finance and Investment, *Annual Reports*, different issues.

Total deposits of the JIB

It may be noticed that the rate of growth of total deposits in 1981 was 118 per cent. This high rate could be explained by the fact that the establishment of the JIB reduced the amounts of savings hoarded by individuals, because many individuals preferred to keep their savings outside the banking system rather than engage in any interest-based dealings (Rawashdeh and Al-Hallaq, 1999). At the same time, those who used to deal with the conventional banks were doing so under the force of circumstances, such as the absence of an Islamic bank. Thus, once a viable Islamic alternative was available, most of these funds are believed to have moved into Islamic banks (Bashir, 1984). The rate of growth of total deposits started to decline afterwards and showed cyclical behaviour.

Iqbal (2001) attributed this decline in the growth rates of total deposits, mainly in the 1990s, to the increase in the number of conventional banks offering Islamic products. The Arab Bank Corporation, for example, which is the biggest financial institution in Jordan, started to offer Islamic products and became a real competitor to the JIB.

Total financing and investment of the JIB

The rates of growth in total investment are highly dependent on the amount of total deposits. In 1981, for example, the rate of growth reached its maximum at 108 per cent (see Figure 9.1). This could be explained by the same reasons as previously mentioned. The JIB attracted savings which were not deposited in conventional banks for religious reasons. In the same way, this rate came down to only 3.4 per cent in 1990, as did total deposits. This low rate could be explained as a direct result of the second Gulf War, which negatively affected the entire region. However, this rate started to fluctuate after 1996 due to the establishment of the Arab Bank Corporation as a real competitor in providing Islamic products.

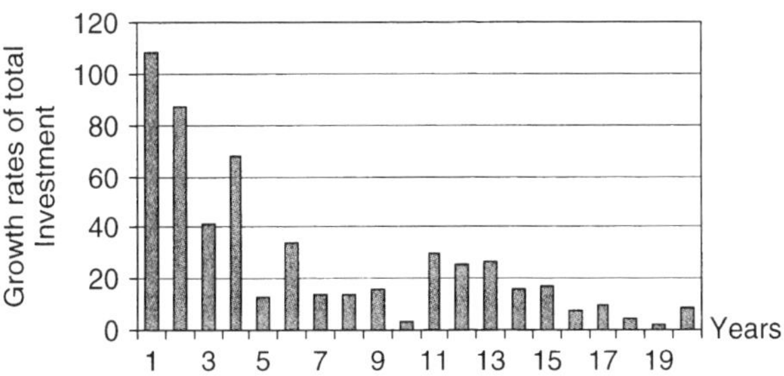

Figure 9.1 Growth rates of total financing and investment by the JIB, 1980–2000

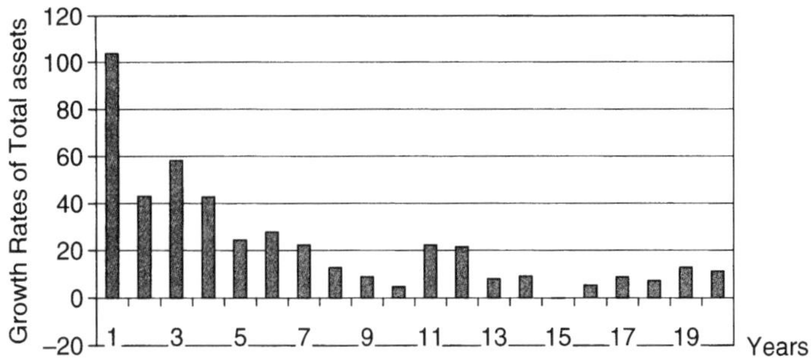

Figure 9.2 Growth rates of total assets of the Jordan Islamic Bank

Total assets of the JIB

The growth rate of total assets of the JIB was 103.8 per cent in 1981. After that, it started to decline, reaching 4.6 per cent in 1990 for the same reasons that affected growth rates of total deposits and total financing and investment (see Figure 9.2).

Theoretical background

Economic growth

Classical economists believed in Say's law, which argues that demand always automatically adjusts to supply. Thus they had no worries about lack of demand, so they discussed growth only in terms of supply. In its simplest terms, classical economists visualized the supply of output as equal to the amount of capital times the productivity of capital (Hunt and Sherman, 1990). The rate of growth is defined as the change in output as a percentage of current output:

Growth rate = change in output/current output

Classical economists, concerned as they were about economic growth, called for as much saving as possible. However, Keynes pointed out that more savings will lead to a rapid increase of capital and, consequently, to more economic growth only if we assume full employment and the rule of Say's law, which claims that demand is always enough for any supply of goods and that all savings are automatically invested (Branson, 1989).

There is no doubt that capital formation is a major determinant of economic growth. However, in developed countries, labour is clearly more productive than the machinery and equipment it has to work with. In underdeveloped countries, on the other hand, the situation is different because these countries tend to increase their capital formation in order to stimulate economic growth with no provision made for repairs or spare parts, and they do not efficiently combine capital with other factors of production. For example, most developing countries were fascinated by the post-Keynesian growth theories. These theories have been quite useful in explaining the optimum growth rate of productive capacity in developed countries but, when economists applied the same analytical tools to developing countries, their conclusions were very misleading (Zuvekas, 1979). Robert M. Solow emphasized the same point (Solow, 2001):

> In my view growth theory was conceived as a model of the growth of an industrial economy. Its parameters certainly could not be regarded as fixed forever, but may be they would need to be considered only over intervals of 30–50 years, long enough, so that the differences between endpoints could not be dominated by demand-driven business cycles. So far as I can remember, I have never applied such a model to a developing economy, because I thought the underlying machinery would apply mainly to a planned economy or a well-developed market economy.

The above discussion indicates that ready-made models could not be applied to developing countries without any modification to suit the country in question. This study will build a simultaneous macroeconometric model to capture both the direct and indirect effects of the Jordan Islamic Bank on economic growth for the period 1980–2000.

Banking systems and economic growth

The importance of the financial system in economic growth has attracted the attention of economists and policy makers ever since the beginning of financial history. The primary purpose of commercial banks is to mobilize idle resources for use in productive investment. As pointed out by Fohlin (1998), a wide array of theoretical models has appeared in the growth and development literature in the past decade to formalize the link between the functions of the financial system and growth of the real economy. In comparison to the traditional growth models, in which output was seen as a function of capital, labour and disembodied technological progress, the current models provide a richer framework for interpreting the potential impact of financial system on economic growth. Pango (1993) provides a simple way to summarize the newer models of finance and growth. He used several simplifying assumptions. The model yields the growth rate of per capita output as a function of three variables: savings rate, return on investment, and cost of intermediation. Thus, according to Pango, the financial institutions may enhance economic growth by raising the total quantity of financial capital available to entrepreneurs, improving the quality of investment and increasing the efficiency of intermediation, lowering costs between the sources and users of funds. On the same lines, Levine (1997) showed that, as financial intermediaries, banks play a crucial role in the operation of most economies. Thus, the efficiency of financial intermediaries can effect economic growth, through the influence of accumulation of physical capital by 'directing funds' to entrepreneurs who wish to invest. Such capital mobilization proceeds in two stages: capital collection through deposit-taking and fund dispersal through loans. By repeating this process, the banking system multiplier expands the money supply and redistributes the economy's capital. These banking functions increase the share of resources targeted to productive investment. Thus, apart from the safe-keeping of valuables, providing fund collection and transfer services and verifying the creditworthiness of their clients, the banks act as pure financial intermediaries who do not get themselves involved in economic activities, such as trading or investment. It is worth emphasizing that the Islamic banks' role cannot be tied only to the role of mobilizing capital; rather, their role can be extended through decisions about how to lend and invest funds (i.e., the quality of investment). An Islamic bank can influence the quality of capital formation.

The model

The suggested model is a simultaneous equation macroeconometric model which includes the growth rate of real per capita income as a proxy variable for economic growth (the dependent variable). The independent variables are: real interest rate (Rt), net transfer from abroad (Re), the total financing and investment made by the Jordan Islamic Bank as a percentage of total credits by conventional banks (RAT), gross investment (It), which is calculated as gross fixed capital formation plus change in stock (I), and gross domestic product (GDP). The structural form of the suggested model consists of two behavioural equations and will be estimated using 2SLS and the data given in Table 9.2.

The economic growth function, measured by the change in the real per capita income, could be explained by the change in the following variables: investment volume, net transfers from abroad, and the total credits by conventional banks (Branson, 1989, p. 528):

$$Per_t = f\,(TCB_{t-1}, Re_{t-1}, I_t)$$

We can write the above function in the power form as follows:

$$Per_t = B0\ TCB^{B1}{}_{t-1} Re^{B2}{}_{t-1}\, I_t^{B3}\, e^{ut}{}_1 \qquad (9.1)$$

where:

Table 9.2 Data for variables used in the suggested model

Financial year	*Real per capita income (Per)*	*Real interest rate (Rt)*	*Net transfers from abroad (Re)*	*Population (POP)*	*Total financing and investments by JIB*	*Total credits by conventional banks (SDCB)*	*Gross investment (I)*	*Gross domestic product (GDP)*
1980	1,065.9	6.5	236.7	2.92	6.8	563.9	493.9	1,151.2
1981	1,352.3	6.5	340.9	3.01	14.2	721.3	701.0	1,426.7
1982	1,530.4	6.5	381.9	3.10	26.5	887.2	679.4	1,638.1
1983	1,592.4	6.5	402.9	3.20	37.6	1,030.9	623.4	1,765.8
1984	1,691.1	6.5	457.0	3.30	63.0	1,184.8	577.6	1,891.4
1985	1,727.8	8.5	402.9	3.41	71.0	1,274.4	426.8	1,969.8
1986	1,754.9	8.5	414.5	3.52	95.5	1,395.4	447.9	2,114.6
1987	1,785.2	7.5	317.7	3.63	109.0	1,513.0	544.6	2,162.7
1988	1,812.9	7.5	335.7	3.75	124.1	1,634.0	569.1	2,218.4
1989	1,944.6	7.5	358.3	3.88	144.1	1,729.2	602.3	2,329.9
1990	2,038.7	8.5	331.8	4.01	148.9	1,863.5	751.5	2,612.5
1991	2,653.6	8.5	424.6	4.15	193.1	1,965.8	667.9	2,779.4
1992	3,770.3	8.5	514.6	4.29	243.1	2,218.3	1,039.4	3,234.2
1993	4,229.3	8.5	666.6	4.35	306.7	2,616.9	1,082.2	3,595.7
1994	4,562.7	8.5	698.7	4.39	356.1	3,248.4	1,451.0	3,857.7
1995	4,943.9	8.5	796.7	4.40	418.2	3,705.7	1,554.4	4,246.9
1996	5,279.3	8.5	1,024.0	4.44	422.1	3,920.3	1,497.4	4,711.0
1997	5,548.7	7.75	1,132.5	4.60	461.8	3,979.7	1,322.3	4,954.8
1998	5,795.4	9.0	983.5	4.75	481.4	4,285.3	1,261.0	5,642.9
1999	6,144.1	9.0	1,035.2	4.90	490.2	4,466.0	1,087.8	5,723.9
2000	6,341.0	9.0	1,268.2	5.04	531.8	4,546.5	1,199.0	5,912.9

Sources: (1) Central Bank of Jordan, *Monthly Statistical Bulletin*, different issues; Jordan Islamic Bank for Finance and Investment, *Annual Reports*, different issues.

Per_t refers to the real per capita income as a proxy for the economic growth;
TCB_{t-1} = total credit by conventional banks;
Re_{t-1} = net transfers from abroad;
I_t = volume of investment;
ut_1 = error term

It must be pointed out that the lag form in the above equation was used to indicate that the effects of the transfers from abroad as well as the total credit by conventional banks takes time to prevail. The logarithmic form will be used for the above equation so as to reflect the change on the dependent variable (Per_t) by the independent variables:

$$\text{Log } Per_t = \log B0 + B1 \text{ Log } TCB_{t-1} + B_2 \text{ Log } Re_{t-1} + B_3 \text{ Log } I_t + U_{t_1} \qquad (9.2)$$

It must be clear that all the coefficients of the independent variables are 'elasticities', such that the partial derivative of the dependent variable with respect to any of the independent variables measures the responsiveness or the sensitivity of change in the dependent variable as a result of the change in the independent variable in question.

Investment function

Investment is measured by the change in gross investment, which could be explained by real interest rate (Rt), GDP, and JIB total financing and investment as a percentage of total credits by conventional banks (RAT).

$$I_t = f\ (R_t,\ \text{GDP}_t,\ RAT_t)$$

The above function in the power form can be written as follows:

$$I_t = A0\ R_t^{A1}\ GDP_t^{A2}\ RAT_t^{A3}\ e^{ut2} \qquad (9.3)$$

where:
I_t = the investment level;
R_t = the real interest rate;
GDP_t = the gross domestic product;
$ut2$ = the error term

This function shows the importance of investment as a major component of aggregate demand. However, the logarithmic form will be used for the two simultaneous equations so as to measure the impact of the independent variables, through their coefficients (i.e., elasticities), on the dependent variables under consideration, which will be used later to determine both direct and indirect effects of these variables.

Table 9.3 Variables used in the model

Endogenous variables	*Exogenous variables*
The change in the real per capita income (Log *Per*).	The change in transfers from abroad (Log *Re*).
The change in total volume of investment (Log *I*)	The change in total credit by conventional banks (Log *TCB*). The change in the gross domestic product (Log *GDP*) The change in real interest rate (Log *R*) The change in JIB financing and investment as a per cent age of total credit by conventional banks (Log *RAT*)

$$\text{Log } I_t = \log A_0 + A_1 \text{ Log } R_t + A_2 \text{ Log } GDP_t + A_3 \text{ Log } RAT_t + U_{t2} \ldots \tag{9.4}$$

There is now a general consensus that the models estimated by standard econometric methods may suffer from the so-called 'spurious regression' problem. This problem is that if the time series variables in the model are non-stationary (which is the case most of the time), the *t*-ratio cannot be used to establish the impact of one variable on the others. By emphasizing the behaviour of the residuals from such models, co-integration analysis is performed which tries to establish the long-run equilibrium between two or more variables (Engle and Granger, 1987). Thus, before estimating the variables in the suggested model, a common practice (which is recommended by Engle and Granger, 1987), is the use of the ADF test. The ADF test showed that the calculated statistics are greater than the critical value at the 5 per cent level. This implies that the error term (*ut*) is co-integrated at 1(0). Based upon that, it may be argued that the use of the 2SLS is valid and will reflect the long-run relationship between the variables.

Variables of the model and their estimation

The model consists of two endogenous variables and five exogenous variables. Table 9.3 describes these variables.

After investigating the problem of identification, both of the above two endogenous equations were over-identified. Thus, it is more convenient to use the 2SLS approach to measure the endogenous variables of the model.

The results of the estimation

The results of the estimation are summarized in Tables 9.4 and 9.5.

From Tables 9.4 and 9.5 we can reach the following conclusions.

Table 9.4 Results of the estimated parameters

Independent variables	*Estimated coefficients*	*t-values*
Total credit by conventional banks (Log TCB_{t-1})	0.50	(1.83)
Gross investment (Log I)	0.22	(4.26)**
Net transfers from abroad (Log Re)	0.24	(8.5)*

Notes: F-test = 179, Constant = 2.2; * significant at 1% level; **significant at 5% level

Table 9.5 The estimated parameters of the investment function (Log I)

Independent variables	*Estimated coefficients*	*t-values*
Gross domestic product (Log GDP)	0.96	(3.43)**
Total financing and investment of the JIB as a percentage of total credits by conventional bank (Log RAT)	0.16	(0.45)
Real interest rate (R_t)	–0.14	(–0.25)

Notes: F-test = 112, Constant = –1.12; **Significant at 5% level

1 Both the change in total investment (Log I) and the change in net transfers from abroad (Re) proved to have a positive and significant impact on the dependent variable (Log Per), such that if gross investment increased by 1 per cent, the per capita income will increase by 22 per cent, whereas the increase in net remittances by 1 per cent will lead to increase in the per capita income by 24 per cent.
2 The impact of total credit by the conventional banks proved to be insignificant, and it shows a positive coefficient. This can be explained by the fact that conventional banks are interested only in getting their predetermined rate of interest regardless of the type of projects borrowers choose to implement. In Jordan, unfortunately, a large portion of investment is devoted to the service sector, where it reduces the chances of increasing job opportunities, and thus reduces the level of employment.
3 The impact of change in financing and investment of the JIB as a percentage of total credit by conventional banks was positive but insignificant. This can be explained by the fact that most of the financing operations of the Jordan Islamic Bank are for the short or medium term, and it has to hold high levels of liquidity in the form of cash to meet any emergencies, while it lacks as many financial instruments as conventional banks.

The reduced form

The structured form is used to explain the direct effect of the independent variables of any model on the dependent variables, but the reduced form explains both direct and indirect effects of independent variables on the dependent variables. This study will use the reduced form to analyse the direct effects of the Jordan Islamic Bank's financing and investments on total investment and the indirect effect of Jordan Islamic Bank financing and investment on real per capita income.

$$\text{Log } Per = 2.23 + 0.50 \text{ Log } TCB\ (-1) + 0.30 \text{ Log } I + 0.34 \text{ Log } Re$$
$$\text{Log } I = -1.11 + 0.96 \text{ Log } GDP + 0.16 \text{ Log } RAT - 0.14\ R_t$$

In order to capture the indirect effects of the independent variables on the change in real per capita income (Log *Per*), we can use the chain rule as follows (Kmenta, 1971):

$$\text{d log } per = \delta \text{ log } I \text{ * d log } Per = (0.96)\ (0.30) = 0.288 > 0$$
$$\text{d log } GDP\ \delta \text{ log } GDP \text{ d log } I$$

It is very clear that total investment will affect positively the level of GDP, which will, in turn, affect the per capita income.

$$\text{d log } per = \delta \text{ log } I \text{ * d log } Per = (0.16)\ (0.30) = 0.048 > 0$$
$$\text{d log } RAT\ \delta \text{ log } RAT \text{ d log } I$$

The indirect effect of total investment as a percentage of total financing and investment by (JIB) is relatively small (only 0.048) on the real per capita income. It must be looked at as a good start. However, the direct impact of total credit by conventional banks is 0.50, which is higher than that of the JIB. This can be explained by the fact of the JIB's small scale of operation and the surrounding economic environment mentioned in the introduction of this chapter (see also Vogel and Hayes, 1998).

$$\text{d log } per = \delta \text{ log } I \text{ * d log } Per = (-0.14)\ (0.30) = (-0.042) < 0$$
$$\text{d log } Rt\ \delta \text{ log } R_t \text{ d log } I$$

The direct effect of real interest rate was negative (–0.14), and this result is consistent with the negative relationship between the interest rate and the level of investment. The indirect effect of real interest rate on the real per capita income is negative and relatively small due to the fact that the real interest rate was fixed and controlled by the monetary authority for a very long period of time (Hallaq al- and Abdulbasit, 1997).

Conclusions

The present study has attempted to investigate the practices of the Jordan Islamic Bank (as a case study) during the period 1980–2000. The 2SLS approach was used to capture the direct and indirect effects of operations of the JIB on the real per capita income, which was used as proxy variable to measure economic growth. Several results were found.

Growth rates of total deposits, total assets and total financing and investment by the JIB in 1981 were very high due to the fact that many individuals were hoarding their private savings outside the formal banking sector rather than engaging in any interest-based financial dealings. Afterwards, these growth rates started to follow a normal pattern of growth. The Arab Bank Corporation in Jordan, the biggest financial institution, started to offer Islamic products in 1995, which brought down the growth of both deposits and total financing of the JIB.

The economic growth function, measured by the change in real per capita income, could be explained by the change in gross investment, net transfers from abroad and total credit by conventional banks. The investment function, measured by the change in gross investment, was explained by the real interest rate, GDP, and total financing and investment by the JIB as a percentage of total credits by conventional banks.

The statistical results showed that both changes in total investment and net transfers from abroad proved to have a positive and significant impact on the change in real per capita income. The total credit by conventional banks proved to be insignificant, even though it shows a positive coefficient. This can be explained by the fact that a large portion of such credits goes to the service sector. Thus, their direct effect on real per capita income was small and insignificant.

The impact of the change in JIB financing and investment as a percentage of total credit by conventional commercial banks on the investment level was positive but insignificant. This is to be expected since most of the JIB financial operations are short or medium term, so that the bank has to hold high levels of cash to meet any contingency in an emergency situation.

The reduced form has been used to explain both the direct and indirect effects of the independent variables on the dependent variable. The volume of investment affects positively the level of gross domestic product, which in turn affects the real per capita income. Thus, the indirect effect of GDP on per capita income will be associated positively with the level of investment.

The indirect effect of total financing and investment made by the JIB as a percentage of total credits by conventional banks was relatively small (0.048) on the real per capita income. But this rate must be looked at as a good start by Islamic banks compared to 0.50 by conventional banks' total credits. The indirect effect of the real interest rate on the real per capita income was negative and relatively small due to the fact that the real interest rate was fixed and controlled by the monetary authority for a very long period of time.

Comment

Ahmed S. Bamakhramah

Economic growth, that magic term, has never stopped attracting and sometimes fascinating researchers and writers in the economics discipline. One wonders why this is the case. I may venture to suggest that it is so due to its macroeconomic effectiveness and ramifications, its susceptibility to measurement and quantification, or the fact that it can be influenced by almost any factor imaginable.

Even when some writers researched into the more 'comprehensive economic development' indicator of macroeconomic achievement, they frequently resorted to per capita growth of income, a measure of economic growth, as the most prominent indicator when it comes to the measurement of economic development. Such emphasis is usually undertaken at the expense of other, sometimes more pragmatic, indicators of achievement such as performance and efficiency.

Associating economic growth with the development of financial systems or institutions (for example, banks and stock markets) is not new in the economic literature; the new thing about this endeavour is its application to Islamic banks. The objective of the study under discussion is to tread this path. The effort, though important academically, raises doubts about whether it serves a practical purpose. One could ask the following question: if Islamic banks were found not to contribute much, or for that matter not at all, to economic growth, does that mean they are not needed? In other words, is it relevant, at least from the practical point of view, to the justification of the existence and development of the Islamic banks whether they contributed to the economic growth of the communities they were established in?

In my view, the answer is no, because there are other paramount, religious and social, reasons for the establishment of such banks, although one would not deny that if the establishment of Islamic banks also contributed to the economic growth of their communities that would help the argument for their establishment and may even encourage support and assistance from governments as well as from the public at large.

However, this kind of reasoning may not stand strongly in the face of the counter-argument that such influence is not specific to Islamic banks. Almost all other financial institutions, and particularly commercial banks, share such influence. What is, thus, particular about Islamic banks that makes their contribution to economic growth worth special attention? The answer to such a question is what, in my view, makes a research paper venturing into such a topic worth the effort. Unfortunately, the study under discussion did not succeed much in this regard, because of three main reasons.

First, the theoretical background was conventional. It applies more to conventional financial intermediaries than to Islamic financing institutions.

The author failed to emphasize the more specific factors that can affect the role of Islamic banks on economic growth, as outlined below:

1 *Delegate monitoring and corporate governance*: Islamic banks, through their particular modes of financing based on PLS, would enhance the monitoring of financed corporations and strengthen their governance, thus stimulating effective resource allocation and productivity growth. A failure by Islamic banks to exercise such responsibility would naturally lead to slower growth.
2 *Enhanced liquidity*: the potential mismatch between (long-term) investment project financing and (short-term) deposits could create liquidity problems for Islamic banks. Because investors cannot easily sell their shares in these projects if they need their savings before the projects mature, it reduces the incentive to invest in long-term projects. Enhanced liquidity therefore encourages investment in long-term, higher-return projects that boost resource mobilization and productivity and therefore stimulate economic growth.
3 *Risk-sharing*: through undertaking long-term, more risky investments, Islamic banks may contribute positively to economic growth. Higher returns and better risk-sharing may induce more investment deposits, thus enhancing resource mobilization and capital accumulation.
4 *Information symmetry*: asymmetric information may lead to adverse selection either due to depositors choosing the best deposit portfolios or the banks selecting among the available investment channels. All this may impede healthy capital accumulation and efficient resource allocation. Asymmetric information is a less serious problem in the kinds of investment modes of Islamic banks.

Second, the statistical results of the study are not conclusive and are riddled with erroneous derivations. In particular, the conclusion about the reduced form effects of the exogenous variables on the endogenous variables derived from the conclusions of the structural form using the 'chain rule' is not statistically legitimate, because some of the effects in the structural form are not statistically significant and thus cannot be relied upon when calculating the reduced form effects through the chain rule.

Third, it is not enough to conclude that Islamic banks promote economic growth. It is even more important to identify which mode or modes of financing contributed most. Islamic banks differ from conventional banks in that their spectrum of financing is more varied. Their investments are more diversified in terms of maturity, liquidity and risk, ranging from the relatively short-term, more liquid and less risky mode of *murābaḥah* to the longer-term, less liquid and more risky mode of equity (or direct *mushārakah*) financing.

Each mode differs in its effect on the capital accumulation capability and resource utilization efficiency of the banks and so the economic growth of the relevant country. The effect of a bank's activities on economic growth will thus depend on which modes of finance and investment the bank undertakes most and how much each one of these modes contributes to economic growth.

In addition, Islamic banks' financing activities tend more towards investment or universal banking compared to conventional (commercial) banking. Thus, they merit different treatment in the analysis of the way they affect economic growth, particularly when dealing with the four above-mentioned factors of influence, which makes comparison with conventional banks unbalanced and less accurate.

Comment

Khalid A. Al Meshal

Islamic banking is a large industry. According to some crude statistics, more than 200 Islamic banks and investment companies are operating in some 50 countries around the world. They manage between them over US$ 200 billion and their growth rate amounts to 15 per cent per annum. The remarkable success and popularity of the Islamic financial products and institutions have attracted a huge number of conventional banks to set up Islamic windows to offer Islamic financial products. In Saudi Arabia, for instance, all operating conventional commercial banks have managed – with varying degrees of success – to introduce Islamic branches or units or have started offering Islamic financial products through existing units. Moreover, some banks have totally transformed the nature of the banks to pure Islamic institutions. The Al-Jazira Bank and Saudi Commercial Bank could be cited as examples.

Although the Islamic banking system has gained an acceptable theoretical basis in the last two decades, the empirical basis is still weak. What is needed at this stage crucially is to evaluate empirically the impact of Islamic financial institutions on major economic variables and on achieving economic and social development goals in Islamic countries. Therefore, empirical studies using advanced econometric approaches should be directed to this line of research.

This chapter is on this important line. It is an attempt to test empirically the claims made on theoretical grounds.

The study concentrates on the role of finance and investment in explaining the behaviour of economic growth in developing countries. It suggests that Islamic investment plays a part in the determination of the economic growth, which is measured by per capita income.

It departs from the Harrod–Domar type framework to using a more realistic model concentrating on the relation between finance and growth, which can be helpful in explaining the trend of economic growth in developing countries.

The model presented in the chapter is highly aggregated and simple in structure. Regarding the data sources, it is not quite clear whether the gross domestic product (GDP) and investment (I) are presented in nominal or real terms.

The behavioural equations of the model should have been econometrically tested, designed for *validity of specification* and *cointegration*. In this regard, it is of crucial importance to adopt a simple *error-correction form* by including at least one-period lag together with the current values for all variables in the model. Those tests are essential before making any recommendations. Also, there is no acceptable justification for keeping insignificant variables, for example (RAT_t) and (R_t), which are considered to be the most important variables in the model. It would be useful if both total credit by conventional banks and total finance and investment by the JIB could be included in the investment equation to compare their impact. On the other hand, in order to have a more realistic model for the purpose of causal analysis, it would be of crucial importance if the data set could be expressed quarterly.

References

Bashir, B. A. (1984), 'Successful Development of Islamic Banks', *Journal of Research in Islamic Economics*, 1(2), 39–54.

Branson, H. William (1989), *Macroeconomic: Theory and Policy*, New York: Harper & Row.

Engle, R. F. and C. W. J. Granger (1987), 'Co-integration and Error Correction: Representation, Estimation and Testing', *Econometrica*, 55, 251–76.

Fohlin, Caroline (1998), 'Banking Systems and Economic Growth: Lessons from Britain and Germany in the Pre-World War Era', *Review, Federal Reserve Bank of Saint Louis*, 80 (3), 27–54.

Hallaq al-, Said and A. Abdulbasit (1997), 'The Role of Social Security Funds in Stimulating Investments: The Case of Jordan', *Al-Balqa Journal*, Amman-Jordan, 4 (4), 13–33.

Hunt, E. K. and Howard Sherman (1990), *Economics: An Introduction to Traditional and Radical Views*, New York: HarperCollins.

Iqbal, Munawar (2001), 'Islamic and Conventional Banking in the Nineties: A Comparative Study', *Islamic Economic Studies*, 8 (2),1–27.

Kmenta, Jan (1971), *Elements of Econometrics*, New York: Macmillan.

Levine, Ross (1997), 'Financial Development and Economic Growth', *Journal of Economic Literature*, 53 (2), 31–67.

Omar al-, Fuad and M. Abdelhaq (1996), *Islamic Banking: Theory, Practice and Challenges*, Oxford: Oxford University Press.

Pango, Marco (1993), 'Financial Markets and Growth: An Overview', *European Economic Review*, 28 (2), 613–22.

Rawashdeh, Mufid and Said Al-Hallaq (1999), 'The Role of Islamic Bank of Jordan in Attracting Hoarded Deposits: An Econometrical and Analytical Study', *Abḥāth Al-Yarmouk*, Jordan: Yarmouk University, 15 (2), 59–81.

Solow, M. Robert (2001), 'Applying Growth Theory Across-Countries', *The World Bank Economic Review*, 15, 283–8.

Vogel, E. Frank and Samuel L. Hayes (1998), *Islamic Law and Finance: Religion, Risk, and Return*, The Hague: Kluwer Law International.

Zuvekas, Clarence (1979), *Economic Development: An Introduction*, New York: St Martin's Press.

Index

Notes: f = figure; n = note; t = table; **bold** = extended discussion or heading emphasized in main text.